Hedge Fund Operational Due Diligence

Founded in 1807, John Wiley & Sons is the oldest independent publishing company in the United States. With offices in North America, Europe, Australia, and Asia, Wiley is globally committed to developing and marketing print and electronic products and services for our customers' professional and personal knowledge and understanding.

The Wiley Finance series contains books written specifically for finance and investment professionals as well as sophisticated individual investors and their financial advisors. Book topics range from portfolio management to e-commerce, risk management, financial engineering, valuation and financial instrument analysis, as well as much more.

For a list of available titles, visit our Web site at www.WileyFinance.com.

Hedge Fund Operational Due Diligence

Understanding the Risks

JASON A. SCHARFMAN

WILEY

John Wiley & Sons, Inc.

Published by John Wiley & Sons, Inc., Hoboken, New Jersey.
Published simultaneously in Canada.

For general information on our other products and services, or technical support, please contact our Customer Care Department within the United States at 800-762-2974, outside the United States at 317-572-3993 or fax 317-572-4002.

Wiley also publishes its books in a variety of electronic formats. Some content that appears in print may not be available in electronic books.

For more information about Wiley products, visit our Web site at http://www.wiley.com.

Library of Congress Cataloging-in-Publication Data:

Scharfman, Jason A., 1978–
    Hedge fund operational due diligence : understanding the risks / Jason A. Scharfman.
        p. cm. – (Wiley finance series)
    Includes index.
    ISBN 978-0-470-37234-0 (cloth)
    1. Hedge funds.   2. Risk management.   I. Title.
    HG4530.S376 2009
    332.64'524–dc22

                                                                    2008023249

Printed in the United States of America

10 9 8 7 6 5 4 3 2 1

I dedicate this book to my wife, Rachel, for her unwavering support, and to my entire family for their constant encouragement.

Contents

Preface

Within the pecking order of the hedge fund world, operational risk professionals have traditionally been thought of as being low on the totem pole. Indeed, many hedge fund investment professionals have at one point or another held the view that operational risk management is one of life's necessary evils and merely a distraction from the "real" business of investing. Yet, ask any hedge fund investor his or her thoughts on the importance of operational due diligence, and you will likely receive a much different response. This book, in part, attempts to reconcile this difference of opinion, by detailing the motivations for comprehensive operational due diligence and outlining a flexible framework to diagnose a hedge fund's operational risks.

This book is not intended to describe how to run a hedge fund; rather it is meant to provide guidance on how to effectively diagnose, evaluate, and monitor a hedge fund's operational competencies. Performing these types of evaluations can unveil certain risks investors may not have been aware they were signing up for when they decided to invest in a hedge fund. Similarly, hedge fund personnel can utilize the techniques in this book to perform a self-diagnostic health check and determine areas in which there is need for operational improvements.

When I first began working with hedge funds, the term *operational risk* was limited solely to back-office concerns. Over time, the term slowly began to encompass more non-investment-related areas. Today, the field of operational due diligence is a diverse and unique area of hedge fund risk management that, partly as a result of several high-profile hedge fund blowups, has gained new prominence. One need only glance at the cover of *The Wall Street Journal* or turn on CNBC to learn about the latest debacle of hedge fund losses due to poor operational oversight and controls. Even as this book is being written, details are emerging surrounding record-breaking losses of over $7 billion at the French bank Société Générale, allegedly caused by trader Jérome Kerviel's manipulation of the firm's internal operational safeguards.

Specifically, this book has three main goals. The first is to provide those who work for hedge funds, as well as those who are invested or are considering investing in hedge funds, with an understanding of the importance and benefits of a comprehensive operational due diligence program. This is accomplished by outlining several arguments in favor of thorough operational due diligence and operational risk management. I have also included an analysis of the failed Bayou Hedge Fund Group to highlight how operational risks can bring down an organization.

The second goal is to provide an understanding of how to diagnose and analyze the operational risks that may be present in a hedge fund. I have outlined the primary, secondary, and blended operational risk factors present in the vast majority of modern hedge fund organizations. I have also included several hypothetical examples that are emblematic of the types of scenarios hedge fund investors might experience in the course of the operational due diligence process.

The third goal of this book is to examine techniques for the modeling of operational risk as well as how to factor the results of this operational risk analysis into the overall hedge fund asset allocation process. With regard to the latter, I have introduced several new concepts in this text, including operational threshold self-assessment, Multivariate Commonality Analysis, the concept of operational drag, and the calculation of the Operational Factor. All of these are powerful techniques that can enable hedge fund investors to extend the value of their operational due diligence efforts beyond that of merely a diagnostic filter.

An underlying goal of this book is to encourage discussion and debate about hedge fund operational risk and the arguments for and against increased transparency. It is inevitable that certain readers will disagree with some of the opinions and conclusions drawn in this book. I welcome the debate, and encourage all those interested in hedge funds to participate in furthering the discussions and research in the field of operational risk.

To summarize, a strong operational infrastructure provides a crucial backbone to the modern hedge fund, without which the smartest money managers in the world could not thrive. I hope that this book both educates and provides the practical tools necessary to produce more adept investors and operations personnel. As a final note, this book reflects my individual opinions and insights, and not those of any of my past or present employers.

Jason Scharfman
November 2008

CHAPTER 1

What Is Operational Risk?

T he world of hedge fund risk can be very broadly bifurcated into two distinct areas: those risks that are directly related to a hedge fund's investments, and all others. These investment-related risks can be classified on a high level as market risk, credit risk, and all derivations thereof. Traditionally, investors have been more familiar with, and subsequently placed more focus on, these investment-related risks. There are numerous reasons for this. The marketplace and academics have developed commonly accepted, time-tested ways to quantify these risks through a host of analytical metrics. Through this quantification, both investors and market practitioners alike have been able to more easily correlate these investment-related risks to actual gains or losses for a specific hedge fund investment. Additionally, this quantification allows investors to aggregate similar risks into the context of a larger portfolio and manage these risks accordingly.

In the early 1990s, during the resurgence of hedge fund investing, non-investment-related risks were largely ignored. There were several likely reasons for this, including the lure of extremely positive hedge fund performance and the regulation of the mutual fund industry, which may have given early hedge fund investors a false sense of confidence in the widely unregulated hedge fund market, coupled with a lack of understanding and research in this area. Another reason most hedge fund investors were not focused on these risks most likely related to the fact that there had not been any direct hedge fund catastrophes to keep operational risks fresh in people's minds. More recently, in the wake of a continuing stream of high-profile hedge fund failures, investors have begun to focus more carefully on the entire gamut of risks—both those directly related to investments and all others—involved when investing in hedge funds. As a result, in recent years, both individual investors and larger allocators alike have begun to bundle these residual non-investment-related risks under the umbrella of a newly defined category called *operational risk*. Before diving into a discussion regarding the current definitions of what exactly this operational risk category includes as it refers to hedge funds, it will be useful to gain some historical perspective on the development of this unique risk category.

BRIEF HISTORY

Since the time of Alfred Winslow Jones, creator of the first hedge fund in 1949, operational risk has always coexisted with investment risk. In Jones's time, though, conceptions of risk were a little different from what they are today. Back then, the definition of *risk* was primarily *financial risk*—such as the risk that the market would decline and deplete the initial capital supplied. At that time, most people were simply risk averse. A few sophisticated investors saw beyond this somewhat limited definition of risk and understood that risk could be strategically taken to produce superior returns, which eventually led to the development of new investment strategies such as Jones's hedge fund. Despite being perceptive enough to allocate capital to Jones, his investors most likely did not acknowledge the non-investment-related risks associated with his hedge fund. It was not their fault; the market simply was not developed enough to focus on these types of risks. Even if it had been, investors most likely did not have the analytical tools and framework necessary to conduct an operational risk review. Why, then, is it only in recent years, almost 60 years since the inception of Jones's fund, that investors have taken such an interest in the subject? In order to understand the current climate that embraces operational risk, we must first understand its origins.

The modern era of operational risk can trace its roots back to the mid-1980s in Washington, D.C. It all began with Michigan Congressman John D. Dingell. Congressman Dingell was, and still is, the chairman of the U.S. House of Representatives' Committee on Energy and Commerce. This Committee is the oldest standing committee of the U.S. House of Representatives and has a broad mandate to investigate a wide range of issues. In the past, this Committee has written legislation on a variety of issues ranging from clear air improvements and toxic waste site cleanup to senior citizen health care. The Committee has several subcommittees, including one specifically designated to oversight and investigations.

Beginning in the summer of 1984, this oversight and investigations subcommittee commenced a series of hearings into the accounting profession. Specifically, the Committee was interested in learning about the effectiveness of audit reporting disclosures that were in place at the time. The Committee's investigation was the offshoot of increasing public concern brought about by a consecutive series of high-profile failures, all with issues of financial reporting integrity at the heart of their collapse. More disturbing to the public was that these failures were not concentrated in any one industry or cluster or individuals; rather, they were occurring at a progressively alarming rate across multiple industry sectors and in companies of varying sizes. Those industry segments focused on by the Committee included defense contractors with large losses, such as Pratt & Whitney and General Dynamics; large thrifts, in particular the $2 billion Beverly Hills Savings and Loan Association; and unregistered investment advisors such as ESM Government Securities. As a result of these hearings, in August 1986, the Committee suggested legislation that proposed increased transparency in financial reporting and new procedures focused on detecting fraud.

Development of COSO

Those outside of the government, and in particular large accounting firms with considerable audit practices, scrambled to produce a unified response. Specifically, in reaction to the Committee's hearings and subsequent recommendations, the National Commission on Fraudulent Financial Reporting was formed in 1985. This commission's formal chairman was a former Commissioner of the U.S. Securities and Exchange Commission, named James C. Treadway, Jr., and so it came to be more commonly known as the Treadway Commission. This commission was sponsored by a number of interested parties from the private sector, including the Institute of Internal Auditors and the American Accounting Association. The goals of the Treadway Commission were twofold. Primarily, the Commission sought to distinguish the essential elements of financial reporting that were considered to be fraudulent. Second, the Treadway Commission was to produce recommendations to curb any instances of such behavior in the future. For this purpose, the Commission studied the system of financial reporting covering the period ranging from October 1985 to September 1987. The Treadway Commission produced its initial report in October 1987, which recommended, among other things, increased coordination among the Treadway Commission's sponsoring organizations to better develop a series of guidelines in order to facilitate the implementation of internal controls. This recommendation led to the formation of the Committee of Sponsoring Organizations (COSO). COSO worked to produce a study on the creation of an integrated structure of internal controls to prevent fraudulent financial reporting, specifically this study, which was published in 1992 under the title *Internal Control-Integrated Framework*. This report contained one of the first mentions of the term *operations risk* in a financial risk management context. This study also focused on developing a common definition of the term *internal control*. This definition focused on monitoring three primary categories:[1]

1. Effectiveness and efficiency of operations
2. Reliability of financial reporting
3. Compliance with applicable laws and regulations

The study went on to identify a series of five interrelated components that formed a framework that could be utilized to diagnose and analyze an organization's internal controls. The five components of this framework are:[2]

1. Control environment
2. Risk assessment
3. Control activities
4. Information and communication
5. Monitoring

In April 1988, in response to the COSO report, the Auditing Standards Board issued ten new Statements of Auditing Standards that focused on increasing the auditor's responsibility to uncover and report failures of a firm's internal control structure, especially when auditing financial statements.

Basel Accords

Turning away from Congress and the accounting industry for a moment, the next major stage in the development of operational risk took place in 1988 in Basel, Switzerland, with the creation of the Basel Capital Accord by the Basel Committee on Banking Supervision. The Basel Committee was founded in 1974 by the governors of the central banks of the G-10 nations (Belgium, Canada, France, Italy, Japan, Netherlands, United Kingdom, United States, Germany, Sweden, and Switzerland). The Committee was created in response to the muddled liquidation by German regulators of a Cologne, Germany–based bank called Bank Herstatt. The purpose of the Basel Committee is to create general guidelines and issue recommendations on banking best practices. The Committee does not have any enforcement authority, but its pronouncements, commonly referred to as *accords*, are considered to be highly influential in the continued development of banking supervision. The primary goal of the 1988 Basel Accord, now commonly known as Basel I, was to establish a methodology in order to determine the requirements for the minimum capital that commercial banks should have on reserve. The purpose of these reserves was to act as a buffer against credit risks faced by these banks.

In the early 1990s, a trend of rogue-trader-type events caused a stir in the world banking community. There were the 1994 losses of Juan Pablo Davila, a copper futures trader, that led to almost $200 million in losses for Chilean mining company Codelco. That same year, Orlando Joseph Jett was ordered by the Securities and Exchange Commission (SEC) to repay over $8 million in bonuses due to allegations by his employer, Kidder Peabody, of creating false profits in order to mask losses in the bond markets. In 1995, it was revealed that Toshihide Iguchi, a trader for Daiwa Bank, had hidden over $1 billion in bond market losses over a period of several years. These losses, followed by subsequent delays on the part of the bank in disclosing their magnitude, led to a series of criminal indictments. Daiwa was subsequently banned from the U.S. markets. Later that year, Nick Lesson, the now-infamous Singapore-based futures trader, caused losses of $1.3 billion, which led to the collapse of Barings Bank. In 1996, over $2 billion in losses were racked up by Sumitomo copper trader Yasuo Hamanaka's attempts to corner the world copper markets. These rogue trader events are summarized in Exhibit 1.1.

EXHIBIT 1.1 Summary of Mid-1990s Rogue Trader Events

Year	Name	Institution	Market(s)	Losses
1994	Juan Pablo Davila	Codelco	Futures (Copper)	$170 million
1994	Orlando Joseph Jett	Kidder Peabody	Bonds	$330 million
1995	Toshihide Iguchi	Daiwa Bank	Bonds	$1,100 million
1995	Nick Lesson	Barings Bank	Futures	$1,300 million
1996	Yasuo Hamanaka	Sumitomo	Futures (Copper)	$2,600 million
	Total reported losses over a 2-year period			$5,500 million

Later that year, primarily as a reaction to these events, the Basel Committee added an amendment to the original Basel Accord I that incorporated a capital charge for market risk. In response to a host of changes and to better reflect the evolving nature of the commercial banking industry, in June 2004 the second Basel Accord, called Basel II, was published. The Basel II framework is divided into three distinct but related pillars. The first pillar focused on requirements for the minimum capital banks must keep on reserve in order to insulate themselves from potential losses in certain pre-defined areas. In addition to the already-mandated minimum requirements for market and credit risk, which were covered in the previous accords, the first pillar added a minimum requirement for operational risk. In particular, the first pillar specified three approaches for quantifying operational risk: the basic indicator approach, the standardized approach, and the advanced measurement approach. The second pillar focused on the regulatory review process and provides commercial banks with a generic framework for analyzing a host of other risks that Basel II places under an umbrella category called *residual risk*. Interestingly, this category includes such things as legal risk, strategic risks, and reputation risk. The third pillar seeks to increase the financial reporting disclosures banks are required to make.

Cadbury, Greenbury, Hampel, and Sarbanes-Oxley

The sentiments voiced by both the U.S. House's Committee and COSO calling for increased transparency in financial reporting and more stringent oversight of internal operational risks were echoed outside of the United States as well. One example of this movement taking hold was in the United Kingdom. In response to a series of public financial scandals throughout the 1980s involving large, publicly listed U.K. companies, the Cadbury Commission was formed in 1991. The Commission's sponsors included a number of large accounting firms, the Financial Reporting Council, and the London Stock Exchange. The following year, the Commission, led by Sir Adrian Cadbury, the previous chairman of Cadbury Schweppes, issued a study entitled *The Report of the Committee on the Financial Aspects of Corporate Governance* that led to the creation of the *Cadbury Code*. This Code provided best practice guidance over a host of issues, including the independence and composition of the Board of Directors of a firm, the length of service contracts with third parties, the compensation of senior management, and oversight of financial reporting and internal controls. The Cadbury Code's finding in regards to both the compensation and level of oversight of senior management were later reiterated by the report of the Greenbury Committee. "The group, which was chaired by Sir Richard Greenbury, focused on the remuneration of directors in large public companies and reported in July 1995."[3]

The Greenbury Report was followed by the formation of the Hampel Committee in 1996. The goal of this committee was to evaluate, consolidate, and update the previous recommendations of both Cadbury and Greenbury. In 1998, the committee produced the Hampel Report. This report was a significant departure from the previous work done by Cadbury and Greenbury in the sense that it focused on espousing the best practices of internal corporate governance ideology as opposed to the somewhat more onerous regulatory burdens suggested by the previous committees. Additionally, the Hampel Report suggested the increased importance of shareholder activism and stressed the need for increased corporate accountability. Later in 1998, a combined code was produced that summarized the suggestions of all three reports.

In 2001, Paul Myners was commissioned by the U.K. government to "consider whether there were factors distorting the investment decision-making of institutions."[4] The Myners report focused on a number of continuing problems that, at the time, continued to plague the implementation of best practices in U.K. corporate governance, with a particular focus on pension fund investing. This report was followed in 2003 by the publication of a report by Derek Higgs that, among other things, suggested several changes to the previous combined code.

Concurrent with the evolution of the global banking industry's development of best practices and the corporate governance advances in the United Kingdom, in 2002 two U.S. Congressmen, Paul Sarbanes and Michael Oxley, seemed to pick up where Congressman Dingell had left off 16 years earlier, with the passage and enactment of the Public Company Accounting Reform and Investor Protection Act of 2002, commonly known as *Sarbanes-Oxley* (SOX). Title I of the Act established the Public Company Accounting Oversight Board, whose charge it was to focus on such issues as auditor independence and internal control assessment. Although SOX does not apply to privately held companies, it marked a significant acknowledgment by the United States of the importance of monitoring internal operational risks within an organization and signified a milestone in a changing climate of enhanced transparency and increased regulatory oversight of the financial markets.

MODERN DEFINITION OF OPERATIONAL RISK IN A HEDGE FUND CONTEXT

The previous historical overview attempted to demonstrate that the development of the modern operational risk framework has been a lengthy evolutionary process influenced by numerous governmental, public, and private interests. As the hedge fund industry has grown, investors have begun to take a page out of history and apply the combined operational best practices culled from the development of audit standards, commercial banking, and the like toward this blossoming industry. What exactly do we mean when we refer to operational risk in a hedge fund context?

Even today, the definition of operational risk is a moving target that is often blurry at best. Operational risk has been referred to as a "time bomb for investors"[5] and "a fear category with a problematic reality and status."[6] Others contend that operational risk is purely a regulatory construct that does not really exist. Certain sources use the terms *business risk* and *operational risk* interchangeably. Indeed, this was the case toward the beginning of the development of the field of hedge fund operational risk. Still others draw a distinction defining *business risk* as those risks that are "not directly related to market movements, such as failure to reach a base level of assets under management or a change in management of the fund."[7] Framing operational risk in a mean-variance optimization framework, some have described operational risk as "risk without reward, as it is the only risk that investors face that is not rewarded with potentially increased returns."[8] The logic of this argument goes on to suggest that investors should not expect to receive additional compensation for taking on additional levels of operational risk, as they would with market risk. However, this should be distinguished from the notion that by intelligent diagnosing and monitoring operational risk investors can potentially minimize certain losses and possibly enhance positive returns. Indeed, notions of operational risk do not fall within the standard conventions of expected risk-and-return tradeoffs.

Some definitions seek to define operational risk in the broadest terms, as any risks not directly related to a firm's investments. Others attempt to limit operational risks solely to *operational failures* in the traditional sense—that is, areas that a firm's *chief operating officer* would oversee, such as trade processing and account reconciliation. In practice, the modern definition of operational risk as applied to hedge funds falls somewhere between the two. One definition that reflects this middle ground defines operational risk as "the risk of loss resulting from inadequate or failed internal processes, people and systems, or from external events."[9]

OPERATIONAL DUE DILIGENCE VERSUS OPERATIONAL RISK

It is worth pausing for a moment to discuss the difference between these two terms, which are sometimes erroneously confused in the marketplace. For the purposes of this text, when utilizing the term *operational due diligence*, we will be referring to the process of collecting operational (i.e., non-investment-related) data about a particular hedge fund. Once this data is collected, an investor can then make a determination as to the amount of *operational risk* present at the hedge fund. Put another way, operational due diligence is method by which we inspect a hedge fund's operational competencies and operational risk is the diagnosis.

KEY AREAS

Primary and Secondary Factors

Regardless of the definition utilized, there are several generally agreed-upon areas that make up the core of any hedge fund operational review. Throughout this book, we will refer to these as *primary factors*. These risks include a wide range of factors, from analyzing the personal and professional background of the personnel of an investment firm to gauging the appropriateness of a fund's valuation techniques. We will also refer to a number of *secondary factors* that, for a variety of reasons, some investors may give only minor importance to or not even consider at all during the course of an operational review. Exhibit 1.2 outlines what are generally believed to be the most important primary and secondary factors of hedge fund operational risk.

The question could be posed as to why we would even bother to draw the distinction between risk factors. After all, one could ask, Should not all

EXHIBIT 1.2   Primary and Secondary Factors of Hedge Fund Operational Risk

Factor	Primary/Secondary
Technology and systems	Primary
Business continuity and disaster recovery	Primary
Legal/compliance	Primary
Regulatory	Primary
Assets and investors concentration	Primary
Quality and length of relationship with tier-one service providers	Primary
Reputation of employees (including senior mgmt.) and firm	Primary
Valuation techniques and pricing sources	Primary
Compensation and employee turnover	Primary
Firm stability including expense analysis	Primary
Operations connectivity	Primary
Trade life cycle	Primary
Fund terms	Primary
Transparency and reporting	Primary
Counterparty oversight	Primary
Cash controls and management	Primary
Insurance	Secondary
Independence and oversight of the board of directors	Secondary
Quality and length of relationship with tier-two service providers	Secondary
Tax practices	Secondary

these factors, as well as a host of others, be analyzed as part of the entire due diligence review being performed on a hedge fund manager? This line of reasoning does have validity in the sense that, depending on the circumstances, the secondary factors can be just as important as, if not more important than, the primary factors. Said another way, a secondary factor can be the missing lynchpin that causes the failure of a hedge fund due to operational reasons and, depending on the unique circumstances of the particular hedge fund under review, can be just as important a factor in the failure of a hedge fund due to operational reasons as a primary factor. However, this does not mean that the delineation of this entire set of risk factors into primary and secondary factors holds no value. These classifications are based both on professional experience of where the greatest magnitude of risks lies within a hedge fund and on a historical review of the importance of these risk factors in hedge funds that have failed for operational reasons. It is often difficult to draw a line in the sand between primary and secondary risk factors. However, for a variety of reasons, including the fact that investors do not have the time or resources to fully vet each risk factor with the same level of diligence, certain factors should be designated as having primarily more importance, and subsequently be given more weight, than others.

Blended Risk Exceptions

As with most things in life, there is of course an exception to the definition of operational risk outlined above. Just as we had difficulty pinning down a definition of operational risk, there is similar debate over certain risk factors that lie somewhere between the realms of investment and operations risk. As illustrated in Exhibit 1.3, it certainly would not be prudent to ignore these overlapping risks, but due to their nature, it is not apparent in which risk bucket they should be placed. An example of such a risk would be the examination of a hedge fund's asset flows over some time period. If assets have recently exited a certain sector, it could be classified as an investment decision to take a view if you feel funds will return to the space. However, there could be a noninvestment or operational element to this analysis, as this could directly relate to a fund's ability to successfully scale up operations, retain talent, and complete existing operations development projects, and the like.

These blended risks should be reviewed in the context of the entire organization and combined with an investor's investment review of a hedge fund when reaching an asset allocation decision. In practice, an operational due diligence analyst should not put on blinders and ignore these *blended risk factors* on principle alone, by reviewing only those risks traditionally defined as operational in nature. Similarly, it would be advisable for an investment analyst reviewing the merits of a hedge fund's investment strategy to weigh

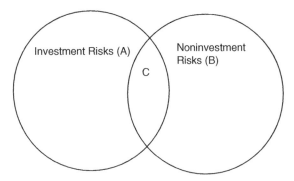

EXHIBIT 1.3 Is Operational Risk Just B, B + C, or A−C?

both these operational and financial risks as well. As is the case in many funds of hedge funds organizations, often an investment analyst is also the same person conducting an operational review. Even in situations where a fund of hedge funds, or similar investment organization, has a dedicated operational due diligence analyst, an active dialogue is advisable to properly vet these blended risks within the context of the entire organization.

Operational Risk Is Both Internal and External   It has been argued that unlike market and credit risk, operational risk is internal to the firm.[10] This thinking presents only half the story. Hedge funds today are exposed to a number of operational risks that are external to the firm across a wide number of areas. Examples of such external risk exposures include hedge funds dependence on third-party service providers and the potential of regulatory oversight. In fact, the distinction between *internal* and *external risk* is where we will begin our discussion of the key areas of operational risk. Most people dive right into the minutia of operational risk by selecting areas of related categories or topics under a broad heading such as "accounting" when determining the major categories of operational risk. There is nothing wrong with this approach, but, for those less familiar with the subject, I find this method tends to confuse some people along the way and lose the forest for the trees, so to speak.

For the purpose of this text, let us start at the 10,000-foot view and get more specific as we go. By taking this approach, we can begin to identify the risks that will be common among the vast majority of hedge funds. This will provide the users of this text, investors and hedge funds, with a baseline set of criteria from which you can begin to evaluate a hedge fund. On the broadest level, we can begin by classifying non-investment-related risks as those that are external to the hedge fund and those that are internal to the hedge fund.

As we begin to outline these risks, it is important to clarify exactly what is meant by external and internal risks. When classifying a risk in these terms, I base the definition on where the preponderance of the source of the risk comes from. Note that the distinctions between external and internal risks are not always starkly contrasted and each contains elements of the other. There are certain risk factors where there is an almost equal allocation of both internal and external sources of risk. As such, we will also discuss a *blended risks* category.

EXTERNAL RISKS

The primary risks that are created external to hedge funds are those that are initiated by third parties. Following the previous classification of risk factors into primary and secondary factors, we can further subdivide these external risks into *primary factor external risks* and *secondary factor external risks*, as summarized in Exhibit 1.4.

EXHIBIT 1.4   Primary and Secondary External Operational Risk Factors

Factor	Primary/Secondary
Regulatory	Primary
Assets and investors concentration	Primary
Quality and length of relationship with tier-one service providers	Primary
Quality and length of relationship with tier-two service providers	Secondary
Counterparty oversight	Primary
Reputation of employees (including senior mgmt.) and firm	Primary

Primary Factor and Secondary Factor External Risks

The four primary factor and one secondary factor external risks fall into categories. They are *regulatory* risk, risks related to an individual hedge fund and investment manager's *assets* and investor base, a hedge fund's relationship with tier-one and tier-two third-party *service providers*, counterparty oversight and *reputational* issues.

Regulatory Risks

Hedge funds are subject to the laws and regulatory regimes of the particular jurisdictions in which they operate. In most cases, the majority of a hedge funds regulatory risks emanate from the laws and rules of jurisdictions in which their funds are domiciled and where their marketing activities are carried out. Certain jurisdictions have financial regulatory structures that require hedge funds to be registered, in one form or another. These registration requirements often come along with ongoing disclosure and reporting requirements. Additionally, such regulatory regimes may potentially expose hedge funds to audits or onsite exams by regulators. If a violation of these regulatory requirements occurs, most regulators have the ability to impose financial penalties, restrict a hedge fund's activity, or suspend it all together.

Asset-Related Risks

There are a number of potential risks related to both the assets under management of both a hedge fund organization as a whole as well as the assets of each individual underlying hedge fund strategy and vehicles managed. While related, these risk factors should be distinguished from the analysis of the firm's continued financial stability, which we will discuss in the subsequent section on primary factors of internal risks.

First, let us turn to assets under management of the underlying hedge fund strategy. We could take a more granular approach toward discussing a hedge fund strategy's assets by focusing on a particular vehicle (e.g., the assets of an onshore fund versus an offshore fund), or, on an even more microscopic level, on the assets of a particular share class within the particular fund (e.g., onshore fund share class A). However, in practical terms, it is most relevant to discuss the assets of an entire hedge fund strategy as opposed to the above-mentioned striations. That being said, for the purposes of this discussion, hedge fund strategy refers to similar hedge fund vehicles managed with materially the same terms and not hedge fund strategies that participate in similar markets but are offered in different versions, say, in terms of leverage applied.

Operational risks pertinent to assets under management can relate to both substantial increases and decreases in hedge fund strategy assets. The word *substantial* here is a relative term. For example, redemption of $50 million from a $300 million long/short fund could be viewed as substantial, whereas the same $50 million redemption from a $2.5 billion event-driven fund would not be viewed in the same light. It is also worth noting that the time frame during which these increases and decreases occur is relevant. Let us discuss substantial asset decreases first.

If a hedge fund strategy begins to lose substantial assets under management, there is often, to borrow a term from technical market analysis, a *signaling effect* that occurs. Similar to dominoes knocking each over one by one, investor fears can begin to spread like wildfire and a run on the bank occurs. The hedge fund community, being conscious of this type of contagious market hysteria, has created several barricades to dam the flow of investors' capital from their funds, including redemption gates, early redemption penalties, and notice periods.

Redemption gate provisions place a predefined restriction on the amount of withdrawals that may occur from a hedge fund during a particular redemption period. The decision to enact the provision, or *lower the gate*, generally lies with the hedge fund manager. Early redemption penalties, also known as *exit fees*, are charges assessed to investors for redeeming capital prior to a previously stated date. This period is typically referred to as a hedge fund's *lockup period*. Exit fees can be distinguished from redemption gates in the sense that their purpose is to discourage investors from redeeming capital as opposed to setting strict limits on capital outflows. Investors should also be conscious of the potential negative implications associated with required redemption notice periods. This period refers to the length of time after investors provide notice to a hedge fund of their intention to redeem capital that they must wait until this redemption is effected and capital is paid out to them by the hedge fund. Some notice periods are as short as 30 calendar days, while others can range as long as 120 business days or longer. When reviewing the terms of notice periods investors should take care to note the distinction between calendar and business days.

Additionally, investors, and their advisors, should be especially conscious of the interaction of these redemption terms and make sure that they are not the last one left standing at the end of a long line for redemptions. For example, a hedge fund with a 10% redemption gate, a two-year lockup with a 10% redemption penalty, and 120-business-days' calendar notice for redemptions poses a greater liquidity risk to investors than a fund with a 30% gate, monthly liquidity (i.e., no redemption penalty or gates), and 30-days' calendar notice.

Similar risk factors exist for a hedge fund strategy that notices marked increases in assets over a relatively short time period. For example, you would expect to see a hedge fund's assets, notwithstanding capacity restrictions, increase over time. A $500 million increase for a $2 billion hedge fund strategy over the course of one-year would not necessarily be viewed as substantial. The same $500 million capital infusion into the $2 billion strategy over the course of two months might be viewed differently. Investors should monitor a hedge fund strategy's asset levels carefully. This analysis can provide insight into such things as remaining strategy capacity, attention the investment manager is paying to a particular strategy (which can also be reflected in performance), and investor confidence in the manager's investment thesis.

Similar risks exist surrounding the assets of the investment manager, that is to say across all underlying hedge fund strategies managed by a particular organization. The analysis of these risks is most relevant in investment managers who follow the general trend of modern hedge fund incubators. Under these structures, a single investment manager houses several related strategies, which are generally seeded through the proprietary capital of the investment manager. The logic behind this type of organization is that there are both investment synergies and operational efficiencies that can be capitalized on as a result of everyone living under one roof. For the purposes of this discussion, let us say that our investment manager, we will call it Jason Capital Management, has $2 billion in aggregate firm-wide assets under management. These assets are divided among the following strategies:

- Jason Credit Opportunities Funds: $1.5 billion
- Jason Emerging Markets Funds: $380 million
- Jason Renewable Energy Funds: $75 million
- Jason Multistrategy Funds: $45 million

It is clear that the Jason Credit Opportunities Funds make up the lion's share of Jason Capital Management's assets under management. If the Credit Opportunities Funds' assets were to decline substantially, perhaps due to poor performance, it is likely that the senior management of Jason Capital Management may elect to close the firm as the revenue generated by the firm's other funds might not make up for the losses of the credit funds. Additionally, since in this example performance was a key driver of redemptions, the fund may be so under water, that is to say, far away from its high-water mark, that the portfolio managers might view closing the fund as more financially attractive than to keep running the business without collecting performance fees. Furthermore, it might not even be financially viable to keep running the firm with these asset losses due to basic overhead and salary expenses. Consequently, investors in the firm's other products should be conscious of both the assets of Jason Capital Management as a whole and its flagship Credit Funds.

Service Providers

Hedge funds rely on service providers for several reasons. Some service providers provide a sense of independent oversight to the firm; others simply provide a service or technology that the hedge fund does not have the expertise to develop internally or where developing such a technology would not be cost effective. The primary service providers utilized by hedge funds are the auditor, administrator, prime broker, legal counsel, custodian, information technology providers, and, more recently, third-party cash-management firms. As the following discussion will illustrate, many of these service providers are beginning to offer a larger array of services outside of their traditional fields, such as administrators offering information technology services, and are evolving into more full-service providers than the single-service relics of the past in order to compete for increasingly demanding, yet lucrative, hedge fund business.

Auditor The traditional role of the hedge fund *auditor* has primarily been to maintain a fund's official books and records and prepare its audited financial statements. Today these are still the primary and most important functions performed by a hedge fund's auditor. That being said, compared to the services provided in the early days of the hedge fund industry, modern hedge fund audit practices offer a wider array of services, including assistance with hedge fund registration and development, assistance with management of the internal accounting function such as providing software for this function, tax planning and compliance with tax reporting requirements, and regulatory compliance. It is worth noting that exempt commodity pool operators and hedge funds that are not SEC registered are not legally required to prepare audited financial statements; but in the modern hedge fund environment, investors would generally not allocate to a fund that has not prepared these financial statements, making the role of the auditor crucial.

Administrator In today's environment, most hedge fund *administrators* either are large standalone firms that have been in the administration business for some time or are newly formed administration companies nestled within large investment banks that typically have large prime-brokerage operations as well. Administrators often have offices across multiple time zones, in order to provide 24-hour rolling coverage, and in certain offshore hedge fund havens around the world such as the Cayman Islands and Bermuda.

In the early years of the hedge fund industry, administrators offered two primary types of services: fund accounting, which includes independent pricing of the portfolio, and shareholder servicing. Within the fund accounting function, the types of services traditionally provided include:

- Trade capture
- Valuations
- Calculation of profit and loss on a daily, weekly, and monthly basis
- Calculation of fees and accruals
- Calculation of net asset value and preparation of financial statements
- Investment accounting
- Fee calculations
- Partnership accounting

- Financial accounting/general ledger maintenance
- Daily profit and loss and net asset value reporting
- Performance measurement
- Tax preparation
- Reporting for investment managers and their investors
- Preparation of weekly/monthly financial statements

The primary services provided by the shareholder services function generally include:

- Overseeing the subscription and redemption processing, which includes receiving and processing all the relevant documentation and complying with hedge fund–specific criteria such as required redemption notice periods, lockups, and potential redemption penalties
- Ensuring compliance with the anti-money-laundering and know-your-client requirements in each jurisdiction
- Tax reporting for investors

Similar to the audit industry, administrators have been eager to meet the growing demands of their hedge fund clients in recent years by both enlarging the suite of services offered and increasing the integration of their traditional administration services with other hedge fund service providers. Other types of services offered by administrators in recent years include:

Corporate Services
- Maintaining minute books and statutory records
- Convening meetings, providing company secretaries, and preparing all necessary filings
- Managing regulatory requirements and liaising with company registrars

Other Types of Services
- Assistance with fund creation and setup
- Maintenance of financial records
- Corporate secretarial services
- Coordination of the audit process and stock exchange reporting
- Prime broker reconciliation
- Structuring of alternative investment instruments and products

There has also been a tendency in recent years for nascent hedge fund managers who do not have the expertise or resources to manage an internal accounting function to outsource this function to the fund's administrator. As a result, several hedge fund administrators have developed technology platforms in recent years that provide straight-through processing and connectivity between a hedge fund and a third-party administrator's front, middle, and back-office functions.

Prime Broker   Commensurate with the exponential growth of the hedge fund industry, the *prime brokerage* business has witnessed substantial growth in the past few years. The following services are typically packaged into the current hedge fund prime brokerage agreement:

- Custodial services including clearing, asset servicing, and custody
- Leverage financing
- Executing the hedge funds trades
- Lending securities short
- Providing short-term financing for leverage

Other types of premium services that have begun to take on more importance in recent years include:

- Capital introduction
- Office space leasing and servicing, which has led to the so-called *hedge fund hotels* in major financial centers around the word
- Consulting services on a wide range of issues from regulatory compliance to operational audits

Legal Counsel   A hedge fund's *legal counsel* serves to provide the core legal advice to the investment manager. Depending on the jurisdictional location of both the investment manager and the underlying hedge fund vehicles, many hedge funds have both domestic (also referred to as *onshore*) and international (commonly called *offshore*) legal counsel. The typical types of basic services offered by law firms to hedge funds include:

- Initial fund creation documentation
- Ongoing legal advice
- Assistance with maintenance of continual legal filing requirements
- Changes in fund documentation

Certain law firms also provide higher levels of service, including:

- Compliance consulting
- Mock regulatory audits
- Employee training on both investment- and non-investment-related issues

Many law firms will also provide a hedge fund with individuals who will sit on the board of either the investment manager or the individual hedge fund or both.

Custodian   A hedge fund utilizes the services of a *custodian*, similar to the way one purchasing a house utilizes the services of an escrow agent to hold the fund's assets, which include both cash and actual securities. Additionally, many prime brokers serve as custodian to the hedge funds they administer.

The typical range of services provided by a hedge fund custodian include:

- Dividend collection
- Addressing corporate actions including exercises of rights and options
- Making margin payments

The important role of a custodian is typically overlooked by many hedge fund investors. Hedge fund assets generally are held with a custodian, including cash in the fund as well as the actual securities. One key point of inquiry for any hedge fund investor when evaluating a hedge fund's relationship with a custodian is whether assets held by the custodian are in the name of the custodian or the hedge fund. Assets which are not held in the name of the hedge fund could potentially expose those assets to other capital commitments of the custodian. If, for example, the custodian were to become insolvent, this could put a hedge fund's investors at greater risk of losing their capital then they would be if the assets were held in the name of the hedge fund.

Information Technology Providers   Hedge funds, like most modern businesses, have a set of basic *information technology* (IT) needs. Large, established hedge funds typically have dedicated in-house IT personnel, whereas smaller, developing hedge funds typically outsource the bulk of this function. Whether the function is maintained in-house or outsourced, all hedge funds rely in some way on some sort of third-party provider for information technology service or support. An example of this on a very basic level would be power for servers from the local utility or reliance on the phone company for Internet connectivity.

On a very primitive level, the infrastructural IT needs of hedge funds include setting up and servicing such basic hardware as desktop computers, networks, servers, and other hardware technologies. Increasingly, IT firms oversee the installation and maintenance of trading systems and platforms, Internet systems, enterprise systems, customer relationship management (CRM) systems, and software development. IT firms also oversee the development of integrated network, computer, voice, and security solutions, including communications room design, electronic communication solutions, and secure remote connectivity.

More recently the bulk of a hedge fund's IT demands focus on software development—both the creation of proprietary technologies for use in investment and non-investment-related matters and the integration of third-party products onto unified proprietary platforms. This type of software and data integration occurs across multiple parts of the firm, including the portfolio management, trading, back-office, compliance, and risk-management functions.

In addition to technology-related business continuity and disaster-recovery concerns, which will be covered in a later section, investors should be conscious of the levels of service being provided to a hedge fund, the appropriateness and scalability of the hardware, and the firm's reliance on service providers (i.e., does the firm rely very heavily on one IT service provider or has the firm diversified this reliance across multiple providers?).

Cash Management Providers   In a world where hedge funds are compared against each other primarily on the basis of investment returns, there has been a trend in recent years to outsource the management of outstanding cash balances to third parties that specialize in generating increased returns from this residual cash through its active management. Proponents of outsourced *cash management* cite several benefits of placing this function in the hands of a dedicated third party, including higher returns on the cash invested in the cash management firm's products through the consolidation of the total amount of investable cash assets, enhanced liquidity management, increased simplification of the cash reconciliation process, and the mitigation of risk to hedge funds of dealing with multiple banks, brokers, and counterparties.

The primary service offered by these cash management firms include the aggregation of a hedge fund's residual cash from multiple sources such as clearing firm accounts, custody accounts, bank accounts, and prime brokers into one aggregate account for centralized cash management. Depending on a number of factors, including a hedge fund's risk appetite, premium placed on liquidity, and trading style, cash management firms invest cash in a wide variety of financial instruments, including short-term commercial paper, foreign currency, investment-grade bonds, and Treasury notes.

Recently, as a result of both the turmoil in the credit markets and the high-profile failures of two large cash management firms, there have been some concerns among hedge fund investors and hedge funds alike concerning the activities of these cash management firms. In particular, both investors and hedge funds are now more than ever focusing on the investment mandates of cash management products and in particular the average maturity of these cash management funds' holdings.

Counterparty Oversight   As outlined above, a hedge fund works with myriad different service providers. Some of the service providers can also be *counterparties*. According to the online glossary of the U.S. Commodity Futures Trading Commission (CFTC), a counterparty can be defined in part as "the opposite party in a bilateral agreement, contract, or transaction, such as a swap." The CFTC glossary further goes on to define *counterparty risk* in part as "the risk associated with the financial stability of the party entered into contract with."[11]

In a hedge fund operational due diligence context, investors should take care to understand how a hedge fund goes about strategically managing its counterparty relationships. Among the main hedge fund counterparties are prime brokers, and this is the example we will focus on. In this context, an example of such a consideration would be where a hedge fund has sourced the majority of its financing requirements from a single prime broker or multiple prime brokers. Often diversity in prime brokerage relationships is preferred for the sole reason that overall counterparty risk is minimized in the event of the failure of one institution. That being said, hedge funds may be able to acquire more beneficial terms if they place a larger piece of business with a single prime broker as opposed to spreading themselves too thin. The hedge fund organization should have processes in place to monitor these counterparty relationships and make such financing decisions, in the case of prime brokers, strategically.

A second major area of hedge fund counterparty risk relates to the contracts typically entered into by hedge funds for derivatives transactions with other parties. The most common agreement in use today was created by the New York–based trade organization, the International Swaps and Derivatives Association (ISDA), and is called the *ISDA Master Agreement*. There are currently two versions of the ISDA Master Agreement, a 1992 edition and a 2002 edition.

The ISDA Master Agreement lists the general terms and conditions of the agreement but does not refer to any specific derivatives transactions between the parties. The preprinted ISDA Master Agreement form can be modified via a manually produced Schedule that allows the parties to make modifications to the Master Agreement. Any details of specific transactions will be included in what is known as the Confirmations entered into by the parties to the ISDA Master Agreement. In addition to the ISDA Master Agreement, the organization also produces a credit support annex. This annex allows parties to an ISDA Master Agreement to reduce their credit risk by requiring the out-of-the-money party to post collateral.

There are a number of issues that a hedge fund may negotiate when entering into an ISDA agreement with counterparties. As part of the operational due diligence process, investors should take measures to understand whether a hedge fund has taken the time to thoroughly vet any ISDA agreements it has entered into and what specific terms it has negotiated for. Investors should also inquire as to the number of ISDAs a hedge fund has entered into and with which counterparties. Some of the more common points of negotiation between hedge funds and counterparties in regard to ISDA agreements include:

- Termination events
  - Scope
  - Notification procedures
- Key person events
- Reporting covenants
- Length of margin locks
- Triggers
  - NAV triggers
  - Supercollateralization triggers
- Cross-defaults
- Setoff
- Collateral:
  - What kind of collateral is acceptable
  - Amount of collateral
  - Whether the agreement is bilateral (both parties provide collateral) or unilateral (only one party provides collateral)
  - Whether rehypothecation is permitted
  - Requirements to be held in separate custodial account
  - Mechanisms for third-party determination of valuations if disputes between parties cannot be resolved
- Thresholds and laddered thresholds
- Minimum transfer amounts
- Length of cure periods
- Tax consideration
- ERISA considerations

Additionally, as part of the operational due diligence process, investors should understand a hedge fund's internal policies and procedures toward approving a new counterparty, monitoring its relationships with existing counterparties, and finally terminating a counterparty.

Reputational Risks

Reputational risk is one of the thorniest issues in modern risk management today. Sometimes referred to as *headline risk*, we classify this as an external risk to the firm because, despite the fact that the action, or the person who had previously been associated with the action that is the source of the reputational risk, comes from within the hedge fund organization, the weight or value given to this action comes from *outside* the firm. The concept is nothing new. Outlandish scandals and the uncovering of skeletons from the past have derailed the careers of many a Hollywood starlet and aspiring politician. For entertainers, the old adage "There is no such thing as bad publicity" cannot be said of the clandestine hedge fund industry. In this realm, perhaps "No news is good news" is more appropriate.

The term *reputational risk* began to gain popularity when it was used in a report by the Bank of England related to an inquiry into the collapse of Barings Bank.[12] The term has subsequently gone on to be defined as "the risk of indirect losses to earnings arising from negative public opinion."[13] With increased focus on operational risk in recent years, so, too, has come a focus on reputational risk. Investors, particularly large allocators, such as pensions and family offices, have become more conscious of the potential negative implications for their reputations should questions arise concerning the reputation of a hedge fund manager to whom they gave money. The flip-side of this equation has been that hedge funds have become very attuned to this risk by more carefully screening the backgrounds of potential employees and cleaning up loose ends that might be lingering in their past. All of this has led to the phenomenal growth of the background investigation industry, which will be discussed in more detail in Chapter 4.

INTERNAL RISKS

We now turn our discussion to operational risk factors whose sources are found within the hedge fund itself. These risks include valuation, personnel, financial stability, operations connectivity, and tax practices. As with our discussion of external risks, we can subdivide these internal risks into primary and secondary factors, as summarized in Exhibit 1.5.

Valuation Techniques and Pricing Sources

The way a hedge fund goes about determining the value of its investments is the most important issue on the forefront of every operational due diligence review. We have classified the risk factors associated with valuation and

EXHIBIT 1.5   Primary and Secondary Internal Operational Risk Factors

Factor	Primary/Secondary
Valuation techniques and pricing sources	Primary
Compensation and employee turnover	Primary
Firm stability (including expense analysis)	Primary
Operations connectivity	Primary
Tax practices	Secondary
Trade life cycle	Primary
Fund terms	Primary
Transparency and reporting	Primary
Cash controls and management	Primary

pricing as internal risks because, similar to our discussion of the classification of reputational risk, while the actual valuation is defined as what the secondary market would pay for a security, the source of this risk is internal to the fund.

There are obvious reasons for the importance of ensuring a fund has appropriate valuation procedures in place. First, there are considerations of fraud. If, for example, a hedge fund portfolio's holdings are claimed by the manager to be worth $20 million, when the market would value them at merely $5 million, the fund manager would be claiming false profits, and subsequently collecting inflated fees, on these mispriced securities. Investors falling victim to this type of scheme would see the value of their investments, which had previously been worth much more, decline to practically nil. Even worse, investors would generally not recover anything from the remaining assets of the fund because the fund would most likely be deemed insolvent and there would be a long line of creditors with greater seniority ahead of these investors. This scenario is similar to the situation in which many investors in Michael Berger's Manhattan Investment Fund found themselves when the fund failed in 2000.

A second reason why the proper valuation of a hedge fund's holdings is of paramount importance relates to the fund's monthly reporting and financial statements. It is a commonly held view that an operational red flag is raised if a fund has to restate its net asset value due to improper valuations in the past. This can have a number of negative repercussions for the fund, including significant financial implications.

As a result, the vast majority of modern hedge funds work with third-party administrators to independently price a fund's holdings. Depending on the size of the hedge fund, as a secondary check, many funds will maintain parallel books internally and determine the prices of their fund's holdings independently from the administrator. Generally, on a daily, weekly, and monthly basis, these hedge funds and the administrators reconcile these two values to determine any discrepancies. This scenario is the typical situation for a hedge fund that primarily trades in highly liquid markets, such as a long/short equity hedge fund.

Investors should be conscious of both the number and appropriateness of pricing sources utilized. Depending on the type of instruments traded, it is considered best practice to have at least two, and generally three, independent pricing sources. If more than one price is utilized, investors should take care to note which pricing sources a hedge fund's policies dictate as the primary and secondary sources. For example, major pricing sources for equities include Bloomberg and Reuters, and you would expect to see one of those sources as a primary pricing source. However, if a fund, for example, holds credit default swaps, an investor would expect to find a source that specializes in this area, such as Mark-it Partners, with Reuters perhaps as a secondary source.

As the worlds of hedge funds and private equity funds begin to converge, many hedge fund hybrids have emerged that hold a certain percentage of their portfolio in illiquid private equity investments. Sometimes, these more illiquid investments are also held in side-pockets which are separate from the hedge fund. An example of such an investment would be an investment in physical assets, such as a fleet of airplanes, or real estate holdings, such as office buildings. Additionally, certain hedge fund styles call for investing in distressed securities. The markets for these types of positions are often very thinly traded, and in some cases there is not even a secondary market for these holdings, which presents certain valuation challenges. Hedge funds in these situations often price these holdings themselves through the use of internal proprietary models. Some funds, depending on the size of the position, will engage third-party valuation consultants with specialized knowledge specific to the holdings in question to independently verify the value assigned by the hedge funds to these positions.

A second consideration is the documentation of and adherence to pricing policies. Hedge funds typically have two pricing policies: one that is maintained internally, and an official pricing policy that is contained in the fund's offering memorandum. A hedge fund's administrator is generally obligated to follow the offering memorandum policy. These official policies are intentionally vague when compared to the fund's internal policies so as to provide administrators with increased flexibility in determining prices. By contrast, internal policies are often very detailed and provide a step-by-step guide as to how a fund will go about determining the prices of all of the different types of instruments that a fund may hold.

There is a wide variety among the pricing techniques outlined in these policies. An example of an area in which this is prevalent is the actual price utilized. Some hedge funds use the last exchange-traded price, whereas others use a midpoint or average price. Still other funds will use the ask or bid price. Understanding the appropriateness of a hedge fund's pricing policies is essential to a review of its valuation techniques.

Contingent on a number of factors including the size of a hedge fund, as indicated by assets under management, and the types of instruments traded, many funds have internal pricing or valuation committees. These committees often consist of senior management throughout the firm and seek to provide another internal check of a hedge fund's valuation techniques. The members of these committees, either via their role on the internal pricing committees, or other related committees, also typically review related matters such as best execution and counterparty approvals. For hedge funds that hold illiquid securities, the oversight of the pricing committee is of particular importance. Investors should attempt to understand exactly what takes place in a particular hedge fund's pricing committee, the powers of the committee (i.e., is it merely an oversight committee or can it exercise certain veto powers?), the frequency of the committee's meetings, and how often the value of illiquid securities is revalidated. In summary, understanding a hedge fund's valuation techniques is of critical importance and investors should carefully vet the techniques applied and pricing sources utilized, and ensure that independence and consistency are prevalent throughout the process.

Compensation and Employee Turnover

It is often said that a business is only as good as its employees. That certainly is true of the hedge fund industry, where intellectual capital is almost always positively correlated with physical capital under management. Hiring and retaining smart, talented, and innovative employees is a constant challenge for the modern hedge fund manager. This is especially true in an increasingly competitive environment. In 2004, there were estimates of approximately 8,500 hedge funds in existence.[14] By 2006, this number had grown to estimates of 9,500.[15] Current estimates place this number at well over 11,000. With this increased competition for talent, star hedge fund employees are making increased demands not just for salary and title but for equity ownership participation as well. Some hedge funds have embraced this top talent and provided these stars with different forms of equity ownership. Equity and compensation that vests over a period of time can be distributed in a number of ways, including various phantom equity arrangements and deferred-compensation structures. This golden handcuffing approach has reaped benefits for some firms but has hurt others as certain trading styles, for instance, have fallen in and out of favor and firms have found themselves attached at the hip to certain individuals. There are potentially substantial monetary and reputational consequences of entering into a poorly structured deal. Investors should attempt to gain an understanding of the nature of any long-term employment contracts and compensation structures in place at a hedge fund and the potential damaging effects to the firm should the terms of these contracts be breached.

Investors should also take care to understand exactly who performs certain duties within an organization. This is not always easy to do, especially in smaller hedge funds, where employees typically wear several hats. However, taking care to understand exactly who does what will allow investors to filter any spin a hedge fund may later put on an employee's role should he or she leave the firm. This is particularly true in the case of the departures of research analysts, who often provide coverage across multiple market sectors.

Employee turnover should be carefully monitored by investors for several reasons. First, in the increasingly competitive hedge fund space, it is becoming more common for teams of people to defect from one hedge fund to another as opposed to individuals. Once again, this is particularly true in the case of research analysts. This often makes sense from the future employer's perspective, because they are inheriting a proven well-functioning unit that can often coexist in a hedge fund's existing structure rather than hiring an individual who will need to acclimate himself to the existing organization. A second reason investors should monitor employee turnover carefully is the signaling effect it creates. This is especially true of more senior management within a firm. From an operational perspective, for example, it raises many more questions in the minds of both existing and prospective investors if a hedge fund's *chief financial officer* (CFO) departs the firm as opposed to the departure of two or three junior staff accountants. Finally, investors should be concerned about employee turnover due to the somewhat secretive nature of the hedge fund industry. Many hedge funds invest substantial amounts of time and money into research and developing proprietary trading models and strategies. Employees intimately familiar with a particular firm's techniques are highly valued by competitors. While many hedge funds do require their employees to sign agreements that prevent them from disclosing this proprietary information, proving a violation of these agreements once employees have left the firm is often difficult. In addition to basic information security measures, such as preventing employees from plugging in external hard drives to personal computers (PCs) and monitoring e-mails to accounts outside the firm, investors should be cautious of who has access to certain types of information within a firm and whether, should they leave, there is potential for this type of valuable information to leave with them.

Key person risk is another factor worth considering. Many hedge fund vehicles contain key person clauses that allow investors to redeem their investment without material penalties, subject to certain terms, in the event that a key person becomes incapacitated or leaves the firm. Investors should take steps to ensure that it is clear who is defined as a key person or persons and what exactly constitutes incapacity or disassociation from the firm. This becomes especially relevant to funds with poor liquidity terms and hard lockups. For example, consider a hedge fund with a two-year hard lockup. If the fund's portfolio manager decides to spend 30% of his time lecturing, rather than managing the fund, would this trigger the key person clause? The answer is probably not, and if the clause is not triggered, investors would be stuck, in this example, for two years before they could get their money out of the fund. What would happen if this percentage were increased to 40%, or even 60%? While it is often difficult to anticipate these types of issues before they happen, investors should try to gain clarity on the specifics of key person clauses prior to subscribing to a particular hedge fund. In addition to asking hedge funds directly about any employee turnover as part of initial and ongoing due diligence, many funds will include the details of any turnover in their monthly or quarterly letters to existing investors.

Firm Stability

A hedge fund is not just a trading desk; it is a business. Just like any other business, hedge funds have a series of basic expenses. These range from the mundane, paying the electric bill and keeping the employee kitchen refrigerator stocked, to the more exotic, legendary large bonuses. While I am not suggesting that investors request to see copies of a hedge fund's phone bills, it is worth gaining an understanding of the types of expenses involved in running the investment management organization on a daily basis as well as the controls in place to monitor these expenses. Additionally, investors should be conscious of which types of expenses are being charged directly to the underlying hedge fund vehicles and which are being charged to the investment management organization. In addition, investors should employ a second level of expense analysis and inquire as to how certain expenses are being allocated among the different funds. Such analysis can alert investors to certain Big Bath accounting practices, where all expenses are inappropriately lumped into one bucket. The classic example of this is marketing and travel expenses. Investors should take note if one particular hedge fund strategy is being charged its appropriate share of marketing expenses for that strategy or if the marketing expenses for other hedge fund strategies managed by the firm are being lumped disproportionately into one fund. If the latter is the case, then investors should question the hedge fund as to why they are footing the bill for the marketing of another fund.

Issues of scalability and capacity should be balanced against the considerations of the length of a particular fund's lockup when evaluating a hedge fund organization's long-term financial viability. This is particularly a concern for newly established hedge funds that expend large amounts of capital on infrastructure and hiring top talent in anticipation of future asset raising. Contingent on performance, these assets may never be raised and, under the pressure of these large expenses piling up, a fund may be forced, by both creditors and investors, to close its doors. Expenditures on certain things such as art or elaborate furniture and office equipment should be monitored as well.

Operations Connectivity

Communication and transparency of information within a hedge fund organization is key. This is especially important for senior management and those in a risk-management role within a hedge fund. If these individuals do not have access to the exposures and daily risks the firm's funds are taking, they cannot begin to manage these risks.

In a well-functioning hedge fund, the engine that drives this transparency lies in the seamless connectivity of a firm's front, middle, and back offices. The front office is primarily responsible for trading operations. The middle office monitors and manages risk exposure. The back office typically focuses on reconciliation and settlement. A competent chief operating officer and chief financial officer should oversee this process so that there is a direct flow of information through this pipeline. Breakdowns in this process often lead to poor reporting and monitoring capabilities. Additionally, lags in this process can deteriorate the real-time monitoring capabilities of risk managers, which can impact the implementation of positions or hedges and subsequently impact performance. Today many hedge funds are relying on third-party platforms to ensure constant connectivity in this process. In the early stages of development, many prime brokers developed platforms that locked their hedge fund clients into front-end systems. Many hedge funds did not like this lack of flexibility and, as a result, newly developed prime broker platforms focus instead on assisting funds in overseeing the connectivity of the middle and back offices while allowing hedge funds to remain flexible in the front-office function. This, in part, has allowed these funds to achieve more competitive pricing for stock loans and financings.

There is an element of communication that is rooted in the organizational culture of a hedge fund. As simple as it may seem, there are certain physical cues investors should be cautious of that may provide insight to gauge an organization. Indeed, a simple example is the functional office space of a firm. Do compliance personnel sit on the same floor as traders, or are they locked away in an office on a different floor?

Tax Practices

As the old adage goes, two things are certain in life: death and taxes. Like all businesses, hedge funds, and their investors, may be susceptible to certain tax requirements. In the United States, for example, there are the many basic taxes that a hedge fund organization will be required to pay, as most employers are, as part of the normal course of business. These include Medicare and Social Security tax and federal and state unemployment taxes. Of more interest to hedge fund investors are the tax implications an investment in a hedge fund may have for them.

One area of consideration for U.S. investors is whether a hedge fund is classified as a trader or investor for federal income tax purposes. Generally, most hedge fund investors will find it beneficial if a hedge fund is designated as a trader. This classification allows several of the hedge fund's expenses, including interest, to be deductible as business expenses. However, if a hedge fund is classified as an investor for tax purposes, then the expenses must be itemized in order to be deducted. There are also a number of limitations to which these itemized expenses may be subject that could have the effect of reducing, or even completely eliminating, a hedge fund's investor's deductions. The classification as either a trader or investor has traditionally been a gray area under negotiation among a hedge fund, its investors, and the Internal Revenue Service (IRS). The risk is that the IRS could challenge a hedge fund's trader status. There are a number of factors that are considered in making the determination as to a hedge fund's trader or investor status, including the nature of the income generated by the fund, the turnover of the portfolio, and the hedge fund's particular investment strategy as outlined in the fund's offering documentation.

A second traditional area of concern to hedge fund investors is whether a hedge fund generates unrelated business taxable income (UBTI). UBTI can be thought of as the tax on income that federal income tax–exempt entities, such as charitable organizations, are required to pay. Income that falls under UBTI is that which is unrelated to the primary business normally carried out by the tax-exempt organization. An example of this would be a university, whose primary business is education, operating a concrete-manufacturing plant. That being said, UBTI does not typically include dividends, gains for the sale of capital assets, or interest. As such, hedge funds will not generally generate UBTI. Consequently, a domestic tax-exempt investor's potential income from an investment in a hedge fund will also not be subject to UBTI. There are a number of specific situations under which a hedge fund may generate UBTI. This is generally considered disadvantageous to a tax-exempt hedge fund investor because, in addition to the investor having to pay additional taxes at a higher corporate rate, there are also additional tax-preparation requirements. Investors should inquire whether a hedge fund has ever generated UBTI and what steps a fund has taken to ensure UBTI will not be generated in the future.

Similar concerns arise for non-U.S. tax-exempt investors surrounding *effectively connected income* (ECI). Foreign investors are not generally required to file U.S. tax returns. The exception to this rule is where they have ECI that is based on the active conduct of a U.S.-based business. It is important to note that the conduct must be active. Passive investments do not generally give rise to ECI. An investment made by a non-U.S. investor in a hedge fund's limited partnership vehicle would generate ECI for a foreign investor. To prevent this, many foreign investors elect to invest in a hedge fund via an offshore blocker corporation. Foreign tax-exempt investors should be careful to review how a hedge fund is structured in order to ensure that unwanted ECI is not generated.

Investors should be conscious of the changing nature of the hedge fund tax environment. Often changes in the external legislative and regulatory tax regimes can have significant effects on both hedge funds and their investors. A recent example of this was the Financial Accounting Standards Board's (FASB) release of Interpretation No. 48 (FIN 48), Accounting for Uncertainty in Income Taxes in July 2006. FIN 48 was an interpretation of FASB Statement 109, and seeks to provide guidance on the recognition of uncertain tax positions. FIN 48 applied to all entities that prepare *generally accepted accounting principles* (GAAP) financial statements, including hedge funds. One effect of FIN 48 on hedge funds was that it caused managers to reconsider the way in which they recognized and measured certain tax benefits in regard to a *more-likely-than-not* threshold of such benefits being sustained by the IRS.

Another, more recent legislative change was the passing of the Tax Technical Corrections Act of 2007 by the House of Representatives. This act, in part, provided clarification in regard to Section 470 of the IRS Code. Section 470 relates to so-called sale-in and lease-out transactions, in particular the loss deferral rules related to property leased to tax-exempt entities. Before the signing of the Technical Corrections Act, under Section 470, hedge funds with certain types of investors such as tax-exempt or foreign partners would have been subject to certain limitations on particular deductions. It should be noted that now Section 470 does not apply to the typical hedge fund.

There are a number of other considerations investors should evaluate when considering both the appropriateness of a hedge fund's internal tax planning and the effect an investment in a particular hedge fund may have on them directly. These other considerations can include how active a role a hedge fund takes in overseeing its tax planning as well as if a fund has taken into account special considerations for different tax treatments for investors from different U.S. states. Examples of other types of questions that could come up during an operational due diligence review of a hedge fund's tax practices include:

- Will full-up/fill-down, which is also known as stuffing clauses in partnership agreements, potentially mitigate the impact of mandatory basis adjustments since hedge funds will most likely not satisfy the electing investment partnership provisions?
- Does the fund adhere to an aggregate allocation method of tax lot layering?
- What is the tax approach taken with instruments such as credit default swaps? Is it mark to market, ordinary income, capital gain treatment, or a different approach? Why was this approach selected?
- In regard to total return swaps for stock baskets, how are wash sale and constructive sale rule triggers treated?
- Could original issue discounts and market discounts apply to distressed investments for tax purposes?

It should be noted that this discussion has primarily focused on the tax implications for both hedge funds and investors in U.S.-based hedge funds that follow GAAP. There are a host of other tax considerations and implications for investors in non-U.S.-based hedge funds that may operate under differing tax regimes. Investors should carefully vet such issues to ensure that a hedge fund has proper tax planning procedures in place and an understanding of trends of potential changing legislation in differing tax regimes so that investors will not incur undue taxes as a result of an investment in a particular hedge fund.

Trade Life Cycle

It is of paramount importance for investors to gain an understanding not only as to the investment thesis of a particular hedge fund (i.e., why it executes certain trades over others at certain times) but also of what happens after the decision is made to execute that trade. Investors should be able to track the life of a trade from the time the trade is placed until it is reconciled at month end and the entire process in between. One thing investors should look for within the life cycle of a trade is independence regarding the trading and reconciliation processes.

Examples of the types of issues that investors should gain an understanding of include:

- Who has authority to place trades?
- Do traders have responsibility for marking these trades?
- What is the average trading volume? How has this changed over time? Is the firm adequately staffed to handle such volume?
- What is the trade documentation process?
- If a blotter is used, who has final authority to review the blotter?
- What oversight is there internally within the hedge fund over individuals with trading authority?
- How are trades executed?
- How are trades allocated among different funds?
- What is the trade confirmation process? What percentage of confirmations are electronic versus paper confirmations?
- Do counterparties, for such instruments as swaps, provide daily position reporting?
- What happens in the event of a trade break?
- How are trade breaks investigated?
- Is there a hard deadline by which all trades must be reconciled?
- Does the third-party custodian hold custody of all the fund's assets or does the hedge fund hold custody of any assets?
- How frequently are cash and position reconciliations performed?
- Are reconciliations performed internally within the hedge fund, by the third-party administrator, or both?
- Depending on the instruments traded, are there dedicated individuals within the firm who focus on certain types of reconciliations that may require special expertise (i.e. bank debt)?

Gaining an understanding of these issues can provide useful insight into the efficiency, controls, and communication across a hedge fund's organization.

Fund Terms

Modern hedge funds have a multitude of different terms for investors. These terms can relate to a number of different facets of hedge fund investing, including the way in which a hedge fund manager is compensated, the timing and amount of investor redemptions, and policies relating to the occurrence of certain events such as key person provisions. The most common hedge fund terms are outlined below:

- Fees:
  - Management fee
  - Incentive fee (high-water mark, hurdle, claw-back, etc.)
- Lockups:
  - Length
  - Hard or soft?
- Redemptions:
  - Notice period
  - Frequency (monthly, quarterly, etc.)
- Gates:
  - Frequency
  - Size

Investors should inquire as to whether a hedge fund has provided certain more favorable terms to particular investors via side-letter arrangements. Investors should also compare the terms among different share classes within an individual hedge fund vehicle and among similar vehicles that are managed in substantially the same manner, which is sometimes referred to as being managed pari passu. It may be the case, for example, that a domestic version of a vehicle may charge a lower management fee but have a longer lockup than its offshore counterpart. If this is the case, and a particular investor does not place a premium on liquidity, then she may consider opting for the domestic vehicle.

Investors should, as part of the operational due diligence process, develop a general understanding as to what terms are generally considered to be within common market practice. When evaluating a new hedge fund for investment, investors should compare a particular hedge fund vehicle's terms against these market norms. If a hedge fund greatly deviates from these norms, investors should question whether there is a logical reason for this deviation. Additionally, if such a deviation is potentially disadvantageous to the investor, as with an overly long hard lockup, investors should consider whether they are being adequately compensated for these off market terms.

Transparency and Reporting

Transparency into a hedge fund organization provided to investors is often placed at premium. This transparency not only relates to gaining clarity into the underlying portfolio of a particular hedge fund, but also applies to gaining an understanding as to the inner workings of the hedge fund organization. Such insights may be gleaned during the course of the year from meetings with the hedge fund manager and reviews of investor letters. On an annual basis, more detailed specifics concerning the particular holdings of a hedge fund can be obtained from the financial statements.

Some larger hedge funds provide only limited transparency to certain large investors. Motivations for this may be well founded. These funds might not want to have word get out regarding their holdings and potentially have other hedge funds learn which positions they are invested in. Similarly, certain quantitative strategies might be concerned that particular approaches they use might be able to be reverse engineered by other market participants if their holdings list was released to too many investors.

Different hedge funds have different standards for the reporting that they provide to investors as well. Some hedge funds provide very detailed statistics on a monthly basis concerning a host of issues, including assets under management, makeup of the investor base, aggregate risk exposures, and top holdings. Others provide general market commentary with few specifics as to the holdings in a particular portfolio. Similarly, in regard to performance estimates, some hedge funds provide timely estimates and others do not. The ability to do this may be impacted by the particular strategy of the hedge fund in question; however, even within particular strategies there is wide variation surrounding the timing and so-called *quality* of net asset value estimates.

Investors may become frustrated by a lack of transparency into both investment processes and holdings and non-investment-related factors. Such transparency and reporting concerns should be vetted before an initial investment in a hedge fund is made. Additionally, investors should track continued transparency, timing, and quality of a hedge fund investor's disclosures and reporting to ensure that they are consistent with initial expectations. Often a delay in reporting, for example, can signify a red flag for other operational problems within an organization.

Cash Controls and Management

As referenced earlier, there had been a growing trend in recent years among hedge funds to outsource the cash management function to third-party cash management firms. However, with the recent turmoil in the markets many hedge funds have focused on bringing the oversight of the cash function in-house. As part of the operational due diligence process, investors should take steps to understand both the amounts of cash held by the fund and the way in which it is managed.

First, consider cash management relating to the hedge fund vehicles. Questions investors should consider include:

- How much cash do the funds typically hold?
- How have these cash levels varied over time?
- How much cash is held by counterparties (i.e., prime brokers)?
- How is cash on hand (also called *unencumbered cash*) managed? Where is this unencumbered cash stored?
- How are margin requirements managed?
- What is the cash-reconciliation process?
- If a third-party cash management firm is utilized, how is this process monitored internally by the hedge fund?

Investors should also be conscious what controls are in place within a hedge fund organization to control the movement of cash. Specifically, investors should address the following issues as part of an operational due diligence review:

- How is cash moved within the organization?
- What wire transfer controls are in place?
- How are bills of the management company paid?
- Who has authority to move cash within the organization?
- Are there multiple signatories required to move cash?
- Are there different levels of cash signatories (i.e., an A list and a B list)?
- Do different movements of different amounts of cash require different levels or numbers of cash signatories?
- Are signatures made electronically or on a physical document?
- Who ensures that the correct number of signatures is received?
- Is there an appropriate segregation of duties internally within the hedge fund as well as third-party oversight into the cash movement process?

Investors will have one less item to worry about by taking steps to properly ensure that a hedge fund is internally conscious of the importance of developing and maintaining proper cash management processes and controls.

BLENDED RISKS

Finally, we will discuss the *blended operational risk factors*. These are risks whose sources are found both within the hedge fund itself and in the external environment. These risks include technology and systems, business

EXHIBIT 1.6 Primary and Secondary Blended Operational Risk Factors

Factor	Primary/Secondary
Technology and systems	Primary
Business continuity and disaster recovery	Primary
Legal/compliance	Primary
Insurance	Secondary
Independence and oversight of the board of directors	Secondary

continuity and disaster recovery, legal and compliance, insurance, and a hedge fund's board of directors. As with our discussion of external risks, we can subdivide these internal risks into primary and secondary factors, as summarized in Exhibit 1.6.

Technology and Systems

Technology is an essential component of every hedge fund. Certain technical trading–based hedge fund strategies, such as managed futures, which traditionally have higher trading volumes, would not be able to function effectively without technology. The category of technology and systems is classified as a blended risk because while the majority of these systems are purchased from third-party vendors, that is to say from sources external to the fund itself, the choice of which systems to utilize, the implementation of these systems, and the ongoing maintenance and potential customization of such systems are all factors that are determined by the firm, which would create a source of risk that springs from inside the fund itself. It is worth noting that the previously mentioned considerations are not by any means limited solely to software. There should be equal, if not more, consideration paid to a hedge fund's choice of hardware as well.

The primary software programs utilized by hedge funds include those that facilitate the following functions:

- Customer relationship management (CRM)
- Fund accounting
- Portfolio management
- Data retention
- Electronic communication monitoring software

Additionally, hedge funds typically interface on a daily basis with such service providers as prime brokers and administrators either via a web-based portal maintained by the service provider or via a proprietary platform provided by the service provider that is installed on the desktop PCs of the hedge fund's employees.

In regard to hardware, the majority of hedge funds today have secure, dedicated server rooms with specialized cooling systems. Investors should take care to understand whether a firm has taken care to design its hardware network in such a way that it both considers the current needs of the firm and is scalable. The goal of such inquiries is to determine whether a hedge fund has the internal competency to make intelligent choices about its information technology requirements or whether it is simply blindly relying on the advice of third parties. For example, investors may wish to inquire as to what network topology a hedge fund has decided to implement. If the response is a bus network, it is worth asking why it selected that topology over a ring network, for example. Even if you are not the most technologically savvy person in the world, asking these types of questions will provide you with the opportunity to both determine whether the fund has thought about these types of issues and learn from its answers. Additionally, many hedge funds now have backup power-generation facilities. These will be discussed in more detail in the Business Continuity Planning and Disaster Recovery section.

Information security recently has become a very important issue in the hedge fund world. Hedge funds maintain a great deal of proprietary information and most go to great lengths to protect it. In addition to maintaining certain compliance policies that prevent employees from sharing such information with people outside the firm, hedge funds have also taken a number of technological and physical security measures as well. In relation to physical access to certain areas of an office, many hedge funds have restricted unauthorized employees from entering certain areas, where personnel records are kept, for example, through the use of access-limited key cards. Other firms have done away with key cards altogether and implemented eye-scanning or fingerprint-reading devices.

From a software perspective, many hedge funds closely monitor employees' Internet activities, e-mail, and personal trading activities via electronic surveillance systems. Specifically in regard to e-mail, firms tend to monitor e-mail correspondence for both message content and the types of files sent. This monitoring can also extend to remote-access devices such as BlackBerrys and cellular phones. Additionally, many firms now ban the use of external hardware devices, such as zip drives, so as to literally prevent people from walking out the door with proprietary information in their pocket. Firms also have begun to keep logs of which employees access certain parts of the firm's systems and the files accessed. By monitoring these electronic footprints, employers have the ability to detect, in the event information or files go missing or end up in the hands of the competition, the last person to access such information. All this may seem a bit cloak-and-dagger, but these firms deal with hundreds of millions of dollars in an age where information has become the printing press of currency.

Within larger hedge funds, the information technology function is generally overseen by a dedicated *chief technology officer* (CTO). At smaller shops, for cost effectiveness, the majority of the information technology function is outsourced to a third-party consulting firm that generally provides basic network administration services and ongoing helpdesk support. The relationship with these information technology consultants is usually overseen internally by a senior operations manager, typically a chief operating officer (COO) or chief financial officer (CFO), from the hedge fund. In evaluating the quality of a hedge fund's CTO or information technology provider, it is essential to ascertain their experience in dealing not just with financial institutions, but with hedge funds in particular. There is a certain set of basic needs all financial services firms have; however, a CTO who has previous hedge fund experience is typically more adept at addressing a firm's current needs as well as planning ahead of future growth.

Business Continuity Planning and Disaster Recovery

Since the tragic events of September 11, 2001, business continuity planning (BCP) and disaster recovery (DR) have been at the forefront of the hedge fund industry. Risks to BCP/DR come from both outside of a hedge fund and within it; consequently we shall classify this as a blended risk. The terms *business continuity* and *disaster recovery* are often erroneously lumped together and thought of as one function. They are indeed related but distinct concepts. Business continuity refers to a hedge fund's ability to continue operations in the event of a business disruption. Disaster recovery relates to a hedge fund's ability to restore itself back from a disaster event to the point where it was before the disaster occurred.

BCP/DR planning is particularly important for both hedge funds that participate in global markets and those that are investors that allocate capital to hedge funds all over the world. Let us consider the example of a hedge fund based in Hong Kong. It is 3 P.M. on Friday afternoon, and there is an earthquake that disrupts Internet and phone connectivity for the region. This prevents the fund from continuing to trade, but the markets stay open while others, who are not affected by the earthquake, are still participating in the market. When connectivity returns the following evening, the fund has realized significant losses and cannot attempt to rectify them because it is the weekend and the markets are closed. If this fund had created BCP/DR plans and activated them, it perhaps could have lessened or avoided these losses.

A disaster event does not need to be as large scale as an earthquake; it can be as limited as an employee spilling a cup of coffee on a server. Generally, we can classify the events that lead to business disruptions as either *exogenous*, coming from outside the firm, or *endogenous*, internal to the firm. Examples of exogenous events include terrorism, weather-related events (hurricanes, floods, etc.), and power failures. Types of endogenous events include hardware malfunction and employee error (i.e., an employee accidentally deleted essential files, leading to a business disruption).

Many funds turn to their information technology service provider to design and maintain the BCP/DR plan for them. In order to ensure that their planning efforts are appropriate, some hedge funds have recently begun to work with specialized consultants to evaluate their BCP/DR plans. The benefit of utilizing such BCP/DR consultants is that they add a degree of objectivity to the planning process and can avoid such things as the technology bias that may result from a third-party service provider utilizing technologies its staff is more familiar with rather than the best technology available.

Business continuity and disaster recovery planning spans all areas of the organization. Successful implementation of a BCP/DR plan requires the coordination of these different functions in order to keep the organization functioning as a whole.

Legal and Compliance

Hedge funds face a variety of risks related to both legal and compliance matters. There is also a separate category of regulatory risks associated with funds where either registration with a financial regulator is required or the fund is subject to oversight from this regulator, such as the Financial Services Authority (FSA) in the United Kingdom. We will bundle these regulatory risks as part of this legal and compliance discussion. The legal and compliance risks a hedge fund faces have their sources both externally, from such sources as the threat of lawsuits by third parties and legally binding contracts entered into by the firm, and internally, from the drafting of internal compliance policies and enforcement of these policies internally within the firm.

The legal and compliance function is generally overseen by a *chief compliance officer* (CCO). As with the chief technology officer role, the CCO role is generally shared in most hedge funds by either the firm's General Counsel, COO, or CFO. For specific legal functions, all hedge funds utilize the services of external counsel in one way or another. Typically, depending on the nature of the vehicles offered, most firms have onshore and offshore counsel. The role of the compliance function has evolved over time. In the early years of the hedge fund industry, compliance personnel traditionally focused on investment-related compliance. That means ensuring that any required regulatory filings were completed in a timely manner and ensuring that a hedge fund did not violate certain trading restrictions (e.g., not investing more than 20% in Chinese equities). Today the modern CCO focuses on a host of both investment and noninvestment issues related to a number of areas, including human resources, anti-money-laundering compliance, electronic communication monitoring, and workplace ethics. One interesting example of the growth of the non-investment-related duties of the CCO is related to human resources training. Many smaller hedge funds traditionally have outsourced this function to third-party providers that consolidate such things as payroll and benefits administration. Certain jurisdictions, however, have specific requirements that a competent CCO should be aware of. In the state of California, for example, there is a requirement that employers, including hedge funds, over a certain size provide mandatory sexual harassment training to employees. A standard benefits administrator might not be responsible for overseeing the implementation of this training and without a diligent CCO this could be overlooked, which could lead to a penalty levied by the state against the firm.

Many hedge funds also utilize the services of third-party compliance consultants. These firms provide a variety of services, including establishing a firm's initial compliance program, assisting with ongoing compliance training, and the conducting of mock audits, often modeled after an actual SEC examination. Depending on the nature of the contract with the fund, these firms also provide hedge funds with ongoing advice and news of regulatory and legal changes that may require revision of their existing policies.

Investors should seek to judge whether a culture of compliance is prevalent throughout the firm. This is often not an easy thing to do. Many firms have detailed compliance policies and procedures but do not actively put such policies into practice. Only through a thorough operational due diligence review can investors effectively gauge whether these funds are practicing what their compliance manual preaches.

Insurance

Hedge funds, like many other businesses, generally carry insurance to protect themselves against certain types of losses. There is no standard list of required coverage necessary for funds to maintain. Indeed, in practice there is no consensus that insurance should be carried at all. The reason for this is twofold. Insurers have been conflicted about offering coverage to hedge funds. On one hand, they are quick to follow suit behind the rest of the financial community to cater to highly profitable hedge fund clientele. On the other hand, they are not yet universally comfortable with the levels of risk, and potential magnitude of losses, associated with hedge funds.

The first question investors should consider is whom the insurance should cover. The typical parties covered by insurance policies are the underlying funds (both onshore and offshore); the hedge fund managers themselves (e.g., portfolio manager); the general partners if there is a limited partnership vehicle; the investment manager and directors, officers, employees; and any related partners of the above-mentioned parties. The standard types of insurance coverage maintained by hedge funds and related parties includes errors and omissions (E&O), directors' and officers' liability coverage (D&O), general partner liability coverage, and employment practices liability coverage. Some hedge funds go beyond these basic levels of coverage. These additional types of insurance typically focus on ensuring the fund against the loss of certain key persons. These types of coverage can include life insurance policies on key persons of the firm. Investors should take care to note to whom these policies are made payable as well as who is paying the premiums on the policies. Some funds also maintain kidnap or ransom insurance. These policies also sometimes cover acts related to extortion and prolonged detention. Ransom insurance had traditionally been utilized to provide the funds to ransom executives traveling in third-world countries, such as those working for oil companies, from captors. This type of coverage gained prominence in the hedge fund industry when portfolio manager Edward Lampert was kidnapped from the parking lot of his firm, ESL Investments, and held hostage for almost two days. Additionally, many hedge fund service providers also maintain liability coverage that protects them in the event they fail to meet the terms of their service agreements with the hedge fund.

Investors should be conscious of any specific policy exclusions that may preclude coverage for certain events. Examples of some commonly used exclusions include claims by regulators, claims arising from violation of anti-money-laundering rules, and bankruptcy of a firm. Investors and hedge funds should also be cautious of overly vague exclusion language that would prevent a hedge fund from filing a claim in the event of "market volatility" or "failure to perform as expected," which are often difficult to defend against. Both investors and hedge funds should take measures to ensure that both the types of coverage provided and the policy limits are consistent with the firm's business model and assets under management. It is considered best practice not to have the investment manager and the underlying hedge fund use one blanket insurance policy with a large policy limit, so as to prevent any potential conflicts of interest in the event that a claim should be filed.

Many hedge funds, particularly the very large ones, often do not have certain types of insurance coverage because of the prohibitively large premiums to provide adequate coverage. They instead have opted to self-insure until policy premiums become more cost effective. Investors should include an analysis of whether a fund can adequately self-insure as part of a financial stability review.

Board of Directors

Boards of directors typically exist in two forms in most hedge fund organizations. There is a board of directors of the investment management company and a separate board of directors for the offshore hedge fund vehicle. The primary role of the board of directors is to provide a layer of oversight. Board members are supposed to represent the shareholders' (e.g., hedge fund investors') best interest. They are supposed to adhere to the guidelines of any jurisdictions in which the underlying fund is domiciled as well as being in accordance with the formal fund documentation, such as the private-placement memorandum.

Board members fall into two categories. There are affiliated or executive board members who are full-time employees of the hedge fund, and nonexecutive or independent members. Nonexecutive members' only involvement with a hedge fund is typically limited to their capacity as board members, although they may also serve as general consultants on a host of issues to the hedge fund. The authority and independence of directors within a hedge fund organization should be a key consideration for investors. This is particularly important within the hedge fund industry, where daily transparency into the inner workings of a hedge fund is increasingly difficult to acquire from an outsider's perspective. Active directors can serve as investors' first line of defense against potentially fraudulent activity. Unfortunately, many hedge funds view the role of directors as simply a statutory requirement and have effectively reduced this role to ministerial in nature. Also contributing to the problem is the development of professional directorship companies that have developed miniature fiefdoms in the offshore hedge fund havens in which they reside. There is nothing wrong with these organizations in principle; indeed they can provide those hedge funds that are looking to gain familiarity with a certain offshore jurisdiction with invaluable local knowledge and insight. Questions begin to arise as to the amount of oversight and familiarity individual board members have with the inner workings of the hedge funds whose boards they sit on when these individuals begin to serve on multiple hedge fund boards.

On a similar note, there are many hedge funds whose boards consist of senior members of the service providers they utilize, such as law firms and administrators. For example, it has not been unheard of for some senior management administrators to have more than 200 directorships.[16] Questions arise as to the independence of these board members. Should questionable practices come to their attention in their capacity as board members, will these individuals speak up at the risk of being asked to leave the board and, even more of concern, lose the business of the hedge fund? Investors should take steps to properly vet the independence and authority of these directors to determine whether they are indeed autonomous or have become captured by the funds they service. In an attempt to curtail this problem and prevent the role of board members from merely serving as a rubber stamp, many offshore jurisdictions' regulatory bodies have begun to suggest they are contemplating legislation that would hold board members accountable for their decisions. Taking a page from Sarbanes-Oxley, this increased board member accountability would hopefully limit the number of hedge fund boards directors choose to sit on and instead focus their efforts on one or two hedge fund boards.

Another point to consider is the number of directors that make up the board. In most jurisdictions, there is no minimum or maximum statutory requirement as to this number. However, certain jurisdictions have begun to implement requirements on the number of independent directors that must be appointed. Similarly, the Irish Stock Exchange, an exchange where many offshore hedge funds are listed, has a listing requirement that a hedge fund company have a least two independent directors.

The typical number of directors is three, but this number can be as many as five or seven. Boards that are too large can be cumbersome and ineffective. Conversely, boards that are too small are often dominated by one or two members. A reduction or expansion in the number of directors could provide clues as to potential changes in independent oversight within a fund.

Investors should inquire as to how frequently the board of directors meet. All boards meet at least once a year; however, questions arise as to the oversight of such a board. More frequent board meetings tend to signal a more active board, and this is generally preferred. Directors' fees should also be considered. High directors' fees should raise suspicions, but so should fees that are too low. Quality board members should be compensated for their time commensurate with their experience and knowledge. If someone will serve on a board for a bargain-basement price, the hedge fund will typically get what it pays for.

THE FIVE CORE THEMES

Now that we have outlined the primary, secondary, and blended risk factors, we can now turn our attention to the last part of our four-pronged approach to operational due diligence analysis. This is themed-based analysis. One of the benefits of thinking in terms of themes is that it allows investors to begin to draw links between the different operational review categories that are often thought of as being distinct. If each of the above-outlined risk factors can be thought of as individual operational risk streams and tributaries flowing through a hedge fund organization, then theme-based analysis can be thought of as evaluating the strength of the bridges cutting across these factors to provide a top-down view of how each of these streams flows together to produce an operationally efficient organization.

There are five core themes that make up the heart of any hedge fund operational review. It is important to note that these core themes should be analyzed in the context of the entire hedge fund organization. The five core themes that serve to effectively link the risk factors outlined above are oversight, controls, connectivity, scalability, and stability. *Oversight* refers to the ability of senior management to monitor what is happening within the organization across all levels. *Controls* refers to policies and procedures in place at the hedge fund to ensure that there is no abuse of authority or overly large risk taking by any one portion of the organization. Controls can be thought of as a detailed system of checks and balances throughout a hedge fund organization. *Connectivity* can be thought of as an extension of the *operations connectivity primary factor*. It refers not only to communication and transparency but also to an environment where the different departments of a hedge fund are not operating as individual units but as a well-functioning team in unison. Connectivity can be measured across multiple levels throughout a hedge fund—from technology and systems being able to interface, to trades flowing seamlessly, through to the reconciliation process, and to a shared employee travel calendar so everyone knows where everyone else is when not in the office.

Scalability is fairly self-explanatory. It refers to the ability of the organization to grow over time. If the organization is only planning for the current environment, then it is not very scalable. If, however, an organization plans in advance of future demand across all levels, then it is scalable. As with the other factors, scalability can be evaluated across all parts of an organization including such areas as staffing, office space, policies and procedures, and server capacity.

Finally, we turn to the last theme—stability. *Stability* can be defined in reference to the organization's ability to continue to be viable over an extended period of time. Stability can be thought of as a larger extension of the *firm stability primary factor*. Rather than focus simply on the expense analysis, the stability theme focuses on the organization as a whole. In this theme context, stability can also refer to such operational areas of the firm as stability of staff, asset growth, and performance.

These core themes are by no means exclusive, but they are a good starting point by which to gain insight into the operational risk culture within an organization. A suggested approach toward evaluating a hedge fund organization is to begin by evaluating the operational competency based on the primary, secondary, and blended risk factors. Once a thorough understanding is obtained for each of these factors, an investor can begin to evaluate the organization as a whole, functioning entity irrespective of any one issue.

Unlike the primary, secondary, and blended risk factors, there are not necessarily a predefined set of criteria on which we can evaluate each of the five organizational themes of a hedge fund. That is because first, each hedge fund is unique and the appropriateness of each factor must be viewed in context. Said another way, there is no one best practice determination for the scalability theme, for example, similar to the way best practices can be defined for each of the primary, secondary, and blended risk factors such as valuation. A hedge fund with a poor valuation policy may have other resources in place that would indicate that it is well positioned to be scalable as a whole entity. That being said, a hedge fund with poor valuation policies will most likely eventually be dragged down by these poor practices; however, the use of themed analysis would highlight this fact in the other theme evaluation areas such as oversight and controls.

In summary, theme-based analysis can be a valuable tool for those performing operational due diligence. When presented with a volume of operational factors to evaluate, investors are sometimes overwhelmed by the minutia of an operational due diligence review. In certain instances, depending on the particular issues presented by the hedge fund in question, getting deep in the weeds to thoroughly vet all aspects of certain issues is very advisable. However, focusing too much on every detail does not facilitate a proper operational due diligence review. Themed-based analysis seeks to allow investors to take a step back and put an entire hedge fund organization in context, hopefully allowing investors to avoid losing the forest for the trees.

Notes

1. See www.coso.org/publications/executive_summary_integrated_framework.htm.
2. See www.coso.org/publications/executive_summary_integrated_framework.htm.

3. See James J. Hughes, "The Greenbury Report on Directors' Remuneration," *International Journal of Manpower*, Vol. 17, No. 1, p. 4, 1996.

4. See www.coso.org/publications/executive_summary_integrated_framework.htm.

5. See "Hedge Fund Operational Risk: Meeting the Demand for Higher Transparency and Best Practice," Thought Leadership whitepaper, Bank of New York, June 2006.

6. See Michael Power, "The Invention of Operational Risk," paper presented at the Said Business School, University of Oxford, March 2002.

7. See Capco, "Understanding and Mitigating Operational Risk in Hedge Fund Investments," whitepaper, Capital Markets Company, 2005.

8. See www.coso.org/publications/executive_summary_integrated_framework.htm.

9. See "Basel II: International Convergence of Capital Measurement and Capital Standards: A Revised Framework," June 2004.

10. See Robert A. Jarrow, "Operational Risk," May 2006, revised June 2007.

11. See International Journal of Manpower, Vol. 17, No. 1, p. 4, 1996; and J. James Hughes, "The Greensbury Report on Directors' Remuneration," MCB University Press, 1996.

12. See Bank of England, "Report of the Board of Banking Supervision Inquiry into the Circumstances of the Collapse of Barings," London, HMSO Publications, 1995.

13. See Philippe Jorion, "Financial Risk Manager Handbook," 2nd ed., Hoboken, John Wiley & Sons, 2003.

14. See Paul F. Roye, "Speech by SEC Staff General Session Speaker at the SIA Hedge Funds Conference: New Regulation—Weighing the Impact," November 30, 2004, www.sec.gov/news/speech/spch113004pfr.htm.

15. See Callum McCarthy, "Hedge Fund: What Should Be the Regulatory Response?," December 7, 2006, www.fsa.gov.uk/pages/Library/Communication/Speeches/2006/1207cm.shtml.

16. See Mark Beames, "The Role of Independent Directors in Offshore Hedge Funds," www.eurekahedge.com/news/04july_archive_news_bearnes.asp.

CHAPTER 2

The Importance of Operational Due Diligence

The goal of this chapter is to provide perspective as to the importance of hedge fund operational due diligence and why it should be an essential part of any hedge fund review. We will start by reviewing several lines of reasoning that establish the importance of this function and finish the chapter with a historical review of a high-profile hedge fund failure, Bayou, taking care to outline the red flags an operational due diligence review would have detected. These red flags perhaps would have provided early warning signs as to these failures.

WHY SHOULD INVESTORS CARE ABOUT OPERATIONAL RISK?

Long-Term Capital Management, Wood River, Bayou, and Amaranth are all examples of highly publicized hedge fund failures that have operational risks at the heart of their collapses. While it is true that each fund did have a unique set of circumstances that led to its ultimate failure, the commonality of operational failures that contributed to these blowups is undeniable. Unfortunately, both investors and hedge funds are quick to forget the lessons of the past. In recent years, it seems that before the newsprint is even dry regarding one failure another takes its place and new names are added to the hedge fund graveyard.

It could be argued that whereas the rate of new hedge fund growth has increased and we have more hedge funds today than we did a year ago, logically the amount of failures should go up. This is a valid argument; however, the operational causes of the failures of the vast majority of these hedge funds were certainly avoidable. With proper controls, these hedge funds that failed for reasons other than pure investment performance could have mitigated these risks instead of aggravating them.

According to recent research in this area, "in the case of blowups, operational risk greatly exceeds the risk related to the investment strategy, with more than half of the hedge fund collapses (i.e., funds that have ceased operations with or without returning the capital to their shareholders) directly related to a failure of one or several operational processes."[1] Indeed, there are a number of reasons why operational risks should be considered equally important if not more important than investment-related risks.

Before detailing the reasons why investors should give equal, if not more, weight to operational risk considerations as compared to market and credit risk, it might be useful to highlight the benefits of performing an operational due diligence in practice. Granted, these reasons are based on backward looking assumptions, but I believe they will illustrate some basic steps that could have been taken by investors to limit their exposure to the operational risk associated with these funds that subsequently failed.

MORTON'S FORK OR A HOBSON'S CHOICE?

Certain groups of investors may consider the operational due diligence process as presenting a Catch-22 or Morton's Fork scenario, in which all reviews will yield the same unpleasant result that there will be a certain amount of operational risk present in a hedge fund. Said another way, there is a misconception that if one performs any amount of operational due diligence, regardless of how much effort is exerted, this is just as good as performing a great deal of operational due diligence. Either way, with the exception of an operationally perfect hedge fund, there will be certain areas where a hedge fund will falter. Some investors foolishly decide to think of these operational risks as diminishing to minuscule levels in hedge funds of a certain size or age. As such, these investors either do not perform operational risk or perform a minimum level of diligence.

Other investors view the decision of whether to perform operational due diligence as a Hobson's Choice, where a choice is offered, but it is the only one available. By this we mean that many investors feel that there is one perfect way to perform operational due diligence. If they do not have the resources or knowledge to perform this task themselves, they are faced with the choice of performing the operational due diligence at a lower standard, which is generally unacceptable to them, or not performing it at all. Like the Sword of Damocles dangling over their heads by a single strand, this can create tensions and anxiety surrounding the operational risk function. Such frustrations can be vetted, perhaps by outsourcing the function or by the more negative *fat-file syndrome*, which will be discussed in more detail in Chapter 4.

Despite the daunting nature of the multitude of operational areas an investor must properly review in order to conduct a thorough operational due diligence review, frustration should not lead to discouragement. Rather, those investors who do not possess the knowledge or resources to adequately vet these issues should either work with professional asset managers, such as funds of hedge funds, or develop a scaled-down operational due diligence framework that is relevant and appropriate for their organizations.

OUTRIGHT FRAUD STILL EXISTS

Embezzlement, inflating profits to mask losses, lying about academic and professional credentials, stealing from retirees and then fleeing the country—these are just some examples of the types of criminal and blatantly fraudulent activities that were carried out by hedge fund managers who, for whatever reason, deluded themselves into thinking they were smarter than everyone else and above the law. Today, these types of activities are in the minority rather than the norm, but as unbelievable as it may seem, outright fraudulent behavior still occurs. That being said, every cart has a few bad apples and this activity is by no means endemic to the hedge fund industry.

By examining the non-investment-related risks of a hedge fund through such methods as background investigations and ensuring independent oversight in areas such as pricing, investors can significantly reduce any exposure they may have to incidences of outright fraud.

Surely, the logical observer may interject, investors will have learned their lesson and such fraudulent schemes would be easily recognized. There are two primary reasons why this argument does not hold water.

First, the nature of fraud is mutable and fraudsters are constantly coming up with new ways to perpetrate schemes. The changing nature of fraud makes it both difficult to predict and even more difficult to prevent. Similar to the practice of law, precedent can serve only as a guide and not as a detailed roadmap to the future. People have different motivations for committing fraud. The nature of fraud is that it occurs on many levels throughout an organization. Both chief executive officers (CEOs) and lowly accountants are susceptible to its temptations. Collusion among parties is another factor that makes the stoppage of fraudulent behavior extremely difficult to predict.

Fraudsters do not necessarily end up in jail forever or ride off quietly into the sunset. Yes, those who are in blatant violation of certain laws can be banned from the industry and even face time in white-collar prisons, but someone who is discovered as lying about his academic qualifications, for example, particularly if he is at a more junior level within an organization, tends to part company with a firm and move on to another one. This is particularly true within the closely knit hedge fund industry. Finally, those on the fringes of fraudulent activity, who were aware of the activity and perhaps even participated in some way but did not take the fall, are still employed throughout the industry. Outright fraudulent activity within an organization is often a fat-tailed event; incidences of it occurring are rare, but when it does it can have severe consequences. Performing operational views allow investors to more adequately detect such risks and better understand any exposures they may have.

HEDGE FUND FRAUD CANNOT BE MODELED

There have been attempts by academicians and practitioners alike, through the utilization of such things as neural networks, to model fraud. These models are generally backward looking and rely on historical data of fraudulent events to develop guesses or patterns of where future fraudulent behavior will occur. As with any model, there are a number of assumptions built into this process. Much academic progress has been made in the field of studying and predicting the nature of credit defaults, in particular the work of Darrell Duffie and David Lando in regard to the theory of incomplete accounting information; however, this does not translate directly into creating models that can predict fraudulent activity within a hedge fund.

Additionally, one general flaw in the application of such models to a hedge fund context is that they do not take into account the changing, innovative nature of fraud.

Indeed, if fraudulent activity could be accurately modeled, we would exist in a society similar to that portrayed in the Tom Cruise movie, *Minority Report*, where criminals are arrested before they commit crimes. I am of the opinion that the attributes of fraud can be modeled and studied, but that the next fraudulent instance is extremely difficult, if not impossible, to anticipate. Conducting operational reviews allows investors to screen for the major areas to determine whether there is an easy opportunity for fraudsters to take advantage; however, an operational review will not predict with 100% certainty that such activities cannot occur.

SMALL DISCREPANCIES ADD UP

Invariably, as one conducts due diligence on a hedge fund, a number of inconsistencies will begin to present themselves. An example of such a common discrepancy relates to the listing of third-party service providers. Most hedge funds prepare detailed due diligence questionnaires that outline basic frequently asked questions about a firm. When a hedge fund adds or removes a new service provider, investor relations personnel sometimes do not take measures to revise these documents in a timely manner. As such, an investor who attempts to contact a service provider listed in the due diligence questionnaire with whom the hedge fund has discontinued its relationship will discover this discrepancy. This is not a lie on the part of the hedge fund, merely a misunderstanding caused by an investor receiving an outdated marketing document. While this speaks to perhaps poor investor relations oversight within the fund, the intention of the fund is not to defraud investors. There are, however, other instances where a hedge fund may not divulge the full details of a certain issue. As any good due diligence analyst will explain, performing due diligence can be equated to peeling away the layers of an onion. In order to get to the center investors must successively peel away layer after layer with subsequent questions and inquiries. As this process progresses, certain statements made by a hedge fund's employees earlier in the process may be proven incorrect. As was the case with the example of the misstated service providers, some of these errors may be made in earnest; others, however, may be representative of creative marketing or a hedge fund attempting to place a positive spin on a certain subject. As previously discussed in Chapter 1, an example of this could relate to the board of directors of a hedge fund. A hedge fund, for example, may tell an investor that the role of the board is merely statutory in nature and that reducing the number of board members does not materially affect the oversight of the funds. I would classify this statement as a partial truth. While it is true that the board of directors is a statutory requirement in certain jurisdictions, the general market consensus is that a reduction in the number of board members represents a decrease in the oversight of the funds as opposed to having no effect.

Another example of such a statement would be in relation to the use of service providers such as administrators. Unfortunately, most people, because of a natural desire to be helpful and responsive, are inherently programmed to want to provide answers to questions that are posed to them. Think about it; when someone asks you for directions, you would probably try to point her in the general direction even if you do not know exactly the correct path. The same is generally true when individuals are questioned during an operational due diligence review.

Consider a scenario where an operational due diligence analyst is questioning a firm's back-office staff accountant. Let us call this accountant George. George is being interviewed and speaking in great detail about the firm's accounting systems and trade capture processes. George is also very adept at describing how the firm has recently implemented changes in anticipation of an accounting pronouncement that will affect how the firm accounts for certain derivatives. In the room with George is his boss, the firm's chief financial officer (CFO), Marvin. Marvin and George seem to make a great team, each complementing the other's answers and describing the trade flow graphs in exhilarating detail. The due diligence analyst conducting the review now asks the pair about their relationship with the third-party administrator. One such question relates to any employee turnover that has occurred at the administrator over the past two years. Marvin, seeking to impress the due diligence analyst, provides glossy answers, stating that "turnover is endemic to the administration industry, but we have not been affected on our end." The due diligence analyst makes a note of this and proceeds with the interview. George, squirming in his chair, however, knows that this is not the case. This is confirmed when the due diligence analyst separately interviews the head of the administration team, Tom, who works with George on a regular basis. Tom informs the due diligence analyst that he joined the firm four months ago and that there had been several problems with George's account due to high employee turnover, but that such problems have been resolved. Now, with Tom at the helm, there is smooth sailing. Was what Marvin said a lie? After all, there are no longer any problems with the administration service. Is George at fault because he did not speak up? Was it, perhaps, a white lie?

By focusing solely on the financial, investment, quantitative, or factually "harder" elements of a hedge fund, a vast number of non-investment-related, softer cues that may pose significant operational risk exposures can be overlooked. One discrepancy or white lie on its own may be harmless. However, by connecting the dots throughout an operational due diligence review, these little discrepancies can aggregate with alarming speed and produce a different picture from what was originally portrayed by the investment thesis or performance of a firm. Ignoring such seemingly minor risks is ill advised and can lead to an unfortunate lack of oversight, as our analysis of Bayou later in the chapter will highlight.

LACK OF STANDARDIZED REGULATION

In the current marketplace, hedge funds are literally located all over the world. While major financial centers such as New York, London, and Hong Kong constitute the bulk of the hedge fund industry, there are many large, established hedge funds that are located in more exotic locations and in offshore tax havens. Each of these different locales may have different regulatory and enforcement agencies, each with their own particularities. Indeed, once you venture outside the United States and continental Europe the uniformity of regulatory oversight and enforcement is the exception rather than the norm. Even with initiatives such as the United Kingdom's Financial

Services Authority Marketing in Financial Instruments Directive (MiFID), which in part is attempting to harmonize the European Union's regulatory and enforcement framework for financial services, lack of global uniformity abounds.

Certain jurisdictions may require a hedge fund that meets a certain criterion (i.e., of a certain size or with a certain number of clients) to register, whereas others may not require such registration. In some parts of the world, even the question of whether hedge funds should be regulated is a hotly debated one. This was exemplified in the United States, with the June 23, 2006, decision of the U.S. Court of Appeals for the District of Columbia that overturned the requirement that hedge funds be registered with the Securities and Exchange Commission (SEC). The court cited a number of reasons for its decision, including the "notoriously difficult" nature of the definition of hedge funds.

Traditionally, hedge funds are thought of as falling into one of a series of broad categories defined by style of investment management. The major style buckets generally include such strategies as equity long/short, global macro, convertible bond arbitrage, fixed-income arbitrage, merger arbitrage, relative-value arbitrage, event driven, and market neutral. Some have argued the need for a single global hedge fund regulator. This was the stance taken by Sandy Weil, the former CEO of Citigroup, during his speech to finance ministers during a 2007 G7 meeting in Germany.[2] Others, such as MIT's Professor Andrew Lo, have suggested that a governmental agency should be established to study hedge fund failures and develop recommendations based on these studies, similar to the way the U.S. National Transportation Safety Board studies airplane crashes.[3] All of these proposals are in the early stages and more research and dialogue will be required in developing a more robust global regulatory framework, if indeed one ever will be created. This lack of standardized oversight and regulation of the hedge fund industry places the onus on investors to understand that different jurisdictional regulatory regimes hold hedge funds to more or less stringent thresholds in terms of such issues as reporting frequency, including nature and frequency disclosures, onsite audit cycle, and so forth.

EACH HEDGE FUND IS DIFFERENT

There are certain operational risk factors that might have more or less importance based on the type of investment strategy pursued by the fund under consideration. Within an operational context, commonality does exist among hedge funds, regardless of style type, with respect to certain broad categories. Take the example of the business continuity and disaster recovery function. As an investor, you would want to see that every hedge fund has thought about and developed a business continuity and disaster recovery plan. That is essentially where the commonality stops. If the firm manages $5 billion and has employees in three different time zones, you would expect a different level of continuity and recovery planning than at a $400 million hedge fund with one office. Turning to strategy, you would expect a manager with a high trading volume to have more redundancy for the trading function than would a distressed manager with merely a few trades per month. These differences among hedge funds highlight the fact that not only does every hedge fund strategy have unique operational considerations, but each hedge fund has its own particularities. It is imperative that investors understand this fact and perform operational reviews of every hedge fund, large or small, because each one has a different operational story to tell.

ABILITY TO GENERATE AN INFORMATIONAL EDGE

Hedge funds closely guard the specific details of the positions held in their portfolios. Some funds, particularly short biased funds, guard these details more closely than others. At times, some market practitioners or hedge fund investment analysts can gain some insight into this type of financial information; but detailed portfolio transparency is generally placed at a premium. The same can be said for non-investment-related data.

Obtaining operational intelligence about a fund can provide investors with unique insights as to how to appropriately manage certain types of non-investment-related risks ahead of certain other investors. In an age where the speed with which investors are able to act on information can directly relate to profits, this type of intelligence can be invaluable. An example of such an operational edge would be news of a defection of a high-profile portfolio manager from a Hedge Fund A to Hedge Fund B. An investor in Hedge Fund A, learning of this news through such an action as ongoing news monitoring (discussed in more detail in Chapter 4), now has the ability to exercise a more informed choice as to whether to remain invested in Hedge Fund A, as opposed to an investor who has not yet learned of this news. This would be especially important in this case, as most likely there would be a long line of investors waiting to redeem and such an information edge would have put this investor at the front of the line had he acted on it quickly.

Conversely, consider the situations where a star trader decides to leave Hedge Fund B and join Hedge Fund A. An existing investor in Hedge Fund A may have great confidence in this trader and believe that he will be a strong profit generator for the fund. Hedge Fund A may be nearing capacity and accepting only a limited amount of new capital. If this is the case, the existing investor could submit her intention to commit additional subscriptions to the fund ahead of other investors, who may be slow to act on this news. As this simple example illustrates, monitoring the non-investment-related factors associated with hedge funds can allow investors to take actions that will allow them, depending on the circumstances, to both hedge against potential losses and capitalize on opportunities for increased profits.

POTENTIAL TO REDUCE LOSSES AND INCREASE RETURNS

Risk management is generally thought of in literal terms—that is, to diagnose risk so that it can be effectively managed and reduced. Operational risk, and the subsequent operational due diligence review performed to diagnose this risk, is no different. The original purpose of this function was to allow investors to evaluate the noninvestment merits of a firm and make a judgment whether to proceed with investment. If we compare the modern hedge fund landscape to a minefield fraught with potential explosive noninvestment risks, an operational due diligence evaluation can be thought of as using a metal detector to assist you in navigating this treacherous path. In addition to allowing investors to sleep better at night, knowing that they have attempted to vet these risks, risk management also provides investors with insight (or red flags) into any problems that may be on an organization's horizon.

The flip side of the traditional risk management thinking is that by intelligently taking certain risks, investors can generate increased returns. In an operational context, let us consider the example of a hedge fund that is about to make major improvements to its existing accounting systems that will provide a better link to the firm's risk management system. This, then, may provide the firm's portfolio managers with real-time transparency into a portfolio and allow them to take more active bets in certain markets, and potentially generate higher returns. Understanding these changes, and the potential ramifications they may have, may prompt an investor to either add more capital to an existing fund or begin to invest.

CONSIDERING OPERATIONAL RISK FACTORS PRESENTS A DIFFERENT VIEW INTO A FIRM

When conducting regular hedge fund due diligence, most investors and analysts meet with a standard cast of individuals in certain operational supervisory roles. These typically include several individuals from investor relations, a portfolio manager or two, and perhaps even the firm's CFO or chief operating officer (COO). As will be covered in greater detail in

Chapter 4, in properly evaluating the *operational risks* associated with a hedge fund, an entirely different group of people will be met with. Yes, this will include the firm's CFO and COO; but it will also involve many different parts of the firm, if not the entire firm. These individuals include representatives from legal and compliance, technology, a myriad of back-office individuals responsible for everything from trade capture and settlements to reconciliation, and so forth. Finally, by combining a review of non-investment-related factors with investment-related factors, investors are able to construct a complete picture, both internally within a hedge fund and externally through contact with a fund's service providers.

COMMON MISCONCEPTIONS

There are a number of common misconceptions, particularly among first-time hedge fund investors, concerning the diligence being performed on hedge funds.

Aren't Other People Performing These Reviews?

One common thought is that if other people are performing both initial and ongoing operational reviews of hedge funds, then there is no need to invest the significant time and resources required to perform these reviews. This Darwinian evolutionary logic reflects the survival-of-the-fittest mentality. Following along these lines of thinking, any operational problems within a hedge fund will have been uncovered by other people and, if they were deemed of enough concern to cause investors to redeem the fund, funds would either fix the problem and retain assets, or go out of business. Unfortunately, it has been proven that ontogeny does not recapitulate phylogeny, and all hedge funds do not go through the same evolutionary stages. One common belief among hedge fund investors, particularly when considering large funds with established track records, is that someone else, more skilled and with more resources than they have, has already turned over every stone and checked every closet for skeletons. This thinking does not take into account several factors. First, the majority of hedge funds have lockups that prevent investors from redeeming early without experiencing a penalty. Consequently, even if an investor uncovers something that causes operational concerns, he is for all intents and purposes prevented from doing anything about it and the fund's assets will remain stable, at least until the lockup period expires. Rather than be hit with the redemption penalty, many investors opt to take their chances.

Second, access to operational risk information is asymmetrical. The marketplace for the exchange of operational risk data is extremely inefficient.

A long-time investor in a hedge fund most likely has better access to both a firm's key operational decision makers and the more junior individuals who perform these tasks on a daily basis. This same perspective and access might not be shared by a potential investor considering a $10 million investment with a $3 billion hedge fund.

Additionally, hedge fund investors do not necessarily talk to each other. If one organization passes on investing in a hedge fund for operational reasons, it does not necessarily spread the word to other potential investors. This is particularly true of investment banks with asset management divisions or among funds of hedge funds that closely guard their hedge fund research from competitors. Sharing this type of information would destroy their competitive edge.

Things That May Be of Concern to One Investor Might Not Be of Concern to Another

Things change within an organization. The value of the operational review conducted yesterday begins to decay with every passing day. This relationship is summarized in Exhibit 2.1. Investors can gain some sense of comfort from the fact that having many organizations each conduct an ongoing stream of operational reviews provides some sort of continual stream of operational oversight.

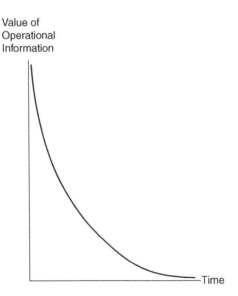

EXHIBIT 2.1 Value of Operational Information Decays over Time

One problem is that if Potential Investor A finds a material operational problem of such concern as to cause her to redeem, this information is not likely to be broadcast to Potential Investor B. Even worse, Potential Investor B might not uncover the same material operational problem that was uncovered by Potential Investor A. Another point of consideration is that different organizations may each have their own definition of what constitutes a material operational concern.

If It Is Not Illegal, Then It Must Okay

Many hedge funds have failed for operational reasons that were perfectly legal according to both the criminal laws of their local jurisdiction and the relevant financial regulators. For example, *it is perfectly legal for a hedge fund to restate its net asset value.* This restatement, which resulted from poor operations planning, has caused many funds to fail. Although it is certainly not illegal, it is definitely an issue of concern to investors.

OTHER CONSIDERATIONS: THERE IS NOT NECESSARILY A POSITIVE CORRELATION BETWEEN ASSETS AND OPERATIONAL QUALITY

One common misconception is that there is necessarily a direct positive correlation between operational quality and assets under management. This relationship is summarized in Exhibit 2.2. This type of belief tends to create a false sense of security that can lead to the performance of lax operational due diligence reviews. Many large institutions with big asset bases have failed. Operational competency cannot be purchased; rather it is a function of well-coordinated management and planning. Larger organizations are susceptible to certain operational risks that a smaller, more nimble organization may be able to avoid. That being said, there are many operational efficiencies that a large organization operating in an economy of scale will be able to take advantage of that would not be present in a smaller organization.

A STUDY IN OPERATIONAL FAILURE: BAYOU HEDGE FUND GROUP

The Bayou Hedge Fund Group was founded in 1996 by Samuel Israel III. The group was made up of the Bayou Superfund LLC, Bayou No Leverage Fund LLC, Bayou Affiliates Fund LLC, and Bayou Accredited Fund LLC. Over the course of the next nine years, the firm raised almost $450 million. It

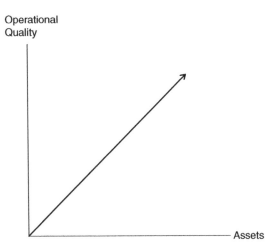

EXHIBIT 2.2   Misconception That There Is Always a Positive Correlation between Assets under Management and Operational Quality

is now public knowledge that the entire organization was a fraud. Mr. Israel, Bayou's former chief financial officer, Daniel Marino, and co-founder James G. Marquez all subsequently pled guilty to conspiring to defraud investors and were sentenced to serve terms of 20 years, 20 years, and 51 months, respectively. Mr. Israel subsequently faked his own suicide and later ran from authorities before turning himself in adding another bizarre twist to an already unbelievable story of fraud and deception. The purpose of this review of Bayou's activities is to highlight the key operational red flags that were overlooked by the vast majority of the firm's investors at the time. Through this analysis, the hope is that the importance of conducting thorough operational reviews will become apparent.

AFFILIATED BROKER-DEALER

The Bayou funds cleared trades through the firm's affiliated broker-dealer, Bayou Securities. The fund cited many reasons for maintaining this affiliated broker-dealer, including reduced clearing costs, the sharing of expenses, and increased quality of execution. The commissions that were generated from Bayou's trading activities were being credited back to the firm's funds. These credits were offsetting losses generated by the funds, making them more difficult to detect. Also contributing to the problem were the fairly large sizes of these commissions due to the Bayou funds' high-volume trading.

Several news sources reported that Bayou's investor marketing materials had attempted to quell investor concerns regarding the affiliation of the broker-dealer by citing that it was registered with security regulators and subject to regulatory examinations. It was also reported that the firm openly acknowledged that this affiliation between the two firms could in certain instances in fact lead to higher clearing costs for the funds and subsequent greater profits for Mr. Israel.

Even before the news of Bayou's failure broke, hedge fund investors expressed trepidation about the firm's affiliated broker-dealer. The majority of investors feel that the potential for conflicts of interest and abuse, as was the case with Bayou, are too great to outweigh the benefits of such affiliation. While all entities affiliated with a hedge fund should be carefully examined to determine the nature of the relationship between the firms, the arrangement in Bayou's case would raise red flags in all modern operational due diligence frameworks. Today, hedge funds with affiliated broker-dealers are increasingly rare.

LARGE DISCREPANCIES IN THE PERFORMANCE OF ONSHORE AND OFFSHORE FUNDS

It was reported that in 2002 Bayou had substantial gaps in performance between its onshore and offshore funds. While it is common for the performance of onshore and offshore vehicles to differ slightly, due to issues such as currency or allocation of trades, in most hedge fund organizations the two vehicles are generally considered to be distinct only for the purposes of the types of investors that may allocate to these vehicles. In Bayou's case, as is the case with most hedge funds, the onshore and offshore vehicles are part of the same hedge fund strategy and are intended to be managed *pari passu*. According to news media, Bayou attempted to explain this discrepancy by claiming that it had transferred trades that had yielded profits from its on-shore fund to the offshore vehicles. This, Bayou claimed, would inflate the performance of the offshore vehicle and assist the firm in attracting larger assets.

Learning of such a practice should have set off a variety of operational red flags. This type of manufacturing of performance raises questions of there being any independent risk oversight within a hedge fund (in Bayou's case there was none), as well as regarding procedures for trade allocation. Additionally, investors in the offshore fund were essentially benefiting at the expense of investors in the onshore fund. Investors such as Tremont Capital

Management realized the early warning signs of such hazardous practices and redeemed capital ahead of the firm's failure.[4]

DECLINING CAPITAL OF BROKER-DEALER

It was reported that the assets of Bayou Securities, the hedge fund's affiliated broker-dealer, were in steady decline during the firm's last year. According to various media sources in early 2004, the firm had a capital position of just under $6 million. By the end of 2004, this position had declined to just under $300,000. This highlights an important point regarding the importance of conducting operational reviews, not just on hedge funds considered for investment but on their service providers and affiliated entities as well. In Bayou's case, the decline in assets of Bayou Securities would have been a good indication that perhaps the Bayou hedge funds were suffering similar hardships (after all, the activities of the Bayou funds were the largest revenue source for Bayou Securities), or that Bayou Securities may have been leaning on the Bayou hedge funds to shoulder some of the burden of its increasing losses. Either way, this red flag would have been detected by a competent modern operational due diligence review.

BOARD OF DIRECTORS: MEMBERS AND ACTIONS

It was reported that the board of directors of the Bayou hedge funds consisted of two individuals: the firm's president, Mr. Israel, and its CFO, Daniel Marino. The small, even number of board members, coupled with the fact that these two individuals were affiliated with the firm and did not have the independent oversight of either a risk manager or an independent director, should have been cause for concern. Unfortunately, these concerns became a reality when, on December 4, 2004, the fund's board, according to sources, enacted a motion that allowed Mr. Israel to maintain $100 million of the firm's money to invest in his own name.

LAVISH EXPENSES OF BROKER-DEALERS

As the financial position of Bayou securities declined, the firm continued to rack up lavish expenses. Media sources reported that the more egregious expenses included limousine services, expensive meals, unusually large legal fees, and the use of a private jet. All told, it is estimated these expenses were ranging close to $25,000 a month. Bizarrely, the firm even utilized the services of a counterespionage consultant at a fee of $20,000. These types of expenses most likely would have been uncovered through a financial stability analysis of the firm or a detailed review of the firm's financial statements including expenses.

FAKE AUDITS PREPARED BY A PHONY AUDITOR

In an attempt to hide increasingly large losses, Bayou created a fake audit firm called Richmond-Fairfield. This firm had only one client, Bayou. Additionally, Bayou's CFO, Daniel Marino, served as Richmond-Fairfield's principal. A modern operational due diligence review would have detected the sham of Richmond-Fairfield for several reasons. First, today most hedge funds are audited by the Big Four accounting firms. Any audit firms outside of the Big Four are scrutinized very closely during a proper operational due diligence review. Second, with Bayou being the only client, Richmond-Fairfield would have been unable to produce any other client references. Today, this would immediately raise an operational red flag. Finally, the fact that Mr. Marino was the firm's sole principal most likely would have been uncovered through basic modern background investigation techniques.

BACKGROUND QUESTIONS

After the dust settled on Bayou, it came out that Sam Israel had made exaggerated claims in the biography he provided to investors. An example of this is the fact that Israel never graduated from Tulane University. The most glaring embellishment was the role he described himself as playing at Omega Advisors, the $4 billion hedge fund run by former Goldman Sachs partner, Leon Cooperman. Specifically, according the media sources, Mr. Israel's biography stated that he had worked at Omega for four years, from 1992 to 1996, and that he was in charge of execution for futures and equities. Omega later clarified that Mr. Israel had worked at the firm for only 18 months and that his role was more administrative. Adding insult to injury, Omega further added that they had received only one phone call attempting to verify Mr. Israel's time at the company. By conducting a thorough operational due diligence review, investors could have easily detected holes in Mr. Israel's biography.

LACK OF INVESTOR COMMUNICATION

It was reported in the media that one reason many of the now-obvious red flags were overlooked by investors was Mr. Israel's ability to communicate with investors in a down-to-earth manner. Investors seemed to like not only his style of communication but the frequency with which he would reach out to them via such methods as investor's letters. According to media reports, several former investors began to redeem their money from the fund when they noticed a decline in the quality as well as frequency of the communications from the firm, particularly in times of poor performance. This type of *signaling effect* speaks to the importance of performing ongoing operational monitoring, which would allow investors to detect these types of issues.

Questionable Portfolio Investments

When performance in the Bayou funds began to decline, it was reported that Mr. Israel and an organization led by Mr. Marino called IM Partners, which was coincidentally headquartered in Bayou's Stamford offices, began to invest in a number of questionable projects. This shift in investment style, both by security type (these new investments were primarily private investments, such as the financing of low budget action films, as opposed to the more equity like positions the firm had been taking) and location (many of these deals were placed in remote locations outside of the United States), should have raised investor concerns. Ironically, one such investment was in the amount of $10 million given to a firm called Kycos, which specialized in performing background investigations. While gaining transparency into the exact portfolio holdings of a hedge fund is generally a challenge for investors, learning about such general exposures as geography or security type should have been made possible. If the fund had refused such requests, which it is believed Bayou did, red flags should have been raised and the issue investigated more thoroughly.

TIES TO PEOPLE BARRED FROM THE SECURITIES INDUSTRY

When Mr. Israel first began to form Bayou, he worked with Stanley Patrick. Mr. Patrick was a technical trader and Mr. Israel worked with him to develop automated trading strategies. In 1990, Mr. Patrick was accused of insider trading. He later pled guilty in 1994, and was barred from the securities industry. The prior relationship between Mr. Israel and Mr. Patrick was not known by many of the firm's investors. Despite the fact that Mr. Patrick was not affiliated with Bayou, this could have posed negative reputational risk to the firm via his association with Mr. Israel. An operational due diligence review coupled with a background investigation would most likely have revealed this relationship and provided investors with the information to make an informed choice about associating with Mr. Israel.

REVISION OF CONFLICTED MARKETING MATERIALS

It has been reported that when the firm began, marketing materials stated that the firm was established in 1996. Later marketing materials indicated the firm started in 1997. This discrepancy was most likely intentional on Bayou's part, in order to shift focus away from poor performance in 1996. In most cases, an operational due diligence review of such materials as audited financials would have detected this error. While I have not personally reviewed these financial statements, we can assume that they would be an unreliable source in this case as they were being fraudulently manufactured by CFO Marino's fake audit firm, Richmond-Fairfield. A host of other sources, however, could have been examined, including hedge fund performance databases, review of a performance track record, and discussions with previous investors or those familiar with the firm.

OTHER ANOMALIES

There were a host of other factors that should have at the very least caused investors to pause when comparing Bayou to other hedge funds at the time. One such feature was the fund's unique fee structure. Bayou did not charge a management fee, as is commonplace for almost every hedge fund. Instead, the fund's profits were solely derived from a 20% incentive fee. Such a structure creates an environment where a portfolio manager may be encouraged to take on unreasonably large risks in order to ensure profits for the firm. This was especially true in Bayou's case as, despite falsely reported positive performance, the firm was actually experiencing significant losses, which further encouraged Mr. Israel to bet more and more of the farm with each successive trade.

A second feature of the Bayou funds that was somewhat unusual, even by today's hedge fund standards, was the low subscription fee. In Bayou's case, the minimum subscription amount was $250,000. The typical hedge fund subscription fee is $1 million, but some funds have minimum subscription fees as high as $10 million. There is nothing inherently wrong with charging a low subscription fee; however, the fact that this fee was outside of common market practice at the time should have caused people to question the motivations for such a low minimum investment. Some hedge funds have valid reasons for charging lower fees, such as attempting to increase the amount of retail assets under management. In Bayou's case, it is not clear that there were such motivations in place. We can only postulate that such low minimums were fueled more by greed and an attempt to prolong a large-scale cover-up as opposed to diversification of the investor base.

There was also a quite telling lawsuit filed in 2003 by a former employee, Paul T. Westervelt Jr., and his son, Paul T. Westervelt III. "According to the complaint, after the elder Mr. Westervelt joined Bayou, he discovered what he considered to be 'possible violations of S.E.C. regulations governing the operating of hedge funds,' and other possible violations."[5] The National Association of Securities Dealers also lobbied a series of fines against Mr. Israel and Bayou.

Notes

1. See Corentin Christory, Stéphane Daul, and Jean René Giraud, "Quantification of Hedge Fund Default Risk," EDHEC Risk and Asset Management Research Centre, EDHEC Business School, January 2007.
2. See Gabor Steingart and Frank Hornig, "Hedge Funds Have to Open Their Books to Regulators," Spiegel Online International, February 12, 2007, www.spiegel.de/international/spiegel/0,1518,465785,00.html.
3. See Gretchen Morgenson, "Clues to a Hedge Fund's Collapse," *New York Times*, September 17, 2005.
4. Ibid.
5. See Gretchen Morgenson, "Connecticut Investigates Hedge Fund for Insolvency," *New York Times*, August 25, 2005.

CHAPTER 3

Who Is Qualified to Perform an Operational Due Diligence Review?

An operational due diligence analyst can be described as being required to be a jack-of-all-trades and master of some. Of course, in a perfect world we could genetically engineer an army of seasoned, gray-haired operational due diligence cyborgs with deep experience and knowledge across all areas of hedge fund non-investment-related risk. Unfortunately, we are bound by the limits of reality, finite resources, and time. This is not to say that by properly allocating resources, employing expertise, and intelligently evaluating the results of a properly conducted operational due diligence review an investor cannot fully understand and manage the non-investment-related risks of a hedge fund. The point is that in practical application, and based on professional experience, one tends to garner better results by leveraging the shared expertise of multiple operational due diligence resources as opposed to one individual. Additionally, as I hope to convey and as will be discussed in more detail in Chapter 4, there are few black-and-white rules when it comes to evaluating the results of an operational due diligence review. Instead, operational due diligence produces a series of *data points* and, depending on a number of factors, the majority of these results can lead to gray areas that are open to interpretation depending on where a particular investor's operational risk threshold lies. Consequently, vetting the results of an operational review through several sources, which may each have specific expertise in particular areas, may provide an investor, who ultimately is responsible for making the final capital allocation decision, with different perspectives against which to evaluate these operational data points.

It is also worth noting that while someone may possess many years of professional experience and insight in a specific area that may be applicable to a primary or secondary operational risk factor, that person might not be necessarily an investor's best choice to perform an entire operational due diligence review. To use a construction analogy, would you say that a plumber is qualified to perform an entire home inspection? The more important question may be, Would you be willing to purchase a home based entirely on his recommendation? This is not to say that the plumber is not extremely qualified to evaluate the nature of all things plumbing related, such as the viability of house sewage systems, quality of kitchen sink fixtures, appropriateness of bathroom faucets, and condition of tub drainage systems. He certainly is. Maybe in the course of many years of working in all kinds of homes, both already built and under construction, the plumber has picked up some knowledge about a few other things such as masonry, electrical work, framing out a room, and the like, but that certainly does not make him an expert in those areas. Just so, someone with detailed knowledge of a hedge fund's back-office operations, such as a hedge fund's controller or chief financial officer (CFO), might not be able fully to evaluate legal perils or off-market terms in an offering memorandum. She may be familiar with the general terms of such documents and may also have an understanding of the language in an offering memorandum related to pricing, but being able to fully evaluate, vet, and suggest ways to change such terms will most likely be out of the scope of her expertise. Most people would probably agree that, in the case of hedge fund legal document review, comparing the legal knowledge of a hedge fund's former controller to that of a full-time hedge fund attorney would not be much of a contest.

From the hedge fund investor's perspective, there are really five levels to any operational due diligence review. The first is knowing what data to gather. The second is the data-gathering process. The third level is to analyze the data. The fourth is to draw a conclusion based on this analysis. As part of this conclusion determining process an investor will evaluate the operational structure of a hedge fund. That is to say, the firm has made choices, conscious or not, to be set up a certain way and to expose itself to, or mitigate, certain operational risks. A potential investor in a hedge fund comes to the table with his own baggage, so to speak. This could be extreme sensitivity to reputational risk or the requirement that a fund enter into a most-favored-nation clause, and so forth. With all this in mind, a potential investor, in coming to an operational conclusion, has to decide if he agrees with the decisions made by the fund with regard to these operational risks. If yes, then a potential investment is in the works and the investor will generally proceed with ongoing monitoring, level five. If no, the two part ways and no investment is made. This process is summarized in Exhibit 3.1.

From a hedge fund's perspective, the operational due diligence process can be broken down into two levels. Traditionally, investors will consider the investment related factors before analyzing the noninvestment factors of

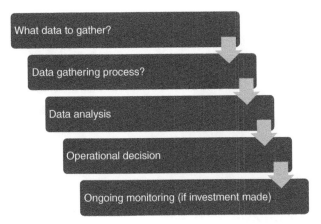

EXHIBIT 3.1 Levels of Operational Due Diligence: Investor's Perspective

a hedge fund organization. But once the initial courting period has ended, and an investor has proceeded far along enough in the investment decision process to consider the non-investment-related factors, the first level of this process is responding to a potential hedge fund investor's operational data requests. These can be via a request for documentation, onsite inquiries, and so on. The second level is to provide additional clarification regarding any questions investors may have as part of an operational review or further to elaborate on the reasons behind why certain operational decisions were made. If an investment is made, a hedge fund will also be responsible for assisting with the ongoing operational due diligence monitoring process as well. This process is summarized in Exhibit 3.2. Exhibit 3.3 shows the combination of these processes.

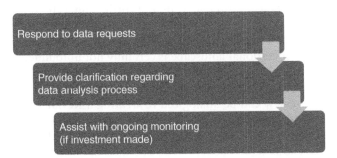

EXHIBIT 3.2 Levels of Operational Due Diligence: Hedge Fund's Perspective

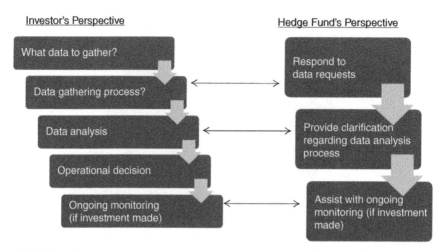

EXHIBIT 3.3   Levels of Combined Operational Due Diligence: Both Perspectives

The purpose of this chapter is to provide an overview of the essential skills necessary to properly analyze the major areas of a hedge fund's operational risks. The process of actually forging these often-disparate skills to allow for the creation of an initial operational due diligence review will be covered in Chapter 4. It should be mentioned that the following discussion of the areas in which those performing an operational due diligence review should have a basic understanding is by no means an attempt to say that someone not possessing expertise in a particular area may not be able to add significant value when conducting operational due diligence. On the contrary, having someone with deep knowledge in one area or surface-level knowledge in all areas still adds infinitely more value, and protects investors more, than not looking at these non-investment-related areas. Nor should potential investors feel intimidated by the forthcoming discussion, feeling that if they cannot cover everything in adequate detail they might as well not try. The fear of missing a small, ticking time bomb in a remote area of a hedge fund's operational landscape is certainly not unfounded but should not act as an all-encompassing deterrent to investors who do not have the resources to build up fully equipped operational risk armies. An operational due diligence review can be analogized to wearing a Kevlar vest. If you are shot in the head, the fact that you were wearing the vest did not do you a bit of good. But if I were going into a shootout, I would rather have the vest on than not. The same can be said of an operational due diligence review. It cannot guarantee your safety, but it can increase the chances of protecting yourself.

It should be noted that the purpose of the following descriptions is merely to provide a base level of competency that should generally be required in each of the functions listed below. It could be the case that a certain hedge fund, for example, has a very intricate network of global legal entities and unique terms in its offering memoranda. Obviously, this type of fund requires a much higher degree of legal scrutiny than a hedge fund manager with a single standalone fund and monthly liquidity. The point is that there are certain basic risk factors that should be examined, regardless of the manager under review. This chapter will describe those basic skills as well as attempt to provide investors with enough of an introduction that they will be able to pursue the in-depth knowledge that each hedge fund under consideration requires.

As alluded to in Chapter 2, this question as to who is qualified to perform an operational review is more difficult to answer than it seems, due to the fact that there is a lack of agreement among both market practitioners and academicians alike as to what constitutes a complete operational review. In recent years, with an increase in the general market consciousness as to the importance of understanding and appropriately managing exposure to hedge fund operational risks, many individuals with knowledge of certain areas have emerged as champions of these non-investment-related issues, albeit they were once confined to the shadows of dank server rooms and the green lampshades of back offices. "The answer to the question: 'What is operational risk?' cannot be separated from the question: 'Who is reinventing themselves in the name of operational risk?'"[1]

Indeed, there are a seemingly limitless number of non-investment-related factors that can be covered as part of an operational due diligence review. There is, however, a general consensus as to the core elements of an operational review, which we laid out as the *primary, secondary, and blended risk factors* in Chapter 1. These are the factors that will guide our analysis in an attempt to answer the question at hand. Before analyzing who can perform an operational review, it is important to consider the essential skills necessary to perform an operational review, and this is where our discussion begins.

ESSENTIAL SKILLS

The primary, secondary, and blended risk factors outlined in Chapter 1 were discussed in such a way as to create a framework that could be overlaid to any hedge fund structure, regardless of investment strategy, in order to provide a starting point from which to gauge an alternative investment manager's core primary and secondary operational competencies. Regarding the way in which the five themes (oversight, controls, connectivity, scalability, and stability) described in Chapter 1, serve to provide some sort of operational connection between the different parts of a hedge fund organization, the same is true of the descriptions of the essential or minimum levels of skills necessary to competently perform an operational review.

It should be noted that the labeling of these skills categories is by no means an attempt to suggest a cookie-cutter approach to operational due diligence. Rather, by outlining these primary, secondary, and blended risk factors, the intention is to focus on the most widely accepted, and generally most important, operational risk factors that exist across all hedge funds, regardless of investment strategies or style. Our discussion of the essential skills necessary to conduct an operational review will build on this framework. Consequently, in describing the core competencies required for hedge fund operational due diligence, we will follow a similar ranking hierarchy of primary, secondary, and blended skills.

As with each of the factors we will discuss below, as part of any operational due diligence review, hedge fund investors should make judgments as to both the competency and appropriateness of the employees in charge of each of the key non-investment-related areas of a firm. Investors should take care in making these judgments to segregate each of a certain employee's individual roles and evaluate each of these roles separately. This is especially important in smaller firms, where senior personnel often wear more than one functional hat. For example, a chief financial officer might also serve as the chief operating officer and even the chief compliance officer of a firm. While the individual in this example may be an excellent CFO, she may not know a thing about compliance and consequently the compliance function should be given more scrutiny and perhaps considered a weaker part of the organization.

PRIMARY SKILLS

In Chapter 1, we outlined the primary factors that are generally covered during an operational due diligence review. The primary skills required in order to perform a review of these risk factors can be summarized as having competency in the following sections. It should be noted that the subsequent discussion of the general types of skills necessary to properly evaluate a hedge fund's operational competencies as part of the operational due diligence process is not a direct corollary to each of the primary categories outlined in Chapter 1. Rather, the outline of these skills serves as a general guidance as to the types of skills required to diagnose the primary operational risk factors of a hedge fund.

Information Technology

Information technology (IT) is an area of operational due diligence that lends itself to getting lost in the minutiae of the subject matter. For example, as a potential hedge fund investor, would you be prevented from investing in a hedge fund with superior returns relative to its peers simply because in order to save some money the organization opted to select a cheaper brand of network router, with a lower-density maximum upstream channel capacity (i.e., bandwidth) for its WAN (wide area network), than a more costly alternative? The more important question for the nontechnorati hedge fund investors is, Do you even know what this means? And more important, should you care? Unfortunately, as with most areas of operational risk, there is no clear-cut yes-or-no answer to such issues.

I would guess that the vast majority of hedge fund operational due diligence reviews are conducted by those with operations and/or legal backgrounds, as opposed to information technology backgrounds. Consequently, in scenarios where a hedge fund does have dedicated in-house IT personnel, as opposed to outsourcing the function to a third party on a primarily on-call basis, many investors and due diligence professionals tend to suffer from the deer-in-the-headlights syndrome. After a few minutes of discussion regarding a general description of the types of hardware and systems utilized by a firm, a tour of the firm's server room is generally taken. Here, server racks are on display with a panoply of wires and hoses running above people's heads and cooling fans whizzing in the background. When presented with this seemingly expensive high-tech architecture and machinery, most investors simply freeze up (like a deer in the headlights), assume all is well, and proceed on with the review.

This is not necessarily a bad thing. Well, let me qualify that remark. It is not the worst case scenario. As discussed above, just as a hedge fund manager cannot say with certainty whether a trade will make money, neither can an operational due diligence analyst predict in which area of information technology a hedge fund will run into problems. However, by discussing the knowledge and skills necessary to conduct a base-level review of the generally most important areas of a hedge fund's IT infrastructure, we can attempt to cover the larger risk-exposure areas.

Technology is one of the most rapidly evolving areas of operational risk. I would say that one of the most important skills necessary to performing an operational review of a hedge fund's information technology function is to keep abreast of the latest trends and technologies available. This can be accomplished in a number of different ways, including reading professional journals, attending conferences, and having continuing discussions with those who work with and invest in hedge funds. Additionally, a number of large software providers that provide systems used by many hedge funds generally offer free webinars and training seminars to both hedge fund clients and those interested in learning more about their products.

Keeping informed about new hedge fund technology is important for two primary reasons. First, a hedge fund may have, for one reason or another, made a decision to implement a technology that is rapidly becoming outdated. The reasons for a technology becoming outdated are numerous, including changing priorities of the software manufacturer, creation of new technologies that are making the existing technology outdated, and so forth. If you, as a potential investor, are not aware of the de-evolution of this new technology, then how can you properly evaluate the fund's decision to implement it? If this is indeed the case, investors should consider whether the fund is aware of this trend of the technology becoming outdated, and question whether it has developed a plan to cope with this eventuality. Is the fund so far along with an implementation of this new technology that it is in effect forced to continue with the transition?

As an aside, when performing onsite interviews with various people in a large organization, you may get different stories from different people. Based on my experience, this happens more often with the IT function, especially when discussing new system implementations. Someone from another division, for example, the back office, will, during an interview, say that the new system is expected to go live in June and run parallel for two months. The chief technology officer will then tell you that the new system will not go live before December and will run in parallel for at least six months as they transition the new system onto the firm's newly purchased servers, because the system requires additional computing power that the firm's existing servers cannot provide. Such a scenario demonstrates that people within the organization are neither communicating nor managing expectations internally. This has very little to do with the information technology function, but it comes up as part of a review of a hedge fund's IT function.

The second reason for keeping abreast of the newest technology is that a fund may not have the insight a potential hedge fund investor may have. By performing operational reviews of multiple hedge funds, investors begin to gain an insight as to the major types of technology systems and platforms utilized by hedge funds. For example, one fund may be implementing new accounting system A while another is transitioning away from system A to install system B.

Each fund may have valid reasons for making these transitions. In this scenario, the hedge fund investor should focus on the negatives pointed out by the fund transitioning away from accounting system A to ensure that the fund transitioning to accounting system A has considered them.

If not, then perhaps this raises questions as to how thoroughly the hedge fund transitioning to system A has vetted the system, and the competency and technical knowledge of those within the organization who selected this system.

In addition to understanding the evolving direction of the technological landscape, hedge fund investors should be able to understand the basic technology choices made by hedge funds about such things as hardware and software. As outlined above, this does not require that a potential investor be an industry expert. Let us consider hardware space. A fund manager tells you that in anticipation of future growth the fund has recently added additional storage capacity to increase the total storage capacity to four terabytes. Let us assume that you have no idea what a terabyte is and that even if you did you would not know whether four is an appropriate number. While lack of knowledge in this area is not ideal, it does not mean that you cannot have a somewhat meaningful conversation about it. You could inquire, for example, how many terabytes of data the firm used to have. Why did the firm decide to upgrade to four terabytes and not five? These types of questions would at the very least allow the potential hedge fund investor to gauge the thought process the hedge fund went through in planning its technology infrastructure.

Of course, the more knowledge you have about a subject, the more perspective you bring to the table, and the types of questions you ask will probe much deeper. So, where does that leave the common hedge fund investors who can have an intelligent discussion, and even form their own opinions, about such things as how the Beijing Olympics will affect the demand for iron ore, but do not know a terabyte from a gigabyte? At the very least, hedge fund investors and operational due diligence analysts alike should know what are the most basic, common types of IT hardware and software utilized by the vast majority of hedge funds. From the hardware perspective, these are the things that most modern offices should have, such as servers, routers, remote connectivity devices (i.e., BlackBerry, cell phones, etc.), phone systems, and so on. On the software side, an example would be electronic communication systems for such things as e-mail and instant messaging.

Some hedge funds outsource such functions as back-office accounting and rely on the technology platforms of their administrators. In these cases, hedge fund investors should attempt to gain familiarity with the common platforms utilized by administrators and understand exactly how these systems may interface with the hedge fund's existing systems. When these functions are not outsourced, or are maintained in parallel with the administrator, investors should ask what systems are utilized for the basic functions of accounting and reconciliation, risk management, client relations, investor reporting, and so on.

As part of a due diligence review, investors should take care to understand what systems are utilized to perform each of the individual functions, as well as how these systems interact with each other and their place in the firm's larger network design. For example, does a risk management system sit on top of the firm's accounting system and pull data from it, or sit alongside of it?

Business Continuity and Disaster Recovery

In the modern hedge fund environment, any review of information technology issues also includes a discussion of business continuity and disaster recovery. Specifically, investors should be able to understand the steps a fund has taken to ensure redundancy of systems and its ability to quickly restore those systems in the event they should be disrupted or crash entirely, as well as its plan to continue operations without these systems, at least temporarily. As with the five themes, business continuity and disaster recovery planning are among the areas that cut across multiple parts of an organization. While certain areas may be considered to be more mission critical than others, almost every part of the firm has an element of essentialness to it. This can range from investor-relations website to having multiple redundant backups of a firm's accounting database. Whereas, on the surface, failure of areas such as back-office operations is obviously more important than the failure of such things as an investor-relations website, it is often surprising to most performing operational due diligence that a failure in either case can have potentially devastating effects. For example, if a firm's website crashes and is out of commission for two days, it could cause a panic among investors who utilize such a website for monthly performance estimates. What are the essential skills necessary to properly evaluate a hedge fund's business continuity and disaster recovery plans? From an IT perspective, the skills necessary are relatively similar to those outlined above. There are a host of other issues that bridge the gap between information technology and other parts of the firm, and some that are wholly unrelated to technology. Among those areas that straddle the fence are such things as alternative power generation capabilities and digital telephony. The knowledge required to properly evaluate such areas generally extends beyond that of the normal techie or IT professional. For example, IT professionals are familiar with different computing capacity speeds, ranges of bandwidth, and the devices that use them. It is all in a common language, so to speak. But the world of backup power generation, for example, deals in such things as diesel, natural gas, megawatts, and hertz, which is an entirely different vernacular.

What is an investor to do? As with most of the topics we discuss in this chapter, there is a certain baseline level of knowledge that one performing an operational due diligence review should have about business continuity planning and disaster recovery (BCP/DR). That being said, BCP/DR is a very large field, which has grown substantially in recent years, and one that has many areas that have no real practical application to the hedge fund industry. For example, most hedge funds will never have to design a full-scale inoculation plan for their employees in the event of a serious flu outbreak. Most hedge funds employ fewer than 50 people, and such a wide-scale disaster event is low on the priority scale. If you are general manager at a factory with 10,000 employees however, inoculating employees in the event of such an outbreak would certainly be a valid concern. (That being said, there was an impact on the financial markets during the SARS breakout, but that is an entirely different issue.)

This minimum amount of knowledge should include familiarity with the essential areas of importance to a hedge fund's BCP/DR. Investors should also be familiar with the common types of systems and procedures utilized for such things as data archiving and recovery, both electronic and physical. They should have enough knowledge to not just accept a hedge fund's canned response when asked about BCP/DR. For example, if a hedge fund's marketing materials do not mention backup power generation, does that mean that the fund has not considered it or that it has reviewed backup power generation options and has made a business decision that it is not worth the expense? Similarly, does a firm have a detailed BCP/DR plan that it never tests? It does not take a disaster recovery expert to tell you that the best plan in the world will not work if people do not have such basic things as each other's BlackBerry numbers to call in the event of a business disruption. When you discuss this issue with a hedge fund manager during an onsite meeting, what kind of answers does he provide?

Law

Despite the host of stereotypes about lawyers and the legal profession, all lawyers are not created equal. Putting aside discussions of evaluating a lawyer's skill and style of practice, there is a certain amount of specific legal knowledge and familiarity with the field that is essential to perform hedge fund operational due diligence. After all, we should remember that a hedge fund's investment management company, like any corporation, is a legal entity, and not a person. Similarly, a hedge fund's investment vehicles are legal entities. Both of these entities are governed by laws and rules, some of which are outlined in a hedge fund's core documentation. This is where we begin our discussion of the legal skills necessary to perform an operational review.

The core legal documentation of a hedge fund, which will be discussed in more detail in Chapter 4, includes a hedge fund vehicle's private placement memorandum, articles of association, subscription and redemption documents, and so on. Most importantly, those performing a review of these types of fund documentation need to have a basic understanding of how to read such documents. This includes familiarity with the basic elements of each of these documents, a general understanding of legal terms, and notions about those terms which coincide with market norms. When applied to hedge fund document review, experience tends to yield significant benefits. In addition to increasing the efficiency with which documentation can be reviewed, it also generally means that a reviewer will be able to properly vet which terminology and structures are consistent with market terms and those that fall outside standard market terms. These off-market terms can include both the inclusion and omission of certain elements, which may place a hedge fund investor in a difficult situation.

Those reviewing documentation need to be conscious of the importance of maintaining consistent terms across multiple fund vehicles offered by the same manager. Consider a hedge fund strategy created under a common master–feeder structure. In this example, assume that there is one master fund and two feeders: one onshore and one offshore. In reviewing the fund documentation, an investor should be conscious of the uniformity of certain terms across the domestic and offshore vehicles. Consider, for example, a key person clause. The offshore fund private placement memorandum may have a key person clause that reads as follows:

In the event that any of the firm's key persons should become incapacitated, investors will have the right to redeem in such a manner consistent with normal market conditions.

Now consider the following language from the onshore fund private placement memorandum:

In the event that a majority of the firm's key persons should become incapacitated, investors will have the right to redeem in such a manner consistent with normal market conditions.

Investors in the offshore fund have an advantage over investors in the onshore fund due to this slight difference in terminology. This difference is not so difficult to spot when comparing these small excerpts of text, but such seemingly slight differences can get lost in a sea of text in private placement memoranda, which can often exceed 100 dense pages.

Even an experienced hedge fund lawyer who may be unfamiliar with the operational due diligence process may be very adept at evaluating the particular document you place in front of him (e.g., just the offshore vehicle's document). However, a thorough operational due diligence reviewer will have the requisite knowledge and skill to ask for, and review, both the onshore and offshore vehicles' documentation, in this case private placement memoranda, for a strategy managed pari passu.

This previous example is just one of the many pitfalls to which hedge fund investors may be exposing themselves where they do not possess the necessary knowledge, experience, and skills to perform a thorough operational review of hedge fund documentation.

Compliance

With the increasing impact of technology across all areas of hedge fund operations, it is becoming increasingly important for those involved in analyzing the compliance function within a hedge fund to understand the recent developments in compliance technology and monitor such trends going forward.

Compliance does not merely include ensuring compliance with external regulations, or regulatory compliance. The compliance function is better summarized as evaluating both conformity with regulatory requirements as well as the system of internal controls and oversight necessary to ensure such agreement. This includes developing an understanding of local regulations.

The relationship between the compliance and legal functions should not be ignored. In addition to the fact that certain hedge fund legal documents may reference certain compliance policies and procedures, and vice versa, these compliance policies and procedures are often drafted by legal personnel.

Vendor Evaluation

Hedge funds' service providers can be almost as important as any policies, procedures, or personnel present within a particular hedge fund organization. As such, it is crucial for an investor performing operational due diligence to be able to make a determination as to the operational risks and competencies of the different service providers. This service provider or vendor evaluation must be primarily approached from two perspectives: quality and appropriateness.

First, a potential hedge fund investor must attempt to gain an understanding of the nature and quality of a third-party service provider in isolation relative to its peers. That is to say, regardless of whether a particular service provider was working with a hedge fund under consideration for potential investment, how would an investor rate it? The second perspective relates to the way in which the hedge fund works with this service provider and whether the service provider is appropriate for the hedge fund in question. Let us begin with a discussion of the first perspective, the quality of the service provider.

The notion of best-in-class vendors or service providers, in the modern era, most likely holds its place within the corporate consciousness in relation to accounting firms. Many investors are familiar with the concept of the Big Four accounting firms (PricewaterhouseCoopers, Deloitte Touche Tohmatsu, Ernst&Young, and KPMG). Unfortunately, there is not necessarily a Big Four list for each industry. Even if there were, with accounting and audit firms as no exception, a service provider's size, however that is defined, is not necessarily representative of its overall quality or appropriateness to service the needs of a particular hedge fund. On the contrary, some hedge funds, even larger ones, may be better served by working with smaller niche players to fill certain needs. At any rate, investors should be able to make a determination as to what are the best practices and common market norms regarding the types of services provided by the different hedge fund vendors.

How is this to be accomplished? One approach is for investors to perform due diligence on the service providers themselves. These service provider reviews can be complemented by the operational data garnered during the hedge fund operational due diligence process. A hedge fund investor's learning curve in regard to understanding and gauging the operational due diligence practices is additive. That is, the more hedge funds and hedge fund service providers and investor reviews, the more knowledge the investor gains in regard to the generally accepted practices in the marketplace. If, during the course of the operational due diligence process, an investor encounters an exception to these common practices, further investigation is required. A hedge fund should be able to succinctly explain why it has chosen to deviate from standard practices by selecting a nontraditional vendor or utilizing a vendor in a certain capacity.

Turning to the second perspective, an investor should be able to determine whether a certain hedge fund has selected an appropriate service provider. An example would be a hedge fund that trades a variety of complex instruments and with a very large asset base and that utilizes a small regional accounting firm. There is nothing inherently wrong with this situation; however, at face value it seems as if there is a mismatch. In addition to investors gaining a sense of comfort from the use of a Big Four accounting firm, often this is where the expertise and resources to properly assist a very large complex hedge fund exist. That being said, if the regional firm in our example employs the leading expert in accounting for collateralized loan obligations (CLOs) and this hedge fund has many CLOs, then this may be an appropriate choice.

In addition to the two primary considerations outlined above, there are a number of other areas in which an investor should evaluate a hedge fund's use of a vendor. These other considerations can include the price charged by the vendor, details of the service-level agreement between the service provider and the hedge fund, and personnel turnover at the service provider, as well as the hedge fund's ability to manage the relationship with the service provider to ensure that the services provided are up to par. The point is that as part of the operational due diligence process investors should take care to question both the quality and appropriateness of service providers rather than simply accept a big name as representative of quality.

Background Investigation and Reputation Management

The skills required to properly evaluate the background and reputation of a hedge fund organization and its principals can be organized into two broad categories. First, as part of the reputation management process, a hedge fund investor should be able to comprehend and follow up on any issues uncovered during a background investigation, which will typically be performed by a third-party firm. While it is impossible to predict every type of issue that will arise during a background investigation, the common issues that come up relate to verification of employment and references and litigation issues. Although most background investigation firms are generally paid to take things such as prior court cases in which a principal of the hedge fund may have been involved and boil them down to a digestible format for investors, this is not often the case. More often than not, an investor performing operational due diligence when confronted with such an issue will find himself turning to the source material (i.e., the text of the case itself) in order to elaborate on the background investigation firm's summary. Additionally, such a review of a court case may require an investor to familiarize himself with certain legal principles and terminology that may be new to him. This does not mean that in order to properly perform operational due diligence an investor needs to be a lawyer. However, having familiarity in reading such documentation is generally considered helpful.

Second, once an investor has made a determination as to the reputation and background of the hedge fund organization and its senior management, the investor should, as part of the operational due diligence process, take steps to understand how the firm continues to protect and manage its reputation. A few larger hedge funds in recent years have hired public relations firms to address such things as media inquiries or to prepare press releases regarding firm-wide announcements. Another area of potential reputational risk to a hedge fund relates to the hiring of new employees. Investors should ascertain details as to the types of reference checking performed on new hires. Additionally, investors should inquire whether background investigations are performed on new hires. Finally, once a new individual is hired, investors must make a determination as to whether they wish to perform a background investigation on these individuals. Having the ability to determine whether a hedge fund properly seeks to protect its reputation, and consequently the reputation of its investors, is an essential skill in regard to minimizing reputational risks.

PRIMARY, SECONDARY, BLENDED, AND OTHER SKILLS

Concerning the skills necessary to properly perform operational due diligence with regard to the other primary risk factors, secondary risk factors, blended risk factors, and any other risk factors not addressed by these three risk-factor categories, we can make some general statements. Considering such things as valuation, trade life cycle, fund terms, insurance, tax practices, counterparty oversight, and all other categories not specifically addressed above, the most important skill set an investor can have is to develop a general competency as to what other hedge funds in the space are doing. As intimated earlier, this research process will allow investors to determine where the market's operational benchmark sits in regard to different operational practices, and will also provide them with insight into the ways in which different hedge funds approach similar problems. In some cases, the majority of hedge funds may be in agreement. For other issues, there may be a wide discrepancy among hedge funds as to how they address certain issues. As each hedge fund is unique, some of these discrepancies may be appropriate; but in other cases a hedge fund may not be implementing what would be considered best practices by the vast majority of hedge fund investors.

Two questions now present themselves: First, what is an investor to do if she is new to alternatives and is considering her first hedge fund investment? Second, what if an investor does not have the resources to visit hundreds of hedge fund managers? The answer to both questions may be that investors should outsource the operational due diligence function to third-party firms that specialize in operational due diligence or to professional money management organizations such as a fund of hedge funds. Alternatively, investors may wish to hold off on allocating a large amount of capital to hedge funds until they have properly developed knowledge about operational best practices and continuing developments in different non-investment-related areas. Under this approach, investors could perform operational due diligence, allocating to those firms that they feel meet a high operational standard, and rebalance capital as necessary if they later learn that a particular hedge fund does not meet the market best practice standard. Additionally, over time, investors will likely develop their own particular views as to which operational practices, regardless of the market's view of them, are acceptable and which are not. This can further serve to refine their asset allocation decisions.

In summary, developing an understanding of what approaches different hedge funds have taken to address different operational risk factors is one of the best ways to determine whether a particular hedge fund is deviating from the market norm. Once investors have enough knowledge to determine whether a hedge fund is deviating from general practices, they can then turn to any issue-specific knowledge they may have to make a determination as to whether the particular hedge fund's approach is appropriate. When faced with a situation which may be beyond the scope of a hedge fund investor's core knowledge base, there are a number of sources where the investor can turn for guidance, depending on the circumstances of the situation, including legal counsel, fellow investors, industry conferences, and perhaps even other hedge funds with which the hedge fund investor has previously invested.

IN-HOUSE VERSUS OUTSOURCING

Now that we have established the importance of conducting operational risk reviews and thoroughly understanding the qualifications of individuals necessary to perform such reviews, the next question a hedge fund investor must consider is whether to outsource this function, perform it internally, or somehow combine the two methods.

There are several factors that go into this decision, including:

- Cost-benefit analysis
- Knowledge and experience of the potential investor (or the investor's employees)
- Who will perform ongoing monitoring
- The goal of the review

Several options include:

- To perform an initial operational risk evaluation
- To more fully protect/vet a specific risk

Options currently in existence in the market (note that these rating services generally don't include background investigations) are:

- Third-party operational due diligence providers that provide customized (one-off) operational reviews, where investors are the clients
- Operational risk rating agencies, where the hedge funds are the clients

EVOLUTION OF INDEPENDENT OPERATIONAL RATING AGENCIES

As a market matures, a number of service providers tend to spring up in order to service this market. Such is the case in the field of hedge fund operational due diligence. In recent years, a number of third-party service providers have emerged in an attempt to meet the increasing investor demand for operational data and operational reviews for hedge funds. One of the more well-developed service provider segments has been the operational risk rating agencies. These rating agencies generally fall into two categories.

The first category of rating agencies provide a seal of approval over hedge funds. These rating agencies do not necessarily focus on evaluating the operational risks of a hedge fund on an absolute or relative scale. Instead, these reviews seek to give funds a "pass/fail" rating. For the purposes of this text, we will refer to such rating agencies as *binary rating providers*, because they seek to provide a binary, yea or nay, evaluation of a fund.

The second group of hedge fund rating providers grew out of the traditional credit rating business. These rating providers primarily attempt to leverage their institutional brand names and take a different approach from that of their binary rating provider counterparts. As an extension of their credit rating methodology, these rating agencies seek to evaluate the operational risks of hedge funds on an absolute scale based on a predefined ratings methodology.

BENEFITS OF THIRD-PARTY RATING AGENCIES

Under the vast majority of third-party operational rating agency models the hedge funds are the clients. This is because, it is not particularly cost effective for an individual client to engage the services of a third-party rating agency to perform an operational review of a hedge fund. Depending on the size of the hedge fund organization under consideration, these operational rating fees can generally begin at $50,000 or more. If we examine the typical portfolio of an ultra-high-net-worth individual investor, which may have 10 to 20 hedge funds, then the cost of operational reviews by such a firm could easily exceed $500,000. When you consider rebalancing and turnover within an investor's hedge fund portfolio, the expense of such reviews could quickly become prohibitive. Consequently, these third-party rating agencies typically have hedge funds as their clients. This provides a substantial savings to hedge fund investors, who no longer have to pay for such ratings. Additionally, operational ratings may provide a good starting point for less-well-resourced investors. This buyer-based model has also faced several criticisms, including questions arising as to the independence of these ratings.

CRITICISMS OF THIRD-PARTY RATING AGENCIES AND OPERATIONAL DUE DILIGENCE PROVIDERS

One criticism of operational risk rating agencies is that the hedge funds themselves are typically the clients. This leads to several other criticisms of this buyer-based model, including that hedge fund clients that are likely to get a good rating are more likely to undergo the ratings process. Specifically, in regard to binary rating providers, who seek to "pass" or "fail" operational risk rating issuers, one question that should be considered is whether these rating agencies will actually fail their hedge fund clients. Indeed, this type of blanket criticism can be applied to all buyer-based models. This criticism perhaps holds more weight in the nascent binary rating provider marketplace, where rating providers often walk a harrowing tightrope between maintaining the credibility of independence in their reviews and pleasing their hedge fund clients.

The activist role of such rating agencies is also unclear. As part of an operational review, if items are found that could be classified as an operational deficiency, questions arise as to whether the rating agency should release its report, and not provide the hedge funds with recommendations as to how to fix the problem, or provide the hedge fund with a series of recommendations, wait until the hedge fund has resolved the problem to some degree of mutual satisfaction between the hedge fund and the rating service, and then issue the report. Instead, this approach appears to lend itself to being classified more as operational risk consulting than as operational evaluating.

An additional criticism of third-party rating agencies is that they often follow generic template methodologies that produce cookie-cutter-type canned reports. Such reports may provide novice hedge fund investors with a false sense of security that all of a hedge fund's operational bases were covered. Each hedge fund is different, and poses unique operational risks that often require a flexible operational due diligence framework in order to properly evaluate all of them. As such, there has been a trend by investors against the homogenization of the operational risk analysis of hedge funds, which for purposes of this text we will refer to as a trend of *hedgemoginization*. Despite the lack of traction in the marketplace among both investors and hedge funds alike, the hedgemoginization culture continues to be fueled by generic operational due diligence methodologies and the canned nature of the operational due diligence reports that are produced by some third-party rating firms.

Another consideration is that background investigations are not being incorporated into the operational ratings process. Without a background investigation, investors rely solely on a third-party operational rating, and perhaps an attached report that may elaborate on some fund-specific operational data points; investors are really only getting part of the picture. Suppose a hedge fund has an extremely strong noninvestment infrastructure, and stringent controls, and would receive the highest operational risk rating possible from all rating providers. Now suppose that this fund's co–portfolio manager was named in several insider trading suits, to one of which he pled guilty, and was fined and sanctioned by the relevant financial regulator. This would clearly alter the potential reputational risks associated with the firm and raise questions concerning the potential oversight of firm management; however, as most operational risk rating agencies do not consider reputational risk, such factors would not negatively impact the operational rating of the hedge fund.

Another common criticism specific to outsourced operational due diligence providers, where the clients are investors as opposed to the hedge funds under review, is that questions arise as to how the proprietary nature of such information can be maintained. Investors looking to establish an operational edge, or who hold themselves out to a different operational benchmark than others, may find such a service unacceptable. These firms, similar to the rating agencies, generally have predefined operational methodologies that they apply to the hedge fund under consideration. It would not be financially feasible for these operational due diligence firms to limit themselves to working for only one client. Consequently, if two clients are interested in having the same operational due diligence firm evaluate the same hedge fund, most firms will accept this business and simply update their previous research. There is nothing wrong with this approach; however, investors should be conscious of the fact that, similar to background investigations, the information they are receiving is essentially equivalent to operational hedge fund research available in the marketplace for purchase.

An additional criticism of these rating agencies is that they are fixed as of a point in time. The majority of these third-party rating agencies do not perform ongoing operational due diligence unless a hedge fund pays for it. As outlined in Chapter 1, operational information has a decaying value over time. As hedge funds change, so, too, do their operational risk exposures and sensitivities. Investors relying on a third-party historical operational risk rating may be relying on outdated or inaccurate data. Let us consider the following example.

Ketchup Capital Management's (KCM) CFO, Duke Nukem, has been with the firm for over 20 years. He recently completed his CFA and has been lured away by KCM's archrival, Mustard Capital (MC). Two months prior to Duke's departure, a large ratings provider, Salt & Pepper Ratings Corp., completed their intensive review of KCM's operational risk factors. KCM scored quite well and was given an A– rating. The highest rating possible from the rating service provider is an A. KCM hastily replaced Duke with Mark Harmony, a highly qualified CFO with a well-respected industry reputation. Mark is qualified for the job, but does not necessarily have the familiarity with the intricacies of KCM funds or policies to effectively oversee the process immediately, and will most likely take six to eight months to get up to speed. Concurrent with Duke's departure, KCM's head of investor relations, Maria Beardsly, is presenting the KCM flagship fund to various endowments and foundations at a capital introduction conference. In addition to talking about KCM's last five successful trades and the pedigree of its senior management, Maria touts the A– rating as a strong indicator of KCM's operational quality. Tom Markson, the manager of the endowment of BigU College, is excited about the prospect of investing with KCM; however, his endowment is particularly sensitive to the issue of operational risk as it had invested in a hedge fund previously that had failed for operational reasons including fraud. A question worth considering is whether KCM would have received the same A– from the Salt & Pepper Ratings Corp. if they had completed their review when Mark had been installed in the role? Also, should KCM disclose that their operational rating may be different as a result of Duke's departure? What about Salt & Pepper—do they have a responsibility, if not some sort of moral obligation perhaps, to openly disclose that the rating given to KCM would be different under their existing framework?

An additional factor worth considering when evaluating the potential benefits of third-party operational risk providers, be it ratings agencies or operational due diligence providers, is the evolving nature of such client-centric diligence firms. Many of these firms, seeking to capitalize on the existing nature of their relationship with hedge fund investors, have begun to offer investment-related due diligence services as well. This raises questions as to the nature of the independence of such reviews.

Another area of yet-uncharted territory for operational reviews is what exactly is being promised by these rating agencies. If, for example, Tom invests with KCM and it does indeed fail for operational reasons, would the endowment of BigU College have any legal recourse over the rating agency?

Some feel that perhaps the true value of such operational risk ratings to the hedge funds is as an investor-relations and asset-raising tool, as opposed to creating a fair and unbiased review of the non-investment-related risks extant within a hedge fund.

FACTORS TO CONSIDER BEFORE PERFORMING AN OPERATIONAL REVIEW OF A HEDGE FUND

Regardless of whether an investor decides to perform an operational review of a hedge fund on his own or outsources the function to a third-party firm, he should first consider the goal of such a review. If the point of an operational review is merely to fill a file folder so that an investor can claim to have gone through the motions, then there are many cheap alternatives available in the marketplace. Similar to Cliff Notes, many of these low-cost, canned third-party reports seem to do the job, and do indeed help investors who know nothing about a fund get up to speed. Unfortunately, many investors tend to confuse report length or cost with thoroughness. However, an investor may perform operational due diligence because he has a genuine interest in determining whether a particular hedge fund meets a certain basic level of overall operational competency. The decision whether to go in-house or outsource the operational due diligence function ultimately comes down to the expertise, resources, and goals of the investor; however, each of these issues should be carefully considered before performing a quick cost-benefit analysis. Every investor has different opinions and operational thresholds regarding what standard of operational competency and level of operational risk he is willing to accept from a hedge fund. An outsourced, one-size-fits-all approach may not be appropriate for every hedge fund under review and for every investor. Such considerations should be carefully weighed and reevaluated throughout the hedge fund investing life cycle.

Notes

1. See Michael Power, "The Invention of Operational Risk," Discussion Paper No. 16, London School of Economics and Political Science, ESRC Centre for Analysis of Risk and Regulation, June 2003.

CHAPTER 4

Creating an Initial Operational Profile

T he previous chapters have described the essential building blocks of hedge fund operational due diligence. Metaphorically speaking, with this detailed blueprint in hand, we can now discuss how to mix the mortar and lay the foundation for our operational review. This process is summarized in Exhibit 4.1. This foundation will come in the form of document collection and analysis, one of the most essential parts of any operational due diligence review. This will allow us to construct the frame for our operational due diligence house. Once our discussion of documentation is complete, we can then discuss the hedge fund manager interview process. This interview process allows us as investors to evaluate the understanding we have developed as a result of the documentation review process. Often it can lead to further questioning, additional document analysis, and fine-tuning of our initial preconception of how certain operational processes are carried out. Once we are sure of the sturdiness of the frame we have constructed, we can then put the roof on the house and come to an operational determination.

WHEN DOES AN OPERATIONAL DUE DILIGENCE REVIEW BEGIN?

We have not yet discussed *when* the operational due diligence process officially begins. One common misconception is that the real meat of a review does not take place until the onsite visit. This could not be further from the truth. Before going to visit a hedge fund, those performing operational due diligence should have a thorough understanding of the firm's core operational competencies as well as who are the key operational players within the organization.

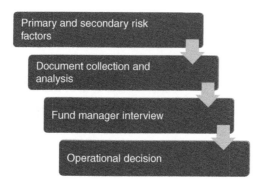

EXHIBIT 4.1 Hedge Fund Operational Due Diligence Sequence Flow

Items that are gathered via more informal communication also factor into the process. These could be answers to preliminary operational questions sent via e-mail, for example, or comments made during the capital introduction process. The operational due diligence clock should start running from the moment you are first introduced to a hedge fund. This approach has multiple benefits, including allowing you to ensure that a hedge fund is not making grand operational boasts in the courting stages, when a thorough subsequent operational due diligence review may paint a less rosy picture. This should factor into the operational decision-making process and is a key element in evaluating the five core themes (oversight, controls, connectivity, scalability, and stability) and in particular a sixth theme, consistency, which we will discuss in more detail in Chapter 6.

The primary purpose of the onsite visit is twofold. First is to confirm the operational story a potential investor has been able to piece together from a hedge fund's documentation. Second is to follow up or clarify any specific issues that were either vague or not discussed in enough detail, or at all, in the manager's documentation. Too many performing operational due diligence go into an operational due diligence review without the proper preparation. This is similar to trying to teach yourself a subject while sitting for the exam. Sure, you might be able to wing it, but it is certainly not the best way to approach the subject.

DOCUMENTATION

The heart of the operational due diligence review of a hedge fund begins with the collection of basic hedge fund documentation. One common misconception held by those performing an operational due diligence review for the first time is that hedge funds know what documentation they are supposed to provide to you. Unfortunately for hedge fund investors, there is no set list of documents they are required to provide to you. This is especially true for unregistered hedge funds. The onus is placed squarely on the investor to be proactive in both requesting and analyzing a hedge fund's documentation. As with most things in the world of operational due diligence, persistence and thoroughness are essential to the document review process. That being said, all things must start somewhere, and we will begin our discussion of hedge fund documentation collection and review with the Piñata Problem.

THE PIÑATA PROBLEM

Beginning an operational review is akin to busting open a piñata—one does not exactly know what is falling out, but it all looks enticing. Organizational charts, audited financials, reams of legal documents, flashy marketing pitchbooks—all are provided by the willing hedge fund manager before a potential investor even has to ask for it. There are hundreds of pages of information at your disposal. It is all really good looking and detailed, and seems to provide a wealth of information about the hedge fund organization with which you are considering making a potential investment.

With all of this document candy lying on the floor, you hurriedly rush over to sort it out. The problem is that no one has gone through with a rubber stamp labeling these documents as *investment related* and *non–investment related*. Even worse, if the rubber stamper had appeared, he would not have told you which documents were more important than others, or better still, what to look for in these documents, or which issue required clarification and further follow-up with the hedge fund manager.

Potential hedge fund investors, with limited resources and/or knowledge, often become intimidated by all of this documentation and are prone simply to throw up their hands. There are generally two types of behavior that follow from this intimidation syndrome. Some potential hedge fund investors performing operational due diligence may decide it is better not to ask for everything. They may feel the documentation is too cumbersome and it is better to focus on smaller, more digestible bites of documentation. A second type of behavior is to ask for everything, throw it in a file, and not thoroughly analyze the majority of the information. This *fat-file syndrome* seems impressive on the surface, or perhaps when the documentation is presented in a lawsuit, but does little to further the operational due diligence effort. It is not that most people collect the documentation with the intention of never reviewing it. It is just that things come up and priorities shift. At the end of the day, it could simply be that a potential investor simply had collected it with the intention of reviewing it but never got to it.

Partially contributing to this fat file syndrome is potential confusion over which documentation a potential investor should be asking for. It may be an instinctive gut reaction to want to request everything. Unfortunately, *everything* is a subjective term. A hedge fund undergoing on operational review may either try to drown you in documents or keep the list short and sweet. When conducting an operational risk review, one approach that is often successful is to have the operational analyst start from a predefined list of topics that you want the documents to address and build from there. This resolves the typical *Anatomy of a Murder* problem that first-year law school students are taught, where document suggestions by a hedge fund in response to a request lead an investor down an errant primrose path, and lends itself to determining the entire shape of the operational elephant before poking about with a flashlight in the dark.

There is no one right answer to the question of which documents to request; however, there are a series of generally agreed-upon documents that each focus on the different major operational competencies of a hedge fund. This list is by no means comprehensive, but rather is proposed as a baseline starting point from which to begin an operational review. Before proceeding in our discussion, two issues should be pointed out. First, not every hedge fund will have prepared the documentation we are about to discuss. Does this mean a potential investor should not even consider the fund? Of course not—some hedge funds do not formalize certain policies or procedures into documents. While memorializing certain procedures is certainly advisable and has numerous benefits to both the hedge fund manager and potential investors, it is by no means an absolute requirement. If a hedge fund manager does not document certain policies and procedures, these procedures can be vetted in person by the potential investor during the onsite review. The point is that even if a physical document does not exist to explain the policies relating to a certain operational function, the hedge fund manager should still be able to explain, or better yet demonstrate, the policies relating to operational areas in question.

The second matter worth noting is that not all hedge fund documentation is created equal. Not all managers call certain policies by the same name. Additionally, certain managers may lump several policies and procedures into a larger document, whereas others may break up this information into several smaller documents. For example, an anti-money-laundering policy is typically found as part of a larger compliance manual. Some funds may break this policy out into a separate document. In this example, if you request only the compliance manual, you will not necessarily get the anti-money-laundering policy.

Similar to the process involved when conducting an onsite manager review, it is advisable that manager document requests not be self-limiting. For example, hedge fund managers will generally provide a potential investor with exactly what she asks for—no more and sometimes less. So if a potential investor submits a request for document X, she will get document X. The problem arises when there are two other documents, Y and Z, that may be crucial to the understanding of X but are not provided by the fund because the investor did not ask for them. The motivations of the hedge fund manager may not be sinister in this instance. Perhaps he was simply complying with the request and did not want to confuse the potential investor with extraneous information. Additionally, documents Y and Z may be primarily focused on some other vehicles that the potential investor is not considering. A better way to request such documentation would be to ask for document X and *all related documents*. This, however, may still not cause the hedge fund to provide such documentation; there are no magic words here. As mentioned earlier, the onus is on the potential hedge fund investor. Only by thoroughly vetting document X, asking additional follow-up questions, and continuing to probe, might an investor be cued as to the existence of documents Y and Z. That being said, if the request itself limits you solely to document X, you may never get to these additional documents.

When performing an operational due diligence review, at least in terms of documentation, it is generally considered better to err on the side of caution. This is to say that, as a rule of thumb, the more documents the hedge fund investor collects and analyzes, the more the investor will be able to learn about a hedge fund's operational processes and risks. So, where do we begin?

There are 15 core documents—18 if Securities and Exchange Commission (SEC) registered—that are generally considered to provide a good starting point from which one can begin an operational due diligence review. This list is by no means all inclusive. Additionally, one central theme that should remain in the back of your mind throughout this discussion regarding hedge fund documentation is that not all hedge funds are created equal. Some work very hard to ensure that their documentation is informative, up to date, and specific to the operations of their funds. Others use stale materials that are confusing at best. This should be a factor in the operational review process, as well. If a hedge fund has the best operational infrastructure in the world but cannot explain how these operational procedures work, you have to wonder what is really going on. Similar to "black-box trading strategies," these black-box operations require a larger leap of faith than most hedge fund investors are comfortable making. That being said, let us turn to the documentation list:

For the Hedge Fund Vehicle(s) Under Consideration:
I. Core fund legal documents:
  1. Offering memoranda
  2. Subscription documents
  3. Articles of association (if applicable)
  4. Limited partnership agreement (if applicable)
II. Other core fund documents:
  5. Audited financials
  6. Hedge fund manager–provided due diligence questionnaire
  7. Samples of recent marketing materials (pitchbook, etc.)
  8. Recent investor letters
  9. Performance track record

For the Hedge Fund Management Company:
  10. Compliance manual, including:
    a. Personal trading procedures
    b. Anti-money-laundering policies and procedures
    c. Electronic communication policy
  11. Organizational chart
  12. Business continuity and disaster recovery plan
  13. Valuation procedures
  14. Certificate of incorporation and/or certificate of good standing
  15. Details of insurance coverage (including copies of insurance certificates)

For U.S. SEC–Registered Funds:
  16. Form ADV Part 1
  17. Form ADV Part 2
  18. Schedule F

A few comments are in order regarding this list of documents. As mentioned earlier, it is essential for those collecting these documents not to be self-limiting in their requests. A common example of where this occurs is in hedge funds organized in a master–feeder structure. In this structure, there are generally two feeder funds: an onshore domestic partnership (typically a *limited partnership*) and an offshore feeder, and a master fund. The feeder funds generally invest substantially all of their assets in the master fund. This is also sometimes referred to as a *hub-and-spoke* system. When submitting an initial document request to a hedge fund, a potential investor may be considering an investment in only the onshore feeder. This does not mean that he should ignore the documents related to the offshore feeder and the master. Valuable information can be obtained from reviewing these documents both in isolation and in conjunction with the domestic feeder documents. If a potential investor is not aware that he should ask for this documentation, he is getting only part of the document story.

If a fund is not registered with the U.S. SEC, it may have been previously and has since deregistered. In this case, a potential investor can generally obtain historically filed documentation from the SEC website (www.sec.gov). Despite the age of such information, it is current as of the most recent filing date before deregistration; it does provide a potential investor with a historical snapshot of a hedge fund at a particular time. Useful information such as the firm's managing principals, former addresses, previously affiliated entities, and so forth can be found in these documents.

In regard to audited financial statements, two points should be mentioned. First, there is the question of how many years of financials should be reviewed. As a general rule, most investors look back at least three years. Following our err-on-the-side-of-caution rule, it is ideal to review financials of the fund under consideration *from inception.* Many valuable pieces of information can be learned and monitored from this historical financial statement review, including such things as auditor consistency, former fund names, different types of investments, any prior terms such as different management or performance fees, allocation of startup costs, and so forth. Of course, for a newer fund, a potential investor may be investing with only one or two years of financial statements. In this case, a potential hedge fund investor should review what is available. Similarly, if a potential seed investment is being considered in a brand-new hedge fund, it may be advisable to review the financial statements of any other funds the portfolio managers may have overseen previously. While it may not have a direct correlation to the firm's financial statements, which have yet to be produced, it may provide you with some insight into the way a certain portfolio manager handles such things as expenses and types of positions held, and so on.

A second point worth noting is who is providing the financial statements to the investor. It is considered ideal to obtain such information directly from the firm's auditor. This would provide an additional level of assurance that the firm is not manufacturing fraudulent financials and claiming a relationship with an auditor that it does not have. Unfortunately, in the current market environment, most auditors will not even confirm the business relationship they have with a hedge fund client, outside of providing their audit opinion on the audit firm's letterhead. This places potential hedge fund investors in an awkward position. Both hedge funds and investors alike realize the importance of third-party independent auditors, but what does one do when the auditors, who charge large fees to the hedge funds for their services, will not speak with potential investors to confirm that they work for the hedge funds? This is an evolving issue; some hedge funds have recently begun to push it back on auditors to confirm their relationships with investors. As with most things, in the world of operational due diligence the onus is on the potential hedge fund investor to confirm this relationship via obtaining the financial statements directly from the auditors. It is by no means an indication of a hedge fund organization's operational prowess if the auditor will not provide such documentation directly, and it must come from the hedge fund. However, you cannot get an answer if you do not ask, and in some cases, particularly outside of the United States, you may be able to obtain the financial statements directly from the audit firm.

Similarly, in regard to legal documentation, obtaining the documentation directly from a third party rather than the hedge fund itself is preferred. This documentation can be provided by the fund's third-party administrator's shareholder services division or the hedge fund's legal counsel. There is, of course, less chance that a hedge fund has something to gain by willfully manipulating its legal documentation as opposed to tampering with financial statements; however, the less opportunity there is for manipulation in the document-collection process, the better. Put another way, the more independent third-party people involved, the more difficult it is to orchestrate false documentation.

In regard to both the certificate of incorporation and certificate of good standing, it is worth clarifying what these documents are as well as the benefits of collecting them. For the purposes of hedge fund investing, a certificate of incorporation is a document that serves to verify that a certain hedge fund vehicle and/or management company was incorporated within a certain jurisdiction. Similarly, a certificate of good standing is a document, generally issued by the place of incorporation of the management company, stating that the management company is in good standing, in legal existence, and that all annual taxes have been paid to date. Often such information can be confirmed via the regulator's website. The question may then be posed as to why it would be useful to collect such a certificate. The answer is twofold. First, websites maintained by certain regulatory authorities are sometimes infrequently updated or contain partial information, making relying on them sometimes difficult. Additionally, a listing on a website, such as pulling up a fund vehicle's name, as a result of a query of registered entities may not provide as complete information as can be found in a full certificate, which includes date of incorporation, type of company registration (e.g., exempt versus nonexempt), and so on. Additionally, certain companion documents may accompany the certificate of incorporation that a potential hedge fund investor would not likely otherwise receive. One example of this would be the document often provided by Bermuda-registered companies, called the

Memorandum of Association of Company Limited by Shares, in conjunction with the certificate of incorporation.

Some may argue that the process of collecting such documentation is overly cumbersome and unnecessary. Ninety-nine percent of the time I would have to agree with them; however, there may be an instance where something an investor reads on one of these documents will cause her to question something on another document and an inconsistency may emerge. It is this unpredictable 1% that can lead to potential problems for investors; consequently, it is advisable to leave no stone unturned in the document review process.

There is a host of other information that may be available, such as 13-F filings, service provider due diligence questionnaires, and so on, from which valuable information can be gleaned and that can provide valuable operational insight into a hedge fund organization. As noted above, collecting and reviewing all such documentation is encouraged and will serve to better hone a potential hedge fund investor's analysis prior to the onsite due diligence meeting.

DUE DILIGENCE QUESTIONNAIRE: TO USE OR NOT TO USE?

There are two opinions as to whether to utilize an operational due diligence questionnaire. Certain hedge fund investors prepare their own, unique due diligence questionnaire, which they have hedge fund managers complete prior to making an investment. Others opt not to use a questionnaire and instead generally rely on the hedge fund's *manager-provided questionnaire*. These manager-provided questionnaires typically follow some sort of pre-defined format based on one of several common industry questionnaires, including the Alternative Investment Management Association's due diligence questionnaire. These investors point to the fact that making a hedge fund manager complete an individual questionnaire specific to the investor's organization places too much of a burden on the hedge fund manager. This was the primary motivation behind the SEC's announcement in March 2008 that it was discontinuing the use of its 27-page questionnaire to monitor insider trading.[1] So, which is the correct approach?

Those who do not use a due diligence questionnaire point to the fact that most hedge fund managers have very detailed due diligence questionnaires that address the majority of issues potential investors would address in their questionnaire. By forcing managers to complete an investor's due diligence questionnaire, these investors are essentially making the hedge fund copy and paste a great deal of information from one questionnaire to another.

This, they feel, is a wasted effort and unnecessary. An additional argument against using a due diligence questionnaire focuses on the surprise element of the operational due diligence review. By providing a hedge fund manager with a list of questions in advance, you are essentially (to borrow a poker analogy) showing your hand before it is played. These people prefer to review all of the hedge fund manager's prepared materials and "surprise" the manager with those questions not covered or that require more detail during the onsite review.

However, those investors who choose to make a hedge fund manager complete their own customized due diligence questionnaire give several reasons for this. First, they cite that a hedge fund manager's due diligence questionnaire is just that, prepared by the manager. It can be argued that all the information in this document contains a certain amount of spin and that it is more focused on marketing than providing information. Of course, this varies from document to document, but it is highly unlikely that hedge fund managers would speak poorly about themselves in their own due diligence questionnaire. Second, a hedge fund manager's generic due diligence questionnaire may not focus in enough detail, or at all, on certain issues that are important to a potential hedge fund investor. A third reason those who insist that a hedge fund manager complete a pre-prepared questionnaire relates to the flipside surprise element referenced earlier. Rather than viewing the element of surprise as to their own advantage, these potential investors prefer to be transparent with the hedge fund managers. They are seeking answers to certain questions and do not place particular importance on putting the hedge fund manager on the spot. Indeed, when performing operational due diligence reviews, potential hedge fund investors will invariably find that they ask certain questions or broach certain issues to which the answer is not immediately available and requires some research by the hedge fund's personnel. This can be something as simple as which release version of a particular software a firm is utilizing or as esoteric as the name of a former employee who departed the firm several years ago. Some investors argue that there is something to be gained by utilizing the surprise element to see how much knowledge and competency certain operational professionals have on the tip of their tongue; however, other investors point out that little is gained by testing these operational personnel on the operational minutiae of their organizations during an onsite interview.

Another reason some investors opt to have hedge fund managers complete their own unique due diligence questionnaires is that forcing the manager to spell out in writing how certain procedures are implemented in a firm serves to create a touchstone to which these processes can be compared during an onsite operational review. If a manager, in a due diligence questionnaire, details that she performs a certain procedure a particular way, but during an onsite interview, when you discuss the same procedure, a completely different set of processes are in place, then something is clearly amiss. Typically, those issues covered in a due diligence questionnaire prepared by the hedge fund manager are more polished internally; however, when investors venture outside these boundaries with their own questionnaires, certain inconsistencies may emerge.

BACKGROUND INVESTIGATIONS

Regardless of the importance a potential hedge fund investor places on such issues as regulatory actions and reputational risk, a background investigation is one of the most important documents that make up part of a complete operational due diligence review package. As with most of the documentation and operational data points collected during an operational review, the importance of the techniques described in this text does not lie in guiding potential investors toward a particular operational decision. Rather, the primary purpose of the techniques described in this text is to be sure that a potential hedge fund investor has the skill to uncover and analyze the non-investment-related risks involved with hedge fund investing. The actual determination made depends on a particular investor's operational threshold. This, too, is the purpose of the background investigation. Regardless of what a hedge fund investor does with the information, without it she is simply making an operational decision with only part of the story and actively choosing to leave certain stones unturned. The purpose of our discussion in this text will not be to teach investors how to perform a background investigation. This is better left to professional investigators and other texts. Rather, here we will discuss the various options those performing operational due diligence have when deciding to place a hedge fund under consideration for potential investment through some type of background investigation process. One key consideration in the process is who the appropriate people are on which to perform the background investigation.

On Whom Are Background Investigations to Be Performed?

Looking across the hedge fund industry, there are a wide variety of answers to this question. As with most things in the field of operational due diligence, once again, the answer is *it depends*. Virtually all those performing background investigation will agree that the hedge fund management company should be investigated. This is where the commonality stops. There are three common approaches hedge fund investors take when determining on whom to perform a background investigation:

1. Equity ownership model
2. Investment decision-making-authority model
3. Risk control model

There is a certain element of overlap among these models; however, each generally has its own unique individuals that will be covered as part of a background investigation search. It should be noted that these models serve as guidelines and not absolute rules. If, when reviewing a hedge fund organization, a potential hedge fund investor wants to have an investigation performed on the firm's administrative assistant, there is nothing wrong with that, if the investor believes he has good reason to perform the investigation.

Equity Ownership Model As the name implies, the equity ownership model suggests that an investigation be performed on all those who have equity ownership in the management company of the hedge fund organization. This is generally feasible from a cost and investigation duration perspective for a small hedge fund organization with two or three owners; however, in larger hedge fund organizations that may have upward of 20 equity owners such searches can become prohibitively expensive and lengthy.

Investment Decision-Making-Authority Model This model focuses on performing background investigations on those individuals who have authority to make investment decisions and act (i.e., trade) on such decisions. This generally includes portfolio managers and traders. This model does not focus on key operational personnel within a firm and instead focuses on vetting the backgrounds of those involved with the investment process on a daily basis.

Risk Control Model This model focuses on all individuals, both investment and noninvestment focused, who control risk within an organization. These can be the portfolio managers and head traders, as well as the chief financial officer (CFO), chief compliance officer (CCO), chief operating officer (COO), and chief executive officer (CEO). Depending on the organization under consideration, this model generally encompasses the most individuals.

When Should a Background Investigation Be Ordered?

At what point, in the overall investment and operational due diligence processes, should a background investigation be ordered? The answer to this question generally depends on the structure of the hedge fund allocation organization. Some funds of hedge funds follow staged- or phased-type approaches, where a background investigation is not initiated until a manager reaches a certain stage or phase in the review process. This is typically in parallel with the operational due diligence process. While they are in the minority, these days, other allocators perform a background investigation only when the entire investment and operational due diligence processes are complete. However, regardless of when the investigation is ordered from a third-party firm, it should be done.

Evaluating Third-Party Background Investigation Firms

Now that we have established the importance of performing a background investigation, we turn to a caveat. Not all background investigations are created equal. Just as with the entire operational due diligence process, there are varying degrees to which a potential investor can investigate a hedge fund management company and its employees.

Before deciding on which type of background investigation to pursue, it is worth considering what the goals of the investigation are. Is the goal simply to determine whether a regulator has ever levied a sanction or fine against the hedge fund's management company or its principals? Are you interested in learning whether a hedge fund has ever been sued by a former employee? Are you interested in learning about anything in the media that may mention a hedge fund in a less-than-favorable light? Perhaps you represent an entity that is opposed to alcohol; would it be important for you to learn whether a hedge fund manager was ever convicted of DUI?

The answers to questions such as these are a way for an investor to gauge how thorough of a background investigation to perform. This brings us to our discussion about how an investor effectively determines the type of background investigation to which to subject a hedge fund. The three factors by which we can evaluate an investigation are:

1. Duration of investigation
2. Depth of investigation
3. Expense

Duration of Investigation   Background investigation firms have a wide range of time frames during which they can complete an investigation. This is contingent on a number of factors, including geographical location of the hedge fund manager, countries lived in and worked in by the subjects under investigation, number of subjects being investigated, whether the background investigation firm has performed previous work on this subject (and how long ago this work was performed), the amount of media available on the subjects under investigation, age of the subjects under investigation, and so on. In a perfect world, an investor reviewing a hedge fund should allow for ample time for the background investigation firm to complete its work prior to making an investment. If anything is uncovered in the investigation that requires further inquiry with the hedge fund manager, this will take additional time to clarify as well. This process can be as short as a few days or take up to several months. To account for this significant time commitment, a background investigation often is ordered in parallel with the start of the operational due diligence process.

Certain background investigation firms promise very detailed reports to be delivered in questionably short turnaround times. It is important for potential hedge fund investors to realize that certain things in the background investigation process cannot be rushed. Courts are open only certain times during the day; company representatives and universities may take a few days to return phone calls to confirm such things as employment and enrollment dates. These things cannot be rushed for want of persistence or money. A competent background investigation firm will not compromise the integrity of its process to provide a quick turnaround.

Depth of Investigation   Similar to the document collection process, there is no predefined list of things that are supposed to be covered as part of a background investigation. For example, some background investigation firms perform credit searches on individuals; others do not. There are several basic areas all background investigations will cover, including searches of a subject's criminal and civil records, bankruptcy records, tax liens, and regulatory filings. If a subject under investigation has lived and worked in multiple countries, a search is required of each jurisdiction. Not all background investigation firms will automatically search each jurisdiction without an investor request. Even if they do, this will generally increase the cost and duration of the investigation. In certain jurisdictions, such searches may prove futile; in places such as Japan, where people do not generally sue each other as they do in the United States, there are limited court records. A competent background investigation firm should be able to provide guidance as to which searches may be worthwhile and which may not. This is especially true when an individual under investigation has only spent brief stints in certain jurisdictions.

Some third-party background investigation firms employ former agents from governmental investigative and intelligence agencies such as the Federal Bureau of Investigation (FBI), Central Intelligence Agency (CIA), and Interpol. Many of these individuals have professional and social networks within local and global police forces around the world and may be able to provide valuable insight into certain types of investigations or watch-lists a subject under investigation may be on. Additionally, certain types of background investigation firms provide multiple levels of service depending on the client they are servicing. These services can include pre-employment screening as well as more extreme litigation support services, including surveillance. In the vast majority of hedge fund circumstances, this type of due diligence is overkill. Certain types of investment banking deals, private equity investments, or investments in emerging markets may require this type of investigative prowess; however, for the vast majority of U.S.-based hedge fund managers, searches of publicly available records and court documentation are considered sufficient. There are an increasing number of background investigation firms that cater to hedge fund investors.

Expense It is important for potential hedge fund investors to understand the process the investigation firm utilized in order to gauge the appropriateness of the costs charged. In regard to background investigations, cost is not always representative of quality, and you do not always get what you pay for. That being said, there is generally a notable difference between a $200 report and a $5,000 investigation. Most third-party background investigation firms that cater to the hedge fund industry will charge a flat fee for their investigative services. Investors should take care to understand exactly what this flat fee is buying them. If a series of issues come up as part of the initial investigation, will the firm investigate them as part of the original fee or will additional costs be incurred? Is the fee quoted the actual fee that will be charged, or is it simply an estimate? Many hedge fund investors do not take the time to ask these questions or understand the background investigator's process and simply view the report as a check-the-box requirement.

The output of such a report should also be considered when pricing out a certain investigation. We can pose the question this way: Would you pay more to a background investigator who is going to provide a potential investor with hundreds of pages of source documentation, media articles, and so on, or to an investigator who provides less source documentation and a summary of findings and analysis of this documentation? While there is nothing wrong with having the appropriate source documentation attached to an investigation, the job of the investigation firm should be to both dig up this information and assist those performing operational due diligence in digesting such information. It is practically useless to provide potential hedge fund investors with hundreds of pages of documentation, media searches, court filings, and so on and leave it up to them to figure out what is important. A competent background investigation firm should assist investors in distilling this information down to its key components. This can be accomplished via a written summary of the key points of the background firm's findings, a verbal discussion, or both. Such an analysis should be included in the price paid for the investigation. If, as a result of this discussion, there are certain issues where the potential hedge fund investor feels that he wants to go to the source and read for himself, he should certainly have access to this documentation from the firm. But the onus should not be on the hedge fund investors to sort through hundreds of pages of additional documentation to find the relevant details. This is why they are paying good money to a competent background investigation firm. Potential hedge fund investors can build such confidence in a firm only after carefully vetting its investigation process, resources, and personnel. Taking the selecting of a third-party investigation firm lightly could lead to disastrous results down the road.

OTHER CONSIDERATIONS

There are a host of other considerations hedge fund investors should be aware of before selecting a third-party background investigation firm. One such consideration is the use of subcontractors. Many investigation firms will accept investigation work for subjects all over the world. That being said, they do not necessarily have the on-the-ground resources to complete this investigation themselves. Consequently, they turn to subcontractors who are regionally based in certain areas throughout the world. A typical example of such a relationship is a U.S.-based background investigation firm that is performing a search on an overseas hedge fund, say in mainland China.

Such subcontracted investigators should have detailed local knowledge; however, their investigative process may not be up to the standards of the home office. Consequently, continuing our example, the level of detail of the search in China may not be as comprehensive as it would be within the United States. Additionally, the subcontractors may not provide translations of source documentation from Chinese into English. This leaves investors receiving a final background investigation report (if they are even provided with the Chinese-language source documentation) scratching their heads while looking at a very expensive page of Chinese characters with no idea what it means.

A final comment on the background investigation process is that there are some hedge fund allocators, small and large alike, who believe they can competently perform the background investigation process themselves. Generally, the in-house individuals performing these searches often have other responsibilities as investment analysts, operational analysts, and the like. Questions arise as to the thoroughness of such investigations and the cost effectiveness of such in-house investigative processes. Typically, these individuals have not been trained in the background investigation process. There is a certain amount of skill involved in being able to properly query certain databases and sort through what is important and what is not. Additionally, professional background investigation firms have subscriptions to many background investigation database services; many individual allocators do not have these because it is simply not cost effective for them to do so. Furthermore, professional investigators are generally much more efficient at reviewing, vetting, and summarizing background investigation information. This is their full-time job. It does not make much sense to expect an investment analyst whose primary job is to pick the best distressed hedge fund to be able to determine whether a database query run on a portfolio manager named John Smith has turned up the same John Smith who was found to have a DUI in his background check. The analyst would not have the training and knowledge to make such a determination. Even if he did, it would not be the best use of his time. That being said, if a hedge fund allocator is willing to invest the resources necessary to properly perform his own internal background investigations, then performing such searches, or a portion of such searches, in house would be perfectly acceptable.

IMPORTANCE OF ONSITE VISITS

Regardless of the type of due diligence being performed, investment or non–investment related, the importance of onsite manager visits cannot be stressed enough. Visiting a hedge fund manager's primary offices is extremely important for several reasons. First, the most obvious reason is to confirm the validity of the hedge fund manager's address. Second, via an onsite inspection, a potential hedge fund investor can confirm physical operational attributes of an organization, such as the suitableness of office space. Is the space too small and will the manager outgrow it in a brief period of time? If so, has the manager secured additional space in advance of this future demand, or will employees be working on top of each other and in conference rooms? Or, is the office space too large for the number of employees in the firm? Has the firm secured this extra space intelligently or simply got a good deal? Does the firm anticipate subleasing this space?

An onsite visit also allows a potential investor to get a sense of the lavishness of a hedge fund's office. There is nothing wrong with having expensive art hanging on the walls or monogrammed coasters if a fund is making money and is conscientious toward overall costs. But, even in the world of hedge funds, extravagance may have its limits. A visit to the office may enable a potential investor to see whether a hedge fund manager is living beyond his means. Other things, such as number of employees, can be verified via an onsite visit. For example, if a hedge fund manager explains in the firm's generic due diligence questionnaire that the firm has

200 employees, and upon visiting the firm's office you are told the vast majority of them are out sick that day, it may be cause for alarm and further investigation. Similarly, a potential investor can attempt to gauge the type of information technology hardware in place during a tour of the firm's server room. Also to be noted during the obligatory office tour portion of the onsite visit with the hedge fund manager are certain things that a hedge fund manager will swear up and down that he does but that may not necessarily be implemented in practice. A good example of this is limiting access to secure rooms, such as sever rooms. For example, if only certain individuals have keycard access to a room, is the room ever locked or is the door left open all the time?

Beyond these seemingly obvious factors, there are several other benefits to an onsite visit, including the nature of the conversations that take place between a hedge fund's employees and potential investors. If an onsite visit is not conducted, due diligence is typically performed via some combination of e-mail and phone and/or videoconference. These types of conversations often take place among large groups of people. When many people are in a room in teleconference, often speaking with their superiors alongside them, the conversation that takes place is very different from a one-on-one conversation between two individuals in person. Related to this point, during an onsite visit there is no mute button available to a hedge fund's employees as there would be on a conference call. People's reactions can be gauged more effectively and in real time, as opposed to allowing for the hesitation of a conference call. Additionally, during an onsite visit potential investors have the option to extend the due diligence process beyond the conference room and onto the trading floor. Employees, both investment and operational, can be shadowed and observed in real time, providing opportunities for potential hedge fund investors to see, in practice, what has been discussed in the firm's documentation and in meetings.

WHICH OFFICE TO VISIT

Given the importance of performing onsite visits, the potential hedge fund investor, when considering a larger hedge fund organization with multiple offices, must now consider the question of which office to visit. Should all offices be visited, or just some? How should the selection be made? I hope you have come to the conclusion by now that operational due diligence is as much an art as it is a science. Consequently, there are no hard-and-fast rules to determine which office should be visited.

Consider the following scenario. A hedge fund manager with which you are considering a potential investment has offices in New York, London, Hong Kong, and Shanghai. The firm's CFO and COO and most of the operational personnel sit in New York, and the majority of functions are carried out from this office. The London and Shanghai offices serve primarily as research offices but are registered with the local regulatory authorities, as some marketing is carried out via these offices. The Hong Kong office is primarily for research as well, but does process some Asian trades overnight when the New York office is closed and has four operations staff members overseeing these trade processing and reconciliation functions. Under such a scenario, in the context of an operational due diligence review, one approach to considering which office to visit is to rank them in order of operational *importance*. Now the question becomes how to define this nebulous term. On a basic level, we can begin to rank the offices by the location of the majority of the firm's operational employees, and perhaps give somewhat more weight to the offices where certain high-ranking operational personnel such as the CFO and COO are located, as well as to the location where the majority of the firm's operational processes are carried out. Using this methodology, we can rank the operational importance of each office in our example as follows:

1. New York
2. Hong Kong
3. London
4. Shanghai

You may be wondering why London was ranked as more operationally important than Shanghai. Note that this operational ranking is purely subjective. The reason for my ranking the office so relates to the nature of the hedge fund regulatory environment. The primary financial regulator in London is the Financial Service Authority. This regulator, as will be discussed in Chapter 10, as a result of a recent trend of multijurisdictional regulator coordination, may reach through to the firm's New York office and vice versa if the New York office is registered with the SEC. There is currently no such reach-through with the China Securities Regulatory Commission, the Shanghai regulatory authority. The point is that there may be other overriding external concerns that may affect the ranking of operational importance; investors should not apply this process as if it were law, but rather dynamically, depending on the particular circumstances of the hedge fund manager's office locations presented before them.

MANAGER INTERVIEW PROCESS

Now that the manager documentation has been reviewed and the decision made as to which offices to visit, we turn our attention to the manager interview process. This process is a crucial part of the operational due diligence review framework. Where a hedge fund's documents attempt to tell a hedge fund's operational story in black and white, the manager interview process fills in the spaces and adds color to the picture. Similar to the document review process, those conducting an operational review for the first time may become quickly frustrated. Once again, many investors are under the misconception that all hedge funds have a universally accepted group of individuals they will put on parade as part of an operational due diligence review. Unfortunately, this is not always the case. As with the documentation collection process, investors must be proactive in stating which individuals they would like to meet with as part of the onsite manager interview process.

The interview process can best be summarized by this quote from the Quentin Tarantino movie, *True Romance,* when mob boss Vincenzo Coccotti (played by Christopher Walken) is interrogating Clifford Worley (played by Dennis Hopper): "Now, what we got here is a little game of show and tell. You do not wanna show me nothin', but you're tellin' me everything." Said another way, a hedge fund manager is generally incentivized to provide those conducting an operational review with only the specific information asked for. Anything more and it could open a virtual Pandora's Box of additional questions and concerns. It is not necessarily that the fund has something to hide; rather from its perspective the primary motivation is to ensure that the hedge fund investor reviewing the firm's operational competencies comes away from an operational review satisfied that the hedge fund organization has successfully developed a control environment to actively mitigate and monitor operational risks. This satisfaction can be measured by the actual investment and subsequent additional allocations from investors. Consequently, as with the document collection and analysis process, the onus is on the investors to be proactive in mandating whom they would like to meet with during an onsite operational review.

The skill with which an interview is conducted is an often-underrated part of the operational due diligence process. As with most things in life, the onsite manager interview process is infinitely more valuable if the interviewer has a plan and a certain goal he wishes to accomplish during the interview. This plan can come in the form of a preliminary meeting agenda that can be developed through the document review process. This is not to suggest that basic operational areas of a firm, such as the trading process, should not be covered during an onsite review; it is to suggest that an interviewer performing an operational due diligence review can use this onsite discussion of the process to confirm basic information, rather than learning it for the first time when the firm's head trader is sitting across from him. Such preparation will allow those conducting an operational review to more intelligently utilize the time allotted to them by focusing on certain specific areas that may not have been clear or were completely omitted from a hedge fund manager's prepared documentation.

WHAT TOPICS SHOULD BE COVERED DURING AN ONSITE REVIEW?

We will begin our discussion of which topics to cover during an onsite operational review by returning to the primary, secondary, and blended operational risk factors defined in Chapter 1. These factors are the generally agreed-upon areas at the heart of any hedge fund operational review. Consequently, these factors should be utilized as the starting point of an operational onsite review agenda.

When performing an onsite review, hedge fund investors typically meet with individuals from various parts of the firm in order to review the firm's operational functions. It makes sense, therefore, to regroup the primary, secondary, and blended risk factors by related category so that these factors can be efficiently covered during the interview process. This regrouping can be organized by the senior operational professional, who should generally be the most appropriate person to discuss a particular risk factor. This regrouping is summarized in Exhibit 4.2.

This regrouping bears pause to discuss who an investor should seek to meet with during an onsite operational review. It is generally considered best practice to meet with a firm's senior operational professionals, including the chief compliance officer, chief operating officer, general counsel, chief financial officer, and chief technology officer. In some hedge fund organizations, one individual may wear multiple hats. Consequently, the chief operating officer may also be the chief financial officer. This is not necessarily a bad thing. In fact, the argument may even be made that having multiple roles exposes the individual to multiple parts of the organization, which allows her to make better-informed firm-wide decisions as opposed to being limited to focusing on one particular function. However, the argument could also be made that by not focusing on one particular function of the firm (e.g., just the COO or CFO function) these functions become diluted. When faced with such a scenario, investors must make the determination, based on the entire operational control environment with the firm, whether having such shared roles exposes the firm to an unacceptable level of operational risk.

When reviewing this regrouping, it is paramount that those performing an operational due diligence review understand that this list is by no means all inclusive. Certain factors, such as valuation, may require significantly more scrutiny during an operational review of managers who trade more

EXHIBIT 4.2 Regrouping of Primary and Secondary Risk Factors by Senior Operational Functional Assignment

Factor	Primary/Secondary	Operations Individual to Discuss Topics With
Assets and investors concentration	Primary	Investor relations
Fund terms	Primary	Investor relations
Transparency and reporting	Primary	Investor relations
Business continuity and disaster recovery	Primary	Chief technology officer/chief operating officer
Technology and systems	Primary	Chief technology officer
Quality and length of relationship with tier-one service providers	Primary	Chief operating officer
Insurance	Secondary	Chief operating officer
Quality and length of relationship with tier-two service providers	Secondary	Chief operating officer
Counterparty oversight	Primary	Chief operating officer/chief financial officer/senior management
Trade life cycle	Primary	Chief operating officer/head trader/chief financial officer
Operations connectivity	Primary	Chief financial officer/chief operating officer
Valuation techniques and pricing sources	Primary	Chief financial officer
Cash controls and management	Primary	Chief financial officer/chief operating officer/senior management
Firm stability including expense analysis	Primary	Senior management/chief financial officer/chief operating officer
Tax practices	Secondary	Chief financial officer
Legal/compliance	Primary	Chief compliance officer/general counsel
Regulatory	Primary	Chief compliance officer/general counsel
Independence and oversight of the board of directors	Secondary	Board members
Reputation of employees (including senior mgmt.) and firm	Primary	Senior management (if applicable)
Compensation and employee turnover	Primary	Senior management and all senior members across each function

esoteric or illiquid securities, such as distressed-hedge-fund managers, as opposed to long/short equity managers, who trade solely exchange-priced equities.

SAMPLE TOPIC QUESTIONS

In order to gain an understanding of how each of these topics is covered during an onsite operational due diligence review, it is useful to examine the types of questions that may be asked. As noted, these questions are by no means all inclusive; rather questions have been included that should provide a flavor for, at a minimum, the depth at which such issues should be covered. I have generally omitted basic generic questions, such as "Describe your firm's strengths," and instead focused solely on those operational issues of fundamental importance. The answers to these questions, as well as the essential follow-up questions required, will vary greatly from one hedge fund manager to the next.

Assets and Investors Concentration:
- What are the current assets under management for the firm? For each fund?
- What were the assets under management a year ago for the firm? For each fund?
- What has been the peak of assets under management? When was it reached?
- What is the breakout of investors by investor type in the firm? In each fund?
- What percentage of assets under management do the following represent (as a percentage of both firm and fund assets under management):

  (a) Largest investor
  (b) Three largest investors

Business Continuity Planning and Disaster Recovery (BCP/DR):
- Does the firm maintain written BCP/DR procedures?
- Is the plan tested? If so, how often? When was the most recent test?
- Who is in charge of updating the plan?
- Does the firm have backup power-generation facilities?
- Has the hedge fund ever had to activate its BCP/DR plan?
- If the hedge fund organization has multiple offices, how are these offices supposed to coordinate with each other in the event of a business disruption in either location?

Technology and Systems:

- What third-party and proprietary systems are currently in place?
- What types of hardware are utilized?
- Have any systems been customized or upgraded by the firm? Are there any plans to do so?
- What are examples of the types of problems that arise with the firm's current systems? What are the firm's information security policies? How are they implemented?

Quality and Length of Relationship with Tier-One and Tier-Two Service Providers:

- How long have you worked with your current service providers?
- What services do you receive from each of your service providers? For example, does the hedge fund utilize an administrator in order to provide a complete net asset value (NAV) calculation (also known as *full NAV* service), provide NAV lite, or something in between? Are you happy with your service providers or are you thinking of switching?
- What are the terms and length of contract with your service providers?
- Have you experienced any turnover of personnel at the service provider that has impacted the level of service the fund receives?

Insurance:

- What types of insurance coverage does the firm maintain?
- What are the terms of this coverage?
- Does the hedge fund self-insure for anything (as opposed to obtaining third-party coverage)?
- Has the firm ever issued a claim on any of its insurance policies?

Valuation Techniques and Pricing Sources:

- What is the valuation process? Can the hedge fund manager describe it in simple terms?
- Is the valuation process documented? Who ensures that the documented policies are being carried out?
- Is there an appropriate segregation of duties between those with valuation responsibilities and those with investment management responsibilities?
- Have any of the funds ever had to restate the net asset value? If so, when and why?
- What is the role of the compliance department in overseeing the valuation process? Is compliance oversight manual or automated? Is any compliance valuation testing performed?

- Does the firm have a pricing committee? If so, who is on the committee? How often does the committee meet? What happens in committee meetings?
- What percentage of the fund's portfolio is priced directly by the hedge fund manager?
- Does the firm work with any third-party valuation consultants besides the administrator? If yes, how often and for what purposes?

Operations Connectivity:
- Who has authority for placing trades at the firm?
- What is the trade flow process?
- What is the settlement and reconciliation process?
- How does the firm deal with trade breaks?
- Who has authority to transfer cash? Is the same process in place for all amounts of cash transfers or are more signatures required for higher-level cash transfers?
- What is the collateral management process?
- Where is excess cash held? Is it held in the name of the fund?

Firm Financial Stability Including Expenses Analysis:
- Does the firm plan to raise assets or are the funds closed? If closed, are they hard closed or soft closed? If open, how much does the firm plan to raise?
- Are the funds being charged for inappropriate expenses (e.g., firm marketing, client services, employee bonuses, etc.)?
- Are current processes scalable?

Legal/Compliance:
- Does the firm utilize compliance consultants? If yes, what is the nature of the relationship (e.g., do they perform regular mock audits or simply advise on certain issues)?
- Provide details of the past regulatory visits.
- Provide details of any previous or current litigation.
- What is the firm's electronic communication policy? Is electronic communication monitored? How and by whom?
- What is the employee trading policy? Is preclearance required? If yes, by whom? Are brokerage statements reviewed and reconciled to employee trades?
- What is the firm's gift policy? How is this tracked?
- Are soft dollars utilized? If so, for what purpose? How is this monitored?

Independence and Oversight of the Board of Directors:

- How long has each director served on the board?
- How much compensation do directors receive for their services?
- Have there been any reductions or increases in the membership of the board? If yes, why?
- Which board members are independent, and which are affiliated with the firm?
- Are any of the board members from service providers of the hedge funds? If so, what is the firm's reason for this?
- Do any of the directors sit on any other boards? If yes, how many other boards?
- How often and where does the board meet?
- What resolutions has the board passed recently?

Reputation of Employees (Including Senior Management) and Firm:

- What is the employment history of the firm's senior management? Did they leave their previous firms on good terms? Can they provide references?
- Is there anything in senior managements past that is noteworthy from a reputational risk perspective (e.g., criminal convictions, sanctions by regulators, etc.)?
- Is senior management involved in any current litigation or disputes that may be distracting (e.g., a messy divorce, dissolution of former business partnerships, etc.)?
- Does senior management have any outside business interests? If yes, what is the nature of these interests? How much of senior management's time do they take?

Personnel and Employee Turnover:

- Provide details of historical employee turnover (additions and departures).
- Does the firm have any additional planned hires?
- If the firm indicates that someone has left on good terms, can you contact this former employee as a reference?
- What does the firm do to ensure retention of key employees? Are non-compete agreements utilized?

Other Questions:

- Are any members of the firm related? Does the firm maintain a policy on relatives working together? If so, how does it prevent potential conflicts of interest?

- What is the alignment of interests between the firm and its investors? Amount of principal and employee capital invested? Deferred compensation structure, and so forth?
- Side letters: Do other investors have them? What are their terms?
- Does the firm have any relationships with any affiliated entities?
- Is the hedge fund management company locked into any long-term contracts, such as office space leases, technology service contracts, and so on?

IN WHAT ORDER SHOULD THESE TOPICS BE COVERED?

Is there a preferred order in which to cover the primary, secondary, and blended risk factors? There is no one correct or generally accepted order by which an onsite operational due diligence review should be completed. Rather, the focus has traditionally been on which issues to cover, with less importance given to the prescribed order. In practice, the order in which the topics are covered generally varies as a result of a number of factors, including availability of different personnel to meet with potential investors during an operational review. One general order that can be suggested is to begin with high-level topics such as assets under management and performance and work down the line into the more detail-intensive subjects such as valuation and compliance.

SERVICE PROVIDER REVIEWS

Reviews of hedge fund service providers can be a valuable complement to the hedge fund manager due diligence process. Throughout the hedge fund operational due diligence process, the nature of the relationship between the hedge fund and its service providers will be discovered. Different service providers, such as administrators, perform services differently. They have different models for managing such things as employee retention and training. Some have dedicated pricing groups; others do not. The service provider due diligence process will allow potential investors to properly vet such issues and determine the appropriateness of the level of service provided to the hedge fund under consideration.

There are two primary goals in performing due diligence on a hedge fund's service providers. First, by speaking with a hedge fund's service providers, investors have the opportunity to confirm what the hedge fund has told them about the nature of their relationship with the service provider. Second, the service provider due diligence process allows hedge fund investors to determine both the suitability and scalability of the service provider's services. Questions may arise when this second element is not appropriately monitored: Will the service provider grow with the hedge fund? Will the hedge fund outgrow the service provider? Will the service provider outgrow the hedge fund and not provide it with the same level of service?

Two questions that are commonly raised in regard to the service provider due diligence process are which service providers to perform due diligence on and how to perform such due diligence. In regard to the first question, ideally, all service provider relationships should be reviewed. Those traditionally viewed as the most important are the hedge fund's independent administrator and auditor. As previously discussed, most hedge funds' auditors will not speak directly with hedge fund investors, so they are essentially ruled out. This leaves the hedge fund's administrator(s). Now we come to the second element of service provider due diligence: how to perform it.

Continuing with our administrator example, similar to the hedge fund operational due diligence process, the service provider review process should start with documentation collection. The types of documentation available from hedge fund administrators are generally more limited than the types available from hedge funds. There is, however, certain documentation that can provide valuable insight into the structure and practices within a hedge fund administration organization.

Most hedge fund service providers generally have their own due diligence questionnaires, typically following a standard format such as those provided by the Alternative Investment Management Association. Additionally, many large hedge fund administrators have undergone third-party internal control assessments such as a SAS 70 review process. Such reports will be discussed in more detail in Chapter 10. Hedge fund administrators will generally provide those considering an investment in a hedge fund with copies of such documentation, which can provide valuable insights into the administrator's organization. Other types of documentation that may be collected include such things as the administration agreement between the hedge fund under consideration and the fund's administrator. Some hedge fund administrators will provide copies of such an agreement; others will not, generally depending on the level of consent provided by the hedge fund they work for. As we have stated many times, as a potential hedge fund investor, you will not know unless you ask. Reviewing such an agreement can provide an additional level of insight into the relationship between the hedge fund and the administrator.

The next stage in the service provider review process is the service provider interview. If a potential hedge fund investor has the resources and time to visit with a hedge fund's service providers, such visits are highly recommended. Similar to the hedge fund manager onsite review process, valuable insight can be gained from visiting an administrator's offices. That being said, in practice it is not often feasible, either from a resources or a time perspective, to perform an onsite administrator review. If this is the case, a telephone or videoconference may suffice. The point is that, as a potential investor in a hedge fund, you will want to allow the service provider the opportunity to tell his side of the story. Typically, in addition to confirming what a hedge fund has described about its relationship with its service providers, by speaking directly with service providers, such as administrators, hedge fund investors can see the other side of the equation and gain a deeper level of insight into both sides of the relationship.

QUALITATIVE OPERATIONAL REPORT: DOCUMENTING THE OPERATIONAL DATA

As investors progress through the initial operational due diligence process, they will begin to develop a number of operational data points. This operational data will be used to make a final determination as to the operational competencies and risks present at a particular hedge fund. A common question investors are faced with is how to best summarize and review this operational data. One approach is to attempt to assign quantitative scores to different operational categories based on the operational data collected. These scorecard approaches will be discussed in more detail in Chapter 8. Another approach, which can be used either in conjunction with or separately from a scorecard approach, is to develop a qualitative operational report.

Qualitative operational reports can take many different forms. Some reports follow a check-the-box method. That is, if a hedge fund meets a certain criterion, an investor will indicate that the criterion is met, provide a brief qualitative description, and move on. Other qualitative operational report templates are more formal and voluminous in nature, requiring an investor to provide a qualitative description of a particular hedge fund's policies, procedures, and practices for a number of predefined criteria. Such approaches ensure that a number of specified criteria will be addressed but may suffer from being self-limiting as a function of their design. Another type of qualitative operational report is more free-form and takes the form of a general memorandum focusing on those issues that are of importance to the investor or the audience who will be reviewing the report.

Regardless of the format selected, preparing a qualitative report after an initial operational review is advisable as it affords investors with the opportunity to summarize the results of the initial operational due diligence review. In addition to providing a written memorialized result of the findings, creating a qualitative operational report will help investors to avoid overlooking certain outstanding items that they may wish to follow up on or monitor over time.

Note

1. See Jesse Westbrook, "SEC Abandons Hedge-Fund Probe Tactic after Complaints," March 14, 2008, www.bloomberg.com/apps/news?pid=20601087&sid =aEHnDyK9iIMA&refer=home.

CHAPTER 5

Evaluating the Gray Areas: Examples

We now come to a discussion of the fourth stage in the operational review process: the operational decision. By this stage in the review process, an investor has collected and reviewed all the relevant fund manager documentation and completed the hedge fund manager interview process. All outstanding questions have been answered and no stone has been left unturned. All of the relevant data points are in hand. After the dust has settled on the operational due diligence process, investors are now faced with a binary decision: to allocate or not. As alluded to in Chapter 4, there are often a number of gray areas that come to the surface as part of a review of this operational data. Depending on a multitude of factors, including where a particular investor's operational threshold lies, reasonable minds can come to different allocation decisions. The purpose of this chapter is twofold. First is to outline several scenarios an investor may be presented with when conducting an operational due diligence review. Second is to provide some perspective on what to do when approaching these operational crossroads. These goals will be accomplished through the analysis of several hypothetical situations. (It should be noted that all situations and persons described are purely fictional and solely for demonstrative purposes.)

SCENARIO 1: "IT WAS NOT ME"—HEDGE FUND MANAGER CLAIMS MISTAKEN IDENTITY

Dom Telonge is the son of Henry and Betty Telonge, and heir to the sizable Telonge family fortune. The Telonges made their fortune, now estimated to be close to $2 billion, by running a successful chain of Bible distributors throughout the Midwest. Sadly, Henry and Betty were killed in a car accident last year, and Dom has inherited the business. Dom does not know anything about the Bible. Indeed, he is not even a religious man and first stepped foot in a church for his parent's funeral. Consequently, he sold the business and is now sitting on a large liquid fortune. Dom meets with Hark Moppus, the firm's attorney and advisor, to discuss his options.

Dom explains to Hark that he wants to spend his life sailing around the world and studying humanity's existentialist nature. Hark, understanding that Dom has had a rough year with the loss of his parents, thinks it would be a good idea for Dom to get away and has agreed to oversee the family fortune in Dom's absence. Dom asks Hark to put something together and e-mail the proposal to him on his yacht in three months' time; by then he will be sailing around the Horn of Africa and will be sufficiently relaxed to review the proposed portfolio. Hark has him sign the appropriate paperwork, so he can manage the funds in Dom's absence. The two part ways, Dom begins to make arrangements for his journey and Hark gets to work on developing an allocation plan.

A few weeks go by, and Hark has been hard at work on the allocation plan. He has decided to put 30% with traditional, long-only managers, 10% in real estate, 30% in bonds and bond funds, and 30% in hedge funds. Hark advises a few other ultra-high-net-worth families and has a good idea which hedge funds he wants to give the money to. One fund in particular is a U.K.-based long/short fund, Buddha Asset Management (BAM), which Hark has previously invested his clients money with and invests primarily in Asian small- and midcaps. Hark is very conscious of protecting his clients' image, and recently began to have background investigations performed on all of the potential hedge funds he is considering for his clients' portfolios. Hark utilizes the same investigators he uses for his litigation practices—a group of former New York Police Department detectives, who are all very well read, called the Atticus Finch Group (AFG). Dom asks AFG to begin work on BAM and several other hedge fund groups he is considering including in Dom's allocation proposal.

It is now two and a half months since Dom set sail. His yacht is docked at the Port of Sudan in the Red Sea, and his crew is preparing for the journey past Ethiopia and into the Gulf of Aden. Hark has been quite busy as well, planning how to best allocate Dom's family fortune. As the three-month deadline is fast approaching, he checks in with AFG to see how their work on BAM is coming. Scott Seynor, a leading investigator for AFG, apologizes for the delay and explains that they are currently in the process of vetting an issue that came up in the background of BAM's lead portfolio manager, Bravis Tarker. Scott goes on to explain that a database search of criminal records revealed that Bravis, who is a U.S. citizen, was accused of, and pled guilty to, criminal possession of a weapon that was subsequently found to be used in a murder. AFG was working on obtaining more specifics. However, the action was filed approximately 20 years ago, and due to the age of the court records, they were having some difficulty.

Hark is shocked by this news, because he has previously allocated a significant amount of his clients' money to BAM. He immediately calls Ferry Jinn, BAM's head of investor relations, and asks him about AFG's findings. Ferry says he has never heard about these allegations and asks to see copies of the court records so BAM can perform its own investigation. Hark puts Ferry in touch with Scott and BAM begins its own investigation utilizing another third-party investigation firm, Macbeth Background Investigation Services. After conducting a series of interviews and visiting local courts in Encitas, California, where Bravis allegedly pled guilty, to review additional documentation, Macbeth's report suggests that this was a case of mistaken identity and that, while not conclusive, someone may have utilized a false name, claiming to be Bravis when indeed he was not. Mr. Tarker vehemently denies the claim, says he knows nothing about this, and has offered to produce a sworn statement to that effect.

Three months have now gone by, and Hark receives an e-mail from Dom. Below a picture of Dom picking Ethiopian coffee beans, is the following text: "Fresh Brewed." Where's the proposal? Dom has completed two versions of the proposal, one including BAM and one not. Which one should he send? If he includes BAM in the portfolio, he exposes Dom to perhaps unnecessary operational risk. On the other hand, BAM may be such a unique investment opportunity that it is worth the risk. By determining Dom's operational threshold, including sensitivities to such things as reputational risk, before such a situation arose Hark could have a potentially more clear-cut decision on his hands.

SCENARIO 2: "IT WAS ME, BUT EVERYONE WAS DOING IT"—ARE REGULATORY WITCH-HUNTS REAL?

BigCo's pension fund has fallen behind the asset-allocation curve in recent years with large allocations to conservative, traditional, long-only equity managers and bond funds. As a result, BigCo's pension performance has suffered relative to peers that have allocated to hedge funds. The problem is that every time BigCo's board of directors decides to get on the hedge-fund bus, another blowup occurs and they are scared off. This has happened three times now, with varying degrees of blowup magnitude, and BigCo's gray-haired board is a bit concerned about being responsible for losing their employees' money on what they have the impression as being very speculative hedge fund investments. After all, the traditional managers to whom the fund has been allocating have not lost money. However, the board finally is facing increasing pressure from the pensioners to generate increased return. As a result, the board recently passed a resolution to allow up to 30% of the firm's $1 billion asset base to alternative investments and hedge funds in particular.

To assist them in this effort, BigCo lured away a high-profile hedge fund consultant, named Marck Blackbox, from a large hedge fund advisory consulting group, the Sauerkraut Group. Marck had a background as a management consultant and over the past few years has made a transition to the asset management field. He has worked for the Sauerkraut Group for the past three years, primarily advising large hedge funds and endowments on allocating to alternative investments. This experience has provided him with a wealth of knowledge about the unique demands and requirements of this group of hedge fund investors. Additionally, Marck has developed a large network of contacts within the hedge fund community. He was excited by the opportunity to join BigCo and has a stable of brand-name soft closed hedge fund managers with which he can leverage his social network and negotiate capacity for the BigCo pension. The board of directors has asked him to produce a plan for the $300 million allocation. Marck is to present this plan at the next board of directors' meeting in two months' time.

One fund in particular is Hot Dog Asset Management (HDAM). HDAM is a well-respected fund in Latin America. HDAM's aggregate assets under management topped $5 billion last year, and the firm's flagship Wiener Opportunities Fund, a long/short Latin American–focused fund, posted a banner 58% return last year. The fund is managed by co–portfolio managers Jon Bunn and Tom Relish. Tom and Jon cut their teeth working as equity analysts at large investment banks in Latin America, and each has his own sector specialties—Jon focuses on mining and Tom on energy.

As part of his mandate with BigCo, Marck was charged with overseeing the pension fund's due diligence efforts, both financial and operational. Marck did not really focus on operational risk while at the Sauerkraut Group, but he did "borrow" the firm's operational due diligence questionnaire before leaving the Sauerkraut Group and has requested that the hedge funds under consideration for the BigCo mandate complete this questionnaire. To Marck's surprise, many of these large firms have refused to complete this questionnaire, simply opting to provide their own due diligence questionnaire. This is quite a different reaction than Marck is used to receiving. At the Sauerkraut Group, each fund manager had to undergo a very detailed, lengthy process to get on the Group's approved advisory platform. Consequently, Marck thought having them complete an operational due diligence questionnaire would not be overly problematic. Indeed, many hedge fund consulting groups and hedge fund database providers alike have a series of hoops that the hedge funds need to jump through before they will consider recommending these funds to their clients—including unique questionnaires, multiple interviews, and sometimes-cumbersome data reporting procedures.

Based on this reaction, Marck has decided that in situations where he feels that the hedge fund's due diligence questionnaire is sufficiently thorough, he will waive the requirement to complete the operational due diligence questionnaire. In fact, Marck really has no choice if he wants to do business with these closed hedge funds, which are in high demand.

HDAM is one of the funds that refused to complete Marck's operational due diligence questionnaire, instead providing their own generic due diligence questionnaire. In reviewing this questionnaire in order to prepare his report for the investment committee, Marck notices the following section:

Has Hot Dog Asset Management or any of its affiliates ever been sanctioned or fined by any regulatory agency?

Yes, in 2001, HDAM was fined approximately $28,000 pesos by the arbitration panel of the Bolsas De Comercia De Buenos Aires as a result of technical violations. All such fines have been paid.

This is a bit surprising to Marck. He was unaware of this fine from his time at the Sauerkraut Group, and has never heard of the Bolsas De Comercia De Buenos Aires. Marck's gut reaction is that this is nothing to worry about. After all, it was a minor violation that the firm paid for an immaterial amount of money. If he were still at the Sauerkraut Group, he would not even bother to mention it to clients if he were advising on the HDAM funds. However, Marck is quick to remember the sensitivities of his new employer, BigCo, and wants to make sure he can answer any questions posed to him about this by the BigCo board. Consequently, he picks up the phone and places a call to his former colleague, Chuck Arriba, at the Sauerkraut Group to see whether he had ever heard of/knew anything about this fine. Chuck, who is from Argentina, primarily focuses on working with the Sauerkraut Group's Latin American clients. He tells Marck that he is unaware of any such fine from reviewing the Sauerkraut database, but explains that the Bolsas De Comercia De Buenos Aires is the Buenos Aires stock exchange and the fine was probably the result of a violation of exchange rules.

Marck decides to follow up with a call to Madrigal Swanson, HDAM's head of investor relations, regarding the fine. The conversation goes as follows:

MARCK: Hey, Madrigal.
MADRIGAL: Hi, Marck. Are we all set with the due diligence on your end? How much can we expect on the first of the month?

MARCK: It's coming along. They are a little more sensitive to certain issues here than we were at Sauerkraut—especially reputational risk.

MADRIGAL: Yes, that's typically what we see with those pension funds. Don't worry; you'll get used to it.

MARCK: Thanks. Listen—I was going through your due diligence question-naire and came across the part about the 2001 fine from the Buenos Aires Stock Exchange. Can you provide me with some more color on this? The board I report to may want more specifics.

MADRIGAL: Sure. This is ancient history. It was the result of a technical violation of exchange rules. On the advice of counsel, we paid a small fine and moved on.

MARCK: What exactly was the activity that triggered the violation?

MADRIGAL: It's related to Argentinean IPOs [initial public offerings]. Back then, everyone, including us, would purchase them early and then dump them when the market opened. The exchange rules at the time didn't ex-plicitly prohibit such activity, and, besides, it was a very small percentage of our book. The fine came about as a result of a crackdown, and on the advice of counsel we paid it.

MARCK: If everyone was doing it, were many people fined? Do you still trade Argentinean IPOs?

MADRIGAL: We were one of a few firms that were singled out. Let's just say that there were certain elements in the regulatory regime at the time we were attempting to target certain activities from hedge funds. Those with less political clout were held up as pariahs as part of a witch hunt. We've since moved away from this, and IPOs as a whole make up less than 5% of the fund.

MARCK: Thanks, Madrigal. I don't anticipate this will be a problem.

The two-month deadline is now a week away. Marck has lined up 25 premier hedge funds, all of whom have been soft closed for at least the past year, with whom he has been able to negotiate capacity. He has prepared a detailed asset allocation plan. In the back of his presentation, he has included summaries of his meetings with each of these managers, including a brief write-up discussing the historical fine at HDAM and his subsequent discussion with Madrigal.

During his presentation with the board of directors, Marck is asked a variety of questions as to the nature of the specific positions held by these hedge funds, his views on the future of the markets these funds are investing in, and why he selected these funds over others. The presentation is moving along smoothly as Marck comes to the part where he runs through a brief summary of each fund to be included in the allocation package. When Marck makes it to HDAM, a feeble hand is raised from the other side of the boardroom. "Excuse me," is interjected, interrupting Marck's fast-moving presentation. It is the voice of Stem Wick, BigCo's general counsel.

Wick, who is in his late seventies, has been with the firm for 36 years and has a reputation for being an extremely conservative stickler for detail. He has not been shy about making it known that he is against the pension fund venturing into hedge fund investing, despite the allure of substantially increased returns. Wick proceeds to inquire as to the HDAM fine. Marck walks through the summary of his discussion with Madrigal and further states, "HDAM is a world-class manager with extremely thorough controls and a culture of compliance."

This response seems to quell Wick's ire; however, his raising of the issue causes board members to quickly flip through the pages of Marck's voluminous presentation in order to read his memo in more detail. A subsequent pile-on effect ensues, and Marck is barraged with questions concerning the fine, the environment in Buenos Aires at the time, and the like. As his discussion continues, although none of the committee members are familiar with Argentinean IPO investing, several board members begin to hypothecate about the scenario, and others question whether this situation can be equated to IPO investing in places like China and Russia. Marck attempts to answer these questions and stresses the current state of the organization and reiterates the regulatory witch-hunt explanation.

Several of the directors express concerns about adding a fund with a "checkered past," as they put it, on the platform. After all, if something goes wrong, the finger will be squarely pointed at them. Marck reminds the committee that this is a highly regarded, large fund and they are doing him and BigCo a favor by giving them capacity. What should the board of directors do? What should Marck advise them to do? Is a historical fine indicative of future problems on the horizon? If the concerns by the board are indeed valid, then why has HDAM raised so much capital from others?

SCENARIO 3: "IT WAS ME, BUT I DID NOTHING WRONG"—MANAGER PROVED NOT GUILTY

In this scenario, we come upon Ketchup Capital Management (KCM) in the early stages of its capital-raising efforts. KCM has recently hired a third-party marketer, Mike Duggan, who has had some success in arranging for a series of meetings with Doodle Incorporated's employee pension plan. Tom Phillips, the manager of the pension plan, is an experienced investor who, over the past two years, has guided the firm to the alternative investment space, and hedge funds in particular, with stellar results. Doodle has gone back and forth with KCM over the past few months and the firm is ready to allocate $20 million to the Ketchup Opportunities Fund. A final hurdle in the Doodle allocation process is the performance of a background investigation on KCM and its principals. Doodle had always primarily relied on its investment analysts performing media searches and checking on a hedge fund manager's reputation, both via manager-provided references and by having analysts check with their own network of contacts for any negative information in a manager's past. As a result of the recent failures of several funds due to fraud and operational failures, Doodle's corporate board has been more sensitive to performing increasingly detailed background investigations in order to both protect against any losses and safeguard the firm's reputation. Doodle recently began utilizing a professional background investigation firm, Hedge Sleuth, which has developed a reputation specializing in background investigations for the hedge fund industry. Hedge Sleuth has also recently begun to branch out into pre-employment screening and litigation support.

Tom informs Mike of their intention to perform this search. As a courtesy, he asks Mike whether there is anything they should know before ordering the investigation to begin. Mike reiterates the statement from KCM's due diligence questionnaire that there has been no criminal litigation (active or pending) and no regulatory sanctions levied against either KCM or its principals. Tom tells Mike that he is sure that this is just a formality and that Mike should expect to receive an allocation from Doodle on the first of the month. Mike tells Tom that he will reserve a capacity slot for him of $20 million.

Hedge Sleuth begins its investigation into KCM's portfolio manager, Giovanni Argonaut and chief financial officer, Trotta Palacio. Hedge Sleuth is renowned for the detailed thoroughness of their work. Their slogan is, "No Stone Unturned." The search proceeds, investigating a number of public databases, confirming university degrees, leveraging the firm's proprietary network of contacts, and the like. Three weeks into the search, former Central Intelligence Agency employee Brick Newton, an investigator for Hedge Sleuth, calls Tom to update him on their research.

Brick informs Tom that a series of court cases were uncovered surrounding Mr. Argonaut from approximately 20 years ago in Phoenix, Arizona. Based on the dates of the cases, Brick determines that they coincide with Argonaut's pursuit of a degree in astrophysics from the University of Phoenix. The cases, which have since been dismissed, were brought by the local Phoenix authorities and alleged that Argonaut had been fraudulently producing and distributing fake driver's licenses to underage college students so that they could appear to be over 21, the legal drinking age. The suit was subsequently dismissed, and no other details were available. A second wrongful death suit was brought by the family of Marcus Thomlinson, a freshman who allegedly had purchased a fake license from Argonaut and subsequently died from alcohol poisoning as a result of the consumption of too much alcohol, which he purchased with this fake license. This suit was subsequently dismissed with prejudice, which indicates that it was most likely settled between the parties. Argonaut had later brought suit against the Phoenix authorities for malicious persecution; however, this suit was subsequently dismissed, as well.

Tom is surprised to hear about this and questions Brick as to whether this could be a case of mistaken identity. Brick informs Tom that he confirmed that it was indeed Argonaut through both his address at the time and his Social Security number. Tom's immediate response is that these issues are in the past, and since Argonaut was found not guilty, this is not something of concern. Tom is conscious of the importance recently placed by the firm's senior management on protecting the firm's reputation, and decides to speak with KCM's people to get their side of the story before raising the issue to Doodle's board.

When Tom first mentions this information to KCM's Mike Duggan, the response at the other end of the line is an uneasy silence. Mike, realizing he needs to formulate a response, asks Tom for specifics regarding the cases, including docket number, party names, and so on. He informs Tom that he was unaware of these issues but will speak with Argonaut and get back to him shortly. Mike is also quick to empathize with Tom's sentiment that Argonaut was found not guilty of these allegations. Mike, half jokingly, adds that even if Argonaut had been found guilty, it was 20 years ago, and not related to the firm or its investment abilities. Tom hesitantly agrees, but mulls the statement over after the call. Would it make a difference if he had been found guilty? Would a guilty conviction mean that Argonaut is a fraud or a bad investor?

The following afternoon, Tom receives a call from Mike. Mike confirms that indeed it was Argonaut who was charged with these allegations. He reiterates to Tom that Argonaut was found to be not guilty, that he is a man of the highest integrity, and that all of these suits were civil and not criminal in nature. Should Tom not invest because of the negative impression people might have of his association with KCM? Put another way, does an acquittal eliminate reputational risk?

SCENARIO 4: THE LOW-PROFILE HEDGE FUND MANAGER—IS NO NEWS GOOD NEWS?

As a boy, Mark Whisper had always kept true to his surname, being a rather quiet fellow. As he progressed through university, he was always more of a thinker than a sportsman. Still waters run deep, and Mark eventually became Dr. Whisper upon receiving his PhD in Analytical Fluid Mechanics from Prinstone University. After working for several years creating financial models for a large bank, Dr. Whisper decided it was time to venture out on his own. After receiving $20 million in initial funding from the Prinstone University alumni association fund, he hired a computer scientist and a secretary to start his new firm, Silentium Asset Management (SAM). SAM was based out of a small townhouse in Sleepy Hollow, New York. After some initial startup time and model tweaking, SAM proudly launched the Quiet Quantitative Opportunity funds (QQO) in early 2004. QQO was a primarily quantitative, high-frequency black-box trading strategy based on Dr. Whisper's proprietary research and models.

Dr. Whisper was fond of sitting in his office for the majority of the day, watching over his models and how they adapted to the markets. Occasionally, he would manually override his models when he saw certain opportunities, but these occasions were rare and more experimental than anything else. Silencio Hushton, the computer scientist, spent the majority of his time monitoring the efficiency with which the models traded, and focused on reducing such things as slippage and creating new software to implement Dr. Whisper's new model ideas. Calm Hope, the firm's secretary, in addition to administrative duties and ordering lunch for Dr. Whisper and Mr. Hushton (they did not leave the office much and often worked through meals), was also responsible for preparing the firm's quarterly performance commentary and monthly performance statistics. Hope had previously worked as an administrative assistant in a law firm. These quarterly updates were more performance analytics than commentary. Dr. Whisper did not often devote more than a half hour to them, instead feeling his investors would be better served by his focusing on the fund's models than by his explaining them. The firm's investors did not mind. They knew and trusted Dr. Whisper, and as long as they were making money, there was no reason to complain.

QQO met considerable initial success and realized net gains of 35% during its first year of operation. This positive performance did not go unnoticed by the wealthy alumni who had allocated to SAM. As a result of these alumni urging their wealthy acquaintances, SAM had received considerable subscription requests and finished the year with $125 million under management. Additionally, it was rumored that Prinstone University's endowment fund was considering allocating $75 million to SAM if its positive performance continued. From a capacity perspective, Dr. Whisper was not the least bit concerned about the prospect of the growth of assets under management outpacing his strategy. From the beginning, Dr. Whisper had thought big. He had designed his models with capacity of $3 billion to $5 billion in mind.

As assets grew, so, too, did Dr. Whisper's interest in shareholder activism in his home country of Moldova. Specifically, his research indicated that many previously state-run enterprises, such as utilities and refineries, were significantly undervalued. Dr. Whisper's main investment hypothesis was to locate these undervalued entities and use his local connections and knowledge to secure seats on the boards of these companies to be an instrument for change. As such, SAM launched the Moldova Infrastructure Fund in late 2005, with an initial capital raise, mostly from existing QQO investors but not Pinstone University, of $40 million. New hire Nikolai Popov would manage the firms from a satellite office in the Moldovian capital of Chişinău.

With the positive performance of the QQO fund and fast-growing assets under management, Dr. Whisper had also been approached by a number of third-party marketing firms and hedge fund consultants seeking to recommend the QQO funds to clients for a referral fee. Dr. Whisper, a born skeptic, had always been suspicious of such referral relationships and preferred to maintain total control over any communications with clients. Additionally, Dr. Whisper did not like the idea of paying someone else fees for his own hard work. After all, he thought, if performance continued to remain positive, investors would find him. Additionally, with his small staff of three and relatively high fees, 2% management fee and 30% incentive fee, he could toil away in virtual anonymity making quite a handsome living for himself without having to give away some of his profits for referrals. Furthermore, Dr. Whisper did not like to talk to investors or be micromanaged, and did not want to be at their constant beck and call. From day one, he vehemently insisted against participating in any conference calls or capital introduction events. He had similarly refused onsite due diligence meetings, thinking that serious investors would let the fund's performance and analytical data speak for itself. He was in charge, investors trusted him to run their money, and that was what he wanted to focus on.

Six months later, Dr. Whisper had accepted the $75 million account from Prinstone University. Additionally, he had received investments from five other midsized institutional clients and several more multifamily offices. Total assets under management now totaled $700 million. Performance over the last six months had been similarly impressive but had begun to experience a recent drawdown. With performance down a bit from last year's 35% return, Dr. Whisper had scaled back risk as a result of what he viewed as a temporary market dislocation and had posted a 12% return for the first six months of the new year. These results were still impressive when compared to other similar funds that had generally posted returns ranging between 7 and 9%, and were in line with Dr. Whisper's model expectations for the QQO funds. From a staffing perspective, SAM had recently hired a full-time trader to oversee his models for overnight trading in Asian markets.

As assets grew, so, too, did investors' demands for new types of performance analytics and reports. Many had become accustomed to SAM's less-than-communicative style; however, with the recent downturn in markets and the more institutional type of investors that were allocating to the QQO funds, many investors felt they needed a better understanding of both how the fund was positioned and where Dr. Whisper thought the markets were going. On several occasions, Dr. Whisper attempted to call several of his larger investors directly to quell their concerns but quickly became frustrated by the barrage of follow-up questions and continuing demands for transparency and estimates that often followed such conference calls. Adding to investor frustration was the poor quality of responses to information, often handled by Hope, who was not familiar with dealing with hedge fund investors. Several small investors eventually redeemed, but Dr. Whisper felt that the investors who remained with him were the ones who "understood what he was trying to accomplish" and was happy to part company with those who did not.

During the next few months, the QQO funds surpassed the $1 billion mark. At the same time, there had been some changes at the Prinstone University endowment. A wealthy alumnus, Tom Oiltown, had recently passed away. Oiltown, who had made a large fortune by creating an innovative design for the household bagel-slicing machine, had always fondly remembered his time at Prinstone as a younger man and had been a very active alumnus later in life. Recently, his most famous donation to the school had been a mini-car fully outfitted with a tail and coated in black paint, resembling the school's cougar mascot, to be driven around the university's football stadium.

Upon his death, he bequeathed $500 million to the Prinstone University endowment fund, a portion of which was to be used to create the Oiltown Center for Bagel Slicing Studies. The University bigwigs were very excited about Oiltown's gift. The Prinstone pension fund had been floundering for sometime and, with the exception of some index and bond funds, had actively allocated only a handful of alumni referral investments, such as Dr. Whisper's QQO funds. Upon the urging of Tan Caminando, the lawyer representing the Oiltown estate, the Prinstone trustees began a search for a portfolio manager to oversee the endowment fund's investments.

The trustees had picked an interesting time to canvass the market for a new portfolio manager. The markets were still in the middle of a downturn, and this had begun to affect a number of the endowment's investments. In particular, the QQO funds were up only 4% in the last quarterly report. At the monthly trustee meeting, several of the trustees expressed concern regarding the QQO funds' returns. Also contributing to the trustees' concern was a series of articles recently published that linked the University to supporting restructuring efforts in Moldova, viewing this as "un-American." The University was surprised by this, as they had not invested any money in this fund but only in the QQO funds. Dan Abrahmson, one of the trustees who had recommended that the endowment invest with Dr. Whisper, assured the trustees of Dr. Whisper's innovative techniques toward asset management and stated that "he was confident that Dr. Whisper had the best interests of his fellow alumni at heart." This seemed to quell any concerns of the investment committee members and the meeting proceeded without further incident.

Dr. Whisper closely guarded the positions in his portfolio. Additionally, he would not share with any investors the details of his model, speaking only in generalities. Some would call it paranoia, but Dr. Whisper was genuinely concerned that others in the market would seek to reverse-engineer some of his techniques or even trade ahead of certain of the QQO funds' positions. Consequently, his investors were unaware that the recent 4% downturn had been the result of increased commodity exposure in his portfolio. This was an investment theme on which he had begun to lean a bit more heavily in recent months as other long-term themes had not yet come to fruition. Dr. Whisper had become frustrated with the time it was taking some of his research themes to yield results and had switched to highly levered, long positions in certain less-liquid commodity markets, such as frozen orange juice, where he thought he could realize some quick profits. These positions had initially yielded large profits, but had reversed sharply later in the month, based on a supply glut due to an unusually warm winter that led to a longer growing season.

Also contributing to Dr. Whisper's frustrations were redemptions of approximately $200 million, bringing total AUM to $800 million, and the departure of his secretary, Calm Hope, due to Dr. Whisper's increasingly worse quick temper, which created an uncomfortable working environment. Rather than hire a replacement, Dr. Whisper had decided to prepare the monthly performance estimates and commentary himself. The month after Hope's departure, the commentary was sent several times to the same investors and was a week late, as Dr. Whisper could not figure out how to automate the distribution and formatting of the performance e-mails. Several investors called to question the lateness in reporting and the multiple email issue. Dr. Whisper's only response was a mass e-mail stating that this was a technical error that would be fixed going forward.

As the months progressed, QQO's performance had returned to its positive ways. Additionally, Dr. Whisper had asked Hushton, the computer scientist, to take over the performance distribution duties. There had been some additional reporting delays, but not more than a few days. The trustees had also made progress on their search for a new portfolio manager, and had recently hired Boisterous Loudly to oversee the endowment's investments. Loudly had a background in managing large endowment funds in traditional asset vehicles and was skeptical of alternative managers such as hedge funds, which he often referred to as "glorified mutual funds." This was part of the reason he was hired, as his conservative views meshed with those of the fund's trustees.

One of Loudly's first tasks was to gain an understanding of the current Prinstone endowment portfolio. As part of this process, he attempted to arrange a meeting with the four hedge fund managers in the portfolio. Dr. Whisper, of course, refused the meeting but did conduct a conference call after much urging by the alumni. The call was a bit awkward; Loudly inquired as to the nature of the QQO fund's current investments and if the nature of the investment mandate had been broadened over time. Dr. Whisper did not reveal any specifics about his portfolio holdings, models, or research. Operationally, his response to questions about infrastructure back-office issues and the like was a blanket "Mr. Hushton handles those issues." Loudly ended the call by informing Dr. Whisper that he would expect a greater level of communication going forward. He then expressed to the trustees his concerns, both operational and investment related. The trustees understood his concerns, but did not want to take action due to both the profits SAM had been generating and the relationship between themselves and Dr. Whisper.

The morning after his conference call with Loudly was an upsetting one for Dr. Whisper. His funds had lost over 20% in the first few hours of trading. Contributing to his woes were a series of Internet connectivity disruptions that had caused some latency between his computers and those of the exchanges. As his business had grown, Dr. Whisper had not thought it necessary to install multiple Internet backup lines. With the decline in the markets, he received several calls from concerned investors to which, as usual, he did not respond. Later that day, Dr. Whisper decided to place a highly levered, short Asian trade overnight, contrary to his models. The following morning, Dr. Whisper was pleasantly surprised to see that his bet had paid off. There was a market reversal overnight, partly as a result of a terrorist bombing in Asia, which had sent the Asian markets into a nosedive. This one trade would put him up 52% for the quarter. He planned to sell out of his positions and sit on 40% cash for the rest of the quarter to protect his gains while running the models as usual. Dr. Whisper immediately picked up the phone to inform Loudly that he would not have to worry and the QQO fund and performance for the quarter would be astounding. Loudly was very surprised to receive this call, and wondered what had inspired Dr. Whisper to start picking up the phone. Was this performance the result of the kind of risks they were paying him to take? Could Loudly's intuition that Dr. Whisper had ventured into new territory have been correct?

Was this a bad thing? After all, he was making money. Does Dr. Whisper pick up the phone only when there is good news to tell? How would Loudly look to the Prinstone trustees if he advised ending the relationship with QQO when they were going to post an outstanding return?

SCENARIO 5: THE INFRASTRUCTURE OUTSOURCER—CAN ONE ADMINISTRATOR DO EVERYTHING?

Canine Capital Management (CCM) runs a global macro strategy fund. Its investment strategy is straightforward, and focuses on making large directional bets on such things as currencies and equities to generate profits. In 2001, Benji Lassie, lead portfolio manager for the Kennel Group (KG), a large multifamily office, allocated $20 million to CCM. At that time, CCM's total asset base was $350 million, all of which was in the global macro funds. Commensurate with its own growth, KG has increased its allocation to CCM over time and now represents clients having over $400 million with CCM. As KG has grown, so, too, has CCM, which now manages approximately $1.5 billion. The firm's core strategy remains global macro, but as a result of a number of compelling investment opportunities, CCM has begun to add side pockets to its funds as well as making an increasing number of private-equity-like, less liquid investments, which now make up 12% of the portfolio. While there is no formal cap on the limits of these more illiquid investments in the fund's offering memorandum, the fund's exposure to these positions has traditionally been around 5%.

KG has not voiced much concern over these positions, as they have yielded handsome results and been significant contributors to the fund's recent stellar performance. Benji has kept a diligent eye on CCM for any potential style drift, and feels that the firm's transition into more illiquid positions is taken intelligently and opportunistically by the funds. He is comfortable with the current positioning of the portfolio, and has even recently advised several existing CCM clients to increase their allocations based on a host of attractive themes the firm anticipates playing out in the next three to six months.

Since their inception, CCM has outsourced the majority of its back-office operations to its administrator, Weimaraner Optimal Operational Factory (WOOF). CCM has a chief financial officer, Pismo Jones, who oversees the relationship with WOOF and the accounting for the management company, but CCM does not maintain any parallel books and records internally for its funds. WOOF was started in 1998 with seed capital from CCM. CCM has since divested itself of WOOF but continues to utilize their services. WOOF has developed into a lower-middle-tier administrator with 20 other hedge fund clients, administering just over \$8 billion in total. WOOF is based in Dublin, and has recently opened a small satellite office in Hong Kong with the aim of providing more time-zone coverage and garnering business from the growing Asian hedge fund market.

During his initial due diligence, Benji thoroughly vetted the relationship between WOOF and CCM. He even visited the WOOF offices in Dublin. His final determination was that CCM's relationship with WOOF was strategic in nature, and the fact that it had divested itself of WOOF in recent years made him more comfortable as to the independence of the relationship. Additionally, the CCM funds were audited on an annual basis by a respected third-party auditor, which gave him a further degree of comfort.

With the firm's increased growth and recent journey deeper into the land of illiquids, Benji has begun to be concerned that WOOF may not be able to meet CCM's needs anymore. Adding to his concerns are CCM's continuous insistence that there is no need to utilize a third-party valuation consultant, instead stating that all valuations are reviewed by WOOF and the external auditors. Benji has been around the block a few times, and is smart enough to see through CCM's initial smokescreen. He knows that CCM is not lying to him; indeed the valuations are reviewed by WOOF and the auditors at year end. He also knows that the service-level agreement between WOOF and CCM is for the fund to provide valuation services for securities for which it can obtain a price from either a third-party pricing source or a broker or multiple brokers. As per the administration agreement, if it disagrees with WOOF, CCM may override the price, which it has never done. In the case of certain illiquids for which no third-party quotes are available, WOOF's only responsibility is to confirm that CCM is valuing these positions in line with its valuation policies.

CCM documents its evaluation of these illiquids via an internal Valuation Committee. The Committee meets on a monthly basis, reviews the valuations of existing positions, and determines whether a revaluation is necessary. As the number of illiquids in the portfolio has increased, it has come to Benji's attention that the CCM global macro fund in which his clients are invested hold majority stakes in two privately held companies. One position is 85% of a Thai microbrewery and the other is 90% of a Finnish stationery manufacturer. These valuations are being determined solely at the discretion of the manager. Any time a change in valuation is made, CCM provides WOOF with a copy of the memorandum outlining this change. Due to its relatively small client base and lack of expertise in this area, WOOF does not have a division that focuses on independently valuing these types of illiquid positions.

Benji has also begun to notice increased delays in the receiving of performance estimates and final monthly net asset values from CCM. CCM explains that this has been the result of employee turnover at WOOF, which is not uncommon for the Dublin hedge fund administration market. CCM's chief financial officer also reiterates that he feels that WOOF is a best-in-class administrator that provides CCM with the attention it needs, something that he feels CCM would not get at a larger administrator. Benji further inquires as to why CCM has not hired any additional back-office staff to maintain parallel books and records and assist in managing the relationship with WOOF. Pismo states that there is no need for an additional accounting support, as CCM runs a plain-vanilla strategy and WOOF is a more efficient and cost-effective alternative.

Also a bit troubling to Benji is the fact that as CCM has grown, the number of accountants working on the CCM accounts has not materially increased, with only one additional headcount being added since 2001. This was confirmed when Benji performed a conference call with Tina Terrier, the senior manager of the portfolio accounting team that works on the WOOF accounts. Terrier also stated that each of these accountants is shared among other hedge funds but the CCM funds take up the majority of the team's time.

It is apparent to Benji that CCM has outgrown WOOF. Are they staying with them out of a sense of loyalty, since they seeded the business, even though they have now divested? Benji has had a business relationship with CCM for several years and believes the firm's management to be of the highest integrity, but he feels the lack of independence in the valuation process makes it prone to potential manipulation. Is this enough of a concern that he should pull his clients' money out of the CCM funds? If he decides to remain invested in the CMM funds, how should he effectively monitor the situation? More specifically, for how many days will NAVs, for example, need to be delayed before he decides to redeem? Ten? Fifteen? Perhaps NAVs will not be delayed, but an NAV restatement could be necessary if an event occurs that significantly alters the valuation of one of the firm's illiquid positions. This could result in a subsequent "run on the bank" and the funds could enact their 10% redemption gate. Under such a scenario, Benji's clients may not be able to get their money out in an orderly fashion. What should he do?

SCENARIO 6: THE MOUNTAIN CLIMBER—CAN PLANS FOR LARGE, FAST GROWTH TRIP YOU ALONG THE WAY?

Bert first started in the hedge fund industry with visions of grandeur. He had started off as a clerk in the mailroom ten years ago, but worked his way through school at night, earned his CFA, and had progressed through the ranks to eventually become a successful trader on the arbitrage desk at large investment bank. One day over dinner with his fellow traders, Bert learned that his colleague and close friend Ernie was going to leave to start his own hedge fund. Ernie's rich uncle had read in the newspaper all about hedge funds and thought his nephew, a successful trader for the investment bank, could be just as successful as everyone he had read about in the *Financial Times*. He decided to give Ernie $10 million and let him run it for him as he saw fit. Ernie viewed this as a chance to prove himself, not only to his family, but to everyone at the investment bank.

Bert had long wanted to spin off on his own and start a firm but did not have the capital or know-how to do so. After all, he thought, he was a trader, not a hedge fund manager. An opportunity to leave the investment bank and join forces with Ernie seemed promising, but he was not sure whether Ernie would go for it. After several weeks of hot pursuit, Ernie agreed to let Bert join his new firm, Sesame Asset Management Group (SAMG) as head trader.

During the first few quarters of operation, performance was impressive. Others began to take an interest in the new firm's ability to generate profits, especially under the poor market conditions at the time. As performance continued to remain impressively positive, more investors began to allocate to SAMG. One such investor was the asset-management arm of The Old Vampires Association of Transylvania, which provided $50 million to the fund and considered itself to be a strategic investor in SAMG.

At The Old Vamps, as they were commonly known, the chief investment officer was Count Duku. The Count had completed his PhD in finance at Transylvania University in Central Kentucky. His investment thesis for hedge funds was that most hedge fund managers produced their best results in the early stages of their life cycles. As such, The Old Vamps had a reputation for allocating very early on to nascent, emerging hedge fund managers who produced early promising results. They were usually well compensated for taking these bets, despite the added risks.

By year's end, SAMG had a net positive performance of 58.5% and had amassed $400 million in assets. Bert was very pleased with himself, as well, and had established quite a name for himself in the hedge fund industry. He had garnered a $15 million bonus and was confident he was just warming up. The firm had also created quite a buzz for itself in the hedge fund community and had been recently nominated for several industry awards.

Over the past year, Ernie had turned his attention to running the business side of SAMG. He had hired various support personnel, including a chief financial officer and a head of investor relations as well as several junior support operations and trading personnel. With the SAMG brand name developing over time, Ernie also began to contemplate letting SAMG spread its wings and launch several new strategies in addition to the core strategy managed by Bert.

As the following year progressed, SAMG's flagship fund reached $1 billion under management and soft closed to new investors. The Old Vamps had been closely monitoring SAMG's growth, and had increased their allocation to $100 million over time. With the soft close, SAMG had also carved out several directional pieces of the flagship strategy and had begun raising assets for these funds, as well. Overall personnel numbers had increased. SAMG now employed 28 total staff including as well as 4 junior analysts, 1 senior analyst, and 10 operations personnel. This increase in staff had made original investors like The Old Vamps comfortable with the organization's stability; however, based on their experiences with investing in emerging hedge fund managers, The Old Vamps had growing concerns that SAMG was growing too large too fast.

In meetings with investors like The Old Vamps, SAMG investor relations personnel were quick to point out the entrepreneurial nature of the firm and the collegial work environment. The increasing size of the firm, the investor relations personnel pointed out, benefited investors like The Old Vamps because it allowed SAMG to capitalize on more promising market opportunities as more of a major player. At the same time, Ernie had continued his plans to grow the business and had recently hired away a senior team of credit analysts to launch their own hedge fund under the SAMG name. This fund would launch with $20 million, seeded by a combination of proprietary SAMG capital and small allocations from other investors. Additionally, the SAMG flagship fund would make a small allocation to this fund.

Six months later, SAMG announced to investors its intention to launch a Japan-focused fund based in Hong Kong. The fund would be run by Bert and Ernie's former investment banking colleague, Hattori Ichimoku Musashi. Similar to the credit fund, the SAMG Japan fund would be seeded with a combination of proprietary capital, investor allocations, and an allocation from Bert's flagship fund.

During the next two years, SAMG continued this growth model. In total, the firm had reached aggregate assets under management of $10 billion across eight strategies, including the SAMG flagship fund. The flagship fund had allocations to SAMG's seven other funds, which accounted for 35% of the fund's total holdings. This allocation percentage had changed over time, depending on which strategies were performing better or worse. Investors like The Old Vamps had made a significant profit since the time of their initial investment; however, they were beginning to grow concerned about what they were actually invested in. Originally, they had allocated to Bert because they believed he showed promise as a young hedge fund manager.

Now they were beginning to feel that Bert's talent was becoming increasingly diluted by the fund's ever-growing allocation to other strategies.

The Old Vamps had also noticed that whenever some of the firm's strategies had begun to realize poor performance and redemptions, the allocation from the SAMG flagship fund to these strategies had increased in an attempt to bolster the funds. Of course, SAMG argued that this was a good opportunity for the SAMG funds to realize profits in these markets (i.e., buy into the market when it is cheap), but The Old Vamps suspected differently. Also troubling to The Old Vamps was the lack of formal limits of the amounts that the SAMG flagship fund could invest in other SAMG strategies. Count Duku was faced with a decision. Should The Old Vamps walk away from an investment that looks to be continually profitable, or continue to remain invested with SAMG and face the eventual loss of Bert's investment edge over time to the talent of others within SAMG? If this was going to be the case, Count Duku thought he could just build his own multistrategy fund of SAMG funds and have more control over the allocation percentages—an idea that SAMG was not receptive to.

Count Duku had several questions to consider:

- How much co-investment is too much co-investment?
- Are there synergies that can be realized by a group of in-house portfolio managers sharing ideas and providing each other with information flow?
- Was SAMG capitalizing on certain economies of scale by designing such things as scalable information technology systems, across each of its strategies?

SCENARIO 7: THE STUMBLING GIANT—CAN A LARGE MANAGER LOSE SIGHT OF SMALL CONTROLS?

D.J. Todd is a large hedge fund organization with over $5 billion under management across four strategies consisting of 15 funds, with the flagship fund being an Asian-focused long/short equity fund. D.J. Todd had founded its business on two main premises: Locate and foster the best, most innovative investment professionals in the market, and provide these individuals with the highest caliber operational support and efficiency. As such, its growth process had been a little slow compared with the meteoric rise of most of the successful hedge funds that had started at the same time.

D.J. Todd's investors, which it selected carefully, have lauded the firm for its transparency and timeliness of reporting. Investor relations personnel were similarly professional. D.J. Todd's service providers also thought highly of the firm. For example, during the month-end reconciliation process, there were hardly any discrepancies between D.J. Todd's internal NAV and the one calculated by the administrator. If there were ever any discrepancies, they were minuscule, never larger than 5 bps, and were always resolved within one business day at the most.

D.J. Todd has also experienced minimal turnover of senior personnel among the firm. As the firm has grown over time, it has promoted from within, but in some instances it has hired external senior operations personnel to oversee new areas that the firm has ventured into, as there was a lack of internal expertise in certain areas. An example of this was bank debt, which the firm had recently begun to trade. D.J. Todd hired Mark Chebechev to oversee bank debt reconciliations.

Another area where the firm had recently hired additional senior-level employees was investor relations. D.J. Todd had never marketed extensively in the Middle East, but recently hired Bob Smith, a U.S. military veteran who was fluent in Arabic and had an extensive network of contacts throughout the Middle East, to assist in client service and raising assets from this region. D.J. Todd anticipated having Bob leverage the firm's substantial marketing materials library and performance reporting software.

As time progressed, D.J. Todd began to notice considerable increases in assets from the Middle East, and was very pleased with Bob's performance. One day, a large client from Saudi Arabia called D.J. Todd's New York offices to request a copy of a marketing presentation. Bob was at a conference in Dubai and could not be reached. Margo Burger, from D.J. Todd's investor relations department in New York, e-mailed the presentation to the Saudi client. A few minutes later, the client called again, requesting that he be sent a copy of the presentation in Arabic. Margo was unclear what the Saudi client meant, as she had never seen a presentation in Arabic before. She inquired with Tim Cutlass, the firm's head of investor relations.

Tim was equally puzzled by the client's inquiry. D.J. Todd had followed a strict policy of not translating any of its marketing materials into other languages. The firm did not have a problem speaking about itself in other languages, such as Arabic; however, it did not want the burden of preparing multiple copies of presentations for different clients in multiple languages. Additionally, Tim had long felt that the firm's marketing materials would suffer if directly translated from one language to another. Instead, he was of the opinion that the materials would have to *rewritten* for each local market in order to properly deliver D.J. Todd's marketing message in a consistent matter across the globe to all clients. Further, Tim felt that the vast majority of investors and prospects understood enough basic English to find the materials useful.

Tim sent an e-mail to Bob to follow up on this issue. Bob received the e-mail on his BlackBerry. He had just finished attended a networking session at the conference in Dubai for Middle Eastern pension funds that were interested in learning about alternatives. He called Tim on his mobile. It was evening in New York and Tim had just gone home.

TIM: Hi, Bob. How's Dubai?

BOB: Good. Meeting some interesting leads here. Sorry to bother you at home, but I wanted to follow up on that e-mail you sent me about the Saudi client.

TIM: Thanks for the call. Yes, he wanted a copy of some presentation in Arabic. Margo explained that she hadn't seen anything in Arabic and brought this to my attention.

BOB: Yeah, that's fine. I'll send him a copy of it.

TIM: What do you mean?

BOB: A copy of the presentation.

TIM: You mean you produced a copy of our presentation materials in Arabic?

BOB: Yes. I've received some really great feedback on it here.

TIM: I can't believe you did this. This is absolutely against our policies.

BOB: What policies? I didn't see anything about this in the employee handbook. Besides, we've been getting some great responses from it and asset flows have been positive.

TIM: I don't care—stop using it immediately. I'll speak to you later.

Tim promptly hung up the phone. He was more angry at himself than at Bob. *How had he let this occur?*, he thought to himself. Why had he not revised the employee handbook? It never occurred to him that Bob would produce his own materials in another language. Tim reflected on a time when the firm was first starting out and everyone was in the same office. Now he had Bob running around all over the Middle East, making his own materials. Perhaps Tim's stance on translating marketing presentations into other languages was incorrect; after all, Bob had received positive feedback. Tim wondered whether other senior managers had faced similar issues as the firm had grown both in terms of number of employees and complexity over time. If so, he had not heard about any such problems at the firm's weekly senior management meetings. Had other senior managers simply buried any issues under the rug? Had D.J. Todd grown too big for its own good? Was there anyone overseeing coordination across the firm, now that it had grown so big? What should Tim do about Bob?

SCENARIO 8: THE APOLOGETIC HEADMASTER—ARE JUNIOR STAFF AS INFORMED AS SENIOR MANAGEMENT?

Kim Jong represents the asset-management arm of the endowment of a large Midwestern university. This university has become an experienced alternative investment allocator over the past few years, as its allocation to alternatives has slowly increased. Kim in particular has focused her efforts on operational due diligence. The firm is considering an investment in a large, established global macro hedge fund, Jelly Bean Asset Management (JBAM).

JBAM has approximately $3.5 billion under management. The firm employs 75 individuals in total, 45 of whom are investment professionals. Over the past six months, the firm has hired several new research analysts to bolster its Asian research capabilities. The most senior hire is Iori Yagami. When he joined the firm, Iori disclosed to the firm's senior management that he received compensation from serving as a director of a large staple manufacturer. Iori had a previous relationship with this firm from the early part of his career in the stapler business. Several other employees in the firm also held outside directorships, the majority of which were with charitable and not-for-profit organizations. During the course of the operational due diligence process, Kim had performed a background investigation on Iori and several other key professionals at the firm. This investigation had revealed details concerning the outside directorships held by these individuals.

During the onsite interview process with JBAM, Kim was hosted by Ritch Aspen, an investor relations employee specializing in the endowment and foundation space. During the onsite meeting, Kim met with a number of senior operations professionals throughout the firm, including the firm's controller and assistant chief operations officer. During each of these meetings, Ritch left Kim with the senior operations personnel to conduct their meeting. Ritch often found these operational due diligence meetings to be boring. He felt he could not add much, as he could speak about the firm's investments but did not really know about the back-office side of things.

Kim also met with Brennan Thurgood, the firm's assistant chief compliance officer. Brennan had been with the firm since inception, and had previously worked in the compliance department of a large law firm. Brennan was not a lawyer, but was generally knowledgeable concerning compliance-related legal matters. Kim began to ask Brennan questions.

KIM: Employees are required to report to you any outside employment or directorships?

BRENNAN: Yes, that is correct, according to policies and procedures outlined in our compliance manual. Have you received a copy of this manual?

KIM: Yes, I have, thank you. What is the process by which employees report such outside directorships?

BRENNAN: As outlined in the compliance manual, employees are required to disclose any other employment or outside directorships they may have when they join the firm. Additionally, they gain preapproval from the compliance department before undertaking any new employment or outside directorships.

KIM: Do you maintain a register of any outside directorships?

BRENNAN: I would, but no one really has any currently.

KIM: I see; thank you.

Kim continued her meeting with Brennan, focusing on other issues. After the meeting, she placed a call to Mark Bean, the firm's chief investment officer. She informed Mark of the discrepancy between her background investigation and the information provided by Brennan. Mark apologized to Kim, and assured her that this was most likely an oversight on his part. Later that day, Brennan contacted Kim and apologized for the oversight. Brennan indicated that he was no longer responsible for maintaining the outside directorship register and these duties had been designated a few years ago to junior compliance personnel. Kim inquired as to whether Brennan could share with her a copy of this register. Brennan indicated he would look into this and provide it to her. Three days later, Kim received the register, which had omitted several of the outside directorships that her background investigation had revealed.

Kim is now faced with a tough choice and a number of open questions. JBAM is a very successful asset manager. Should this oversight, which some investors might consider nonmaterial, be enough of a reason not to allocate to this manager? Despite Mark's apology, was the firm not taking the compliance function seriously? What if Kim had worked for the Securities and Exchange Commission or another regulator? How would such an oversight be viewed in this instance? Was senior management not diligent in overseeing operational issues that it felt were less important? Did JBAM bring out senior personnel, such as the chief compliance officer, only for what it considered to be large investors? What if Kim had not performed her own background investigation and taken what Brennan had said on good faith? What incentive would Brennan have had to lie to her? Was this simply an oversight? Should this be viewed as a red flag, or merely a mistake? Has the firm taken any corrective action to remedy this and ensure that this junior investor relations individual does not make similar mistakes? Was anything else Kim was told—by either the investor relations employee or other junior, or perhaps even senior, individuals in the firm—not 100% accurate?

CHAPTER 6

Ten Tips for Performing an Operational Due Diligence Review

There are a number of common mistakes both investors and large hedge fund allocators make when first approaching the operational due diligence process. The purpose of this chapter is to provide guidance and some best practices for conducting a more efficient operational review. This list is by no means inclusive, and is meant to further the discussion of operational due diligence standards.

Oversight of certain issues can lead to disastrous results. The biggest mistake people make when performing an operational review is not following up on outstanding issues that result from the operational due diligence process. Of course, this phenomenon is not specific to the operational due diligence process; it is characteristic of almost all sectors of the hedge fund due diligence process and, I venture to guess, the civilized world in general. Unfortunately, it is basic human nature. People promise to do something and, for a variety of reasons, they do not do it. It could be laziness, forgetfulness, procrastination, lack of comfort in sharing certain types of information—the list is endless.

All investors and hedge fund managers should be conscious of this central theme. If you say you are going to do something, do it, and in a timely manner. In the field of operational due diligence, continuing to make false promises is like opening a can of worms. Parties on both sides of the operational due diligence equation begin to take things personally and have doubts about doing business with each other. I have seen this scenario play out multiple times. Many potentially lucrative hedge fund deals go awry simply because of lack of follow-through and false expectations. My advice is to follow through; it will make the due diligence process go much more smoothly for both investors and hedge funds alike.

TIP 1: AVOID MEETING WITH THE WRONG PEOPLE OR THE WRONG GROUPS

As discussed in Chapter 5, onsite visits at a hedge fund manager's offices are a crucial part of the operational due diligence process. These visits can be compared to a game of chess. A shrewd player knows not to reveal his true strategy too early in the match. This applies to setting up an operational due diligence review. In addition to raising, and retaining, assets from clients, most investor-relations employees are hired to serve as a buffer and, in some instances, a proxy for a portfolio manager or other key personnel in the firm. It is not that portfolio managers or senior analysts do not meet with investment analysts or important clients; rather they do not need to do a lot of the basic legwork and handholding certain clients require.

One common mistake first-time hedge fund investors make is that they fail to set the tone of such onsite visits from the get-go. This generally happens in two ways. First, when arranging a meeting through an investor-relations employee, they do not specify the individuals with whom they want to meet. They rely on the hedge fund to dictate whom they will be seeing. A second way this happens is through ambiguity, as when potential investors in a fund make broad statements such as, "We want to meet with someone who can talk about the back office." Is this the firm's controller, or chief financial officer, or chief operating officer? All of these individuals can most likely speak about certain back-office procedures in varying degrees of detail and most likely an investor would want to meet with all three. These approaches are a mistake. While there is nothing wrong with receiving suggestions from an investor-relations person as to who might be the most appropriate people to meet, the ultimate decision should be the investor's. Ambiguity is the enemy of those performing operational due diligence and, to quote U.S. Supreme Court Justice Louis Brandeis, "Sunlight is the best disinfectant."

A common pitfall first-time hedge fund investors fall into in failing to properly set the tone of an onsite visit is combining investment-related and operational due diligence reviews. These are two separate meetings, with two separate agendas, that require meeting with entirely different sets of people. Additionally, as discussed in Chapter 2, investment analysis and operational due diligence are two different subjects with two different skill sets required. Despite any overlap, investors are better off segregating the two processes, at least for the purposes of onsite meetings, and then comparing notes afterward.

Now that we have established that investors should be *proactive* in determining whom to meet with during an operational due diligence review, we come to the question of who are the appropriate people to meet with. This is not so easy to answer. Potential investors should attempt to meet with the key people in each of the functional areas of operational risk, including the chief compliance officer, chief operating officer, and chief financial officer. Sometimes, however, certain operational individuals have multiple roles with a hedge fund. Other times, the roles are not clearly defined.

Regardless of what certain individuals' titles are, once they are meeting with them, investors have to be cautious that they are getting the full story and all the facts as to what is really going on within an organization. A common mistake hedge fund investors make is to meet with people in large groups.

Many operational due diligence analysts request to meet with certain individuals one-on-one so that their answers are not influenced by others in the room. This is especially important, for example, when you are questioning a controller, and her boss, the chief financial officer, is sitting in the room with you. Typically, employees are less candid about certain things when their immediate supervisors are within earshot. Additionally, similar to interrogating the suspects of a crime, when two people do not hear each other's explanations of certain things, sometimes you get two different stories.

For example, an investor-relations employee may tell you that the firm is very happy with its administrator and his team if the fund administrator has experienced no material turnover. This may be true from the investor-relations employee's perspective, or she may be putting a positive spin on the situation. Regardless, a potential investor may get a different story from a controller, for example, who deals with the firm on a more regular basis and may have been more directly impacted by any personnel turnover at the administrator. By making intelligent, proactive choices, both about whom they meet and how they meet with them, hedge fund investors can greatly enhance the effectiveness of operational due diligence reviews.

TIP 2: GET OUT OF THE CONFERENCE ROOM

In addition to meeting with the wrong people or groups, a second common mistake many hedge fund investors make is that they do not understand, or take advantage of the fact, that they have the ability to venture outside the walls of the conference room when conducting an operational due diligence review of a hedge fund. Unfortunately, many onsite operational due diligence reviews begin and end behind the walls of a conference room. This defeats part of the purpose of an onsite review. Regardless of whether you meet with someone (e.g., a hedge fund's chief financial officer) in a conference room or an office, you still generally have a much richer discussion by being face-to-face than you would over the phone or via videoconference. It is not this point that we argue here. The same goal of face-to-face interaction is as surely accomplished in a conference room as it is in a chief financial officer's office. Rather, the crux of this operational due diligence tip is that by venturing outside the conference room, those performing an operational review afford themselves the opportunity to view an organization in its most natural state. (This can be contrasted with reviewing summaries in due diligence questionnaires about a certain process or merely hearing a description of how a certain operational process takes place.)

Some of this can be accomplished during a tour of the hedge fund's office space. A common example is the firm's server room. Most hedge fund manager tours involve the firm's chief technology officer walking investors into frigidly cold server rooms and describing the firm's technology infrastructure over the loud buzzing of server cooling fans. However, some things cannot be accomplished by a tour. An example of this is *shadowing*. The most common example of shadowing is in the job marketplace, and is called *job shadowing*. Under one version of this concept, students shadow a job to see whether they have an interest in working in that field. As part of the shadowing process, students spend the day, almost like a fly on the wall, following someone who does the job they might be interested in doing one day. People who participate in these programs find it is a great way to gain a first-hand perspective on the daily routine involved in performing certain jobs.

When added into the standard conference room question-and-answer onsite operational due diligence review session, shadowing can yield surprising insights. The best way to illustrate this concept is via an example. Let us consider a common element of every operational due diligence review, the trade reconciliation process. In preparing for an operational due diligence onsite review, a potential investor has done all the previous steps described in this text. He has reviewed the firm's due diligence materials, performed some of his own research into the accounting systems utilized by the firm, and feels he has a good understanding of how things work at the hedge fund. He confirms this during the onsite question-and-answer session by discussing the reconciliation process with the firm's chief financial officer. Typically, this is where the conversation would end.

Now let us assume that this investor adds a shadowing component to his review. He leaves the conference room and takes a chair next to one of the firm's junior accountants, who is responsible for trade reconciliation among other duties. At present, this accountant is working on reconciling a trade break. The investor observes the accountant on the phone with several brokers, attempting to verify the original quote provided to the fund and then with the fund's administrator in an attempt to resolve the situation. The accountant then pulls up the trade blotter, books several trades, and walks the investor through how these are transmitted from the trade blotter into the firm's accounting system.

This investor may not have learned anything new, but he did get to see the systems in action. By seeing all of the distinct, moving parts in action, rather than simply hearing descriptions about them or seeing flowcharted diagrams of how these systems interact, it is highly likely that the investor will develop a much deeper sense of how these systems work in practice. Additionally, observing these systems in operation in real time provides an investor with a third data point, in addition to what was garnered from the firm's documentation and conference room interview, to see whether things are actually happening the way the firm describes its operations in its marketing materials and in meetings. Also, while not demonstrated in our example, in practice there may be certain procedures or policies that are not described in much detail, or at all, in the firm's materials or by personnel. These could be additional proprietary software applications or workarounds, certain individuals performing multiple roles, or certain individuals performing specifically designated roles within a function (such as an accountant focused on bank debt within a larger accounting team).

TIP 3: LITTLE WHITE LIES CAN TURN INTO BIG PROBLEMS

When analyzing the various operational risk data points collected as part of the hedge fund due diligence process, ranging from how a hedge fund values mortgage backed securities to when was the last time the e-mail server crashed, it is important to remain cognizant of the way in which these somewhat seemingly distinct data points interact with and support each other, or, in some instances, contradict one another. This is part of the purpose of the five-theme framework (oversight, controls, connectivity, scalability, and stability) described in Chapter 1. There is another global factor that, while not a direct outgrowth of any one core operational function itself, can be thought of as a sixth theme that should always be in the back of a potential hedge fund investor's mind. This is the trait of *consistency*.

Consistency can take many forms as part of an operational due diligence review. It can be as basic as having historical performance figures in a marketing presentation match the figures in a due diligence questionnaire, or noting that a portfolio manager's biography in a pitchbook does not include the same employment history as that contained in his biography on the hedge fund's website. It can also be a little more complex. A firm's new investor-relations employee might tell a potential investor that the hedge fund has never switched third-party service providers. Yet, during an onsite visit, the firm's general counsel informs you that the firm has followed its favorite attorney twice in the past five years as he has changed law firms. The newly arrived investor-relations employee may genuinely not have known about the switch; or maybe the general counsel is less than communicative with her on these types of issues. These are perfectly logical explanations for this inconsistency and absolve both the investor-relations employee and the general counsel of any illicit motives; yet the fact remains that they are telling two different stories and, as part of the due diligence process, you as the investor are doing a certain amount of legwork to get people within the firm on the same page. This is not necessarily your job as an investor. A competent hedge fund in the modern investing environment should be adequately prepared for an operational due diligence review. A key part of this preparation is ensuring that all relevant employees are on the same page. If they are not, the hedge fund organization should make them feel comfortable enough to state, "I am not sure about the answer to that, but I will get back to you," rather than simply present their best guess as fact. If this is not the case, and investors do uncover such inconsistencies, they absolutely should be noted and considered as part of the operational review process.

Consistency can be evaluated not only as internal to a hedge fund but in the way in which a hedge fund organization interacts with external service providers. For example, if when performing due diligence a hedge fund's chief financial officer tells you that net asset value (NAV) estimates are normally produced within two business days after month-end, and a representative from the fund's administrator tells you it has been running more like seven days for NAV estimates, these two bits of information are clearly inconsistent. Is it that the firm's chief financial officer is attempting to pull the wool over the unsuspecting investor's eyes? Perhaps it used to be seven days, and now it is closer to two days. A hedge fund investor would have to do some digging to get to the bottom of the issue, but the hedge fund should be penalized for this inconsistency when making a final operational determination. Is this penalty severe enough to warrant not allocating capital? Perhaps it is; but it has to be considered in conjunction with the rest of the operational data points. This and other small "lies" or "inconsistencies" should not be overlooked simply because they seem trivial in isolation. Consider this: Following our previous example, what if the potential investor had not followed up with the administrator? That would have left the investor simply taking what the chief financial officer said at face value, and perhaps allocating under false pretenses. If the investor allocated, and NAV estimates were being delivered closer to every seven days, as opposed to the two days indicated by the chief financial officer, the investor clearly would be unhappy. This investor might not be unhappy enough to redeem, but others might. Hedge fund investors tend to follow the adage, "once bitten twice shy," and are often reluctant to reallocate to a manager with whom they previously have had a bad experience—and why should they? As with restaurants in New York City, there is no shortage of options in the hedge fund universe. Sure, there are some superstars out there, but the waiting lines are often long and people still need to eat, so they will go around the corner where the food is not as fancy but the service is better.

TIP 4: BE WARY OF PHANTOMWARE

As mentioned several times throughout this text, hedge funds are heavily reliant on technology. Often they are the first users of new software and adapters of new versions of existing software. The use of this software runs the gamut from performing back-office accounting functionalities to trade allocation and risk management. In the current hedge fund environment, many hedge funds have sought to increase their technological edge through large investments in proprietary software development. This is particularly true for largely technically based trading strategies.

Phantomware can be defined as "a hyped product that is delayed, never released, and costs the company and its investors millions of dollars."[1] Similarly, *vaporware* can be defined as "a computer-related product that has been widely advertised but has not and may never become available."[2] Regardless of the terminology used, for the purposes of this text I would like to suggest an alternative definition be added to phantomware/vaporware as it applies in the hedge fund operational risk context: software purchased by a hedge fund organization that is not being effectively utilized by the processes for which the software was primarily designed. As outlined in the following, there are a number of motivations for such a practice, none of which I condone, and potential hedge fund investors should be conscious of not falling victim to phantomware.

One common mistake many investors and hedge fund professionals make is simply writing down the names of software packages utilized rather than understanding the nature and appropriateness of their use. Unfortunately, this is often where the discussion of this topic stops. Many hedge fund investors do not delve deeper into such issues as why a hedge fund selected a certain software package or whether they have recently reevaluated the way in which such software is used.

There are several possible reasons for this, including a lack of knowledge about specific software applications and the false sense of security that accompanies certain large brand-name software packages. Hedge fund investors should realize that whereas such software packages may be impressive in terms of both efficiency and functionality, they may not be an appropriate fit for the particular hedge fund organization in which they are considering an investment.

In the early years of the hedge fund industry, as many successful managers were raising large amounts of capital, there were several reports of phantom manual practices hidden behind the shadow of larger, off-the-shelf software packages. The classic example of this is the purchase of an expensive risk management system. The names of such systems are plastered all over a firm's due diligence questionnaires, but are the hedge fund managers effectively utilizing such risk analysis tools, or are they simply sticking to their knitting and analyzing risk the way they used to before they purchased such a system? Is a large, expensive software package sitting in a box somewhere while a risk manager continues to manipulate a Microsoft Excel spreadsheet? If so, most hedge fund investors would most likely have preferred that the firm not lay out the significant amount of capital required to install and maintain this phantomware and rather reinvest the capital in the firm.

To illustrate, consider the function served by accounting software. There are certain large third-party accounting software packages that most established hedge funds utilize. Once a hedge fund reaches a certain size and the organization feels the need to upgrade its accounting system, it often selects one of these large, off-the-shelf, enterprise-wide accounting packages. Unfortunately, there is a subliminal Pavlovian mechanism in the majority of investors' and hedge fund chief operating officers' brains that releases the "everything's okay" endorphins once they hear the name of one of these well-known accounting packages.

Potential hedge fund investors can learn a great deal by engaging a hedge fund's operational personnel in discussion about such software. Continuing with our accounting package example, investors are well advised to ask the following questions:

- What other accounting software systems did the firm consider?
- What did they like/not like about these other systems?
- Why did they select the system they did?
- What are the terms of their license agreement?
- Can employees in other offices use the software, or does the license limit usage to one office?
- Are they planning to load historical data into the system or just populate it with new data?
- How will this system be integrated into the firm's existing network architecture?
- Will the installation of this system require changes to other systems?
- Will the firm perform any customization on this system?
- Will this system be run in parallel with any other systems?

By focusing in detail on the information technology systems in place at a hedge fund, and then taking time to understand how these systems are actually utilized, hedge fund investors can more adequately ensure that a hedge fund is making intelligent operational decisions and not simply purchasing a system to quell investors' concerns about technology.

TIP 5: FOCUS ON DOCUMENTATION AND NEGOTIATION

The more operational due diligence reviews one performs, the more one begins to notice similarities among hedge funds. Once these patterns or common practices are recognized, the search for *outliers* or *irregularities* will fuel the operational due diligence process. This is especially true when it comes to reviewing hedge fund managers' documentation.

As discussed in Chapter 4, hedge fund documentation, especially legal documentation, can be somewhat intimidating. This is especially true for investors who do not have a background in legal issues. Even those with legal training might not be familiar with common market hedge fund documentation terms or with terms that could be considered *off-market*.

Due to the voluminous and intricate nature of such documentation, many beginning hedge fund investors spend the majority of their due diligence efforts attempting to decipher these documents and understand how a fund's terms will apply to them. This is a crucial part of the document review process, but it should not end there. Investors should take care to ensure that hedge funds are proactive in understanding, monitoring, and updating their own documentation. This applies to both core fund documentation, ongoing documentation that is created during the course of normal business operations, such as vendor agreements, and international swaps and derivative agreements.

Hedge fund investors should engage hedge funds in active discussions about such documentation. In many cases, hedge funds will not provide full transparency with regard to such things as administration agreements, but they may provide potential investors with a summary of the terms of their administration agreement. By digging a little deeper, investors can then determine whether these are common market standard fees. If a fund is particularly large, or has been a client of a certain administrator for a long time, has it actively renegotiated this contract in the past few years to its advantage, or has it simply accepted that administrator's status quo? Even once potential investors are able to determine the answers to such questions, they can dig deeper by asking such questions as how long it took to negotiate the administration agreement and who was involved in the negotiation process. These seemingly innocuous questions can provide valuable insight as to how seriously the firm takes the negotiation process. This can provide insight into not only how consciously a firm focuses on costs, but also how competent legal counsel is (both internal and external), whether senior management is involved in understanding and reviewing such commitments, and so on. For example, if a fund took two weeks to negotiate a first-time administration agreement, this would seem a bit quick, and a potential hedge fund investor should raise questions with the fund about the documentation review process. Such questions might include:

- Who reviewed the terms of the document? Was it one party, or multiple parties, both internally and externally?
- Did the firm source bids from other vendors? If so, how many were there? How long ago were these other bids sourced?
- Who at the hedge fund ensures that the level of service a vendor says it is providing in the contract is actually being delivered?
- Are there any punitive damages or increased levels of service that the vendor is supposed to provide in the event that it does not deliver the service expected?
- What if key people who service the client's account depart the service provider? Does the firm have the option to terminate its contract or renegotiate?

In addition to the documentation review process, investors should be conscious of factors such as the length of the agreement entered into. The shorter the length of the agreement, the more beneficial it is considered to be for the hedge fund, as it will have the opportunity to renegotiate when the contract comes up for renewal. That said, hedge funds that are willing to enter into longer-term contracts with certain vendors may be able to secure higher levels of service and reduced fees. There is no one perfect solution for all hedge funds. The point is that investors should take care to understand whether a hedge fund has the proper controls and review processes in place to make these decisions intelligently and negotiate favorably on its own behalf.

TIP 6: READ THE FINE PRINT (FINANCIAL STATEMENT NOTES, ETC.)

Most hedge fund investors would like to believe that highly paid professionals with impressive academic credentials know what they are doing. It is generally true that such professionals, particularly in terms of operations, have many years of experience and are very knowledgeable and capable of performing their jobs with consistency and accuracy. Unfortunately, this statement cannot be made universally for every hedge fund, and consequently we have yet another reason for operational due diligence reviews.

In some cases, it is not really anyone's fault. When an operational professional, such as a chief financial officer, begins to work at a firm, he is not necessarily involved, in any way, in constructing such things as basic fund documentation. This is the lawyer's job, and a firm's general counsel is supposed to oversee this process. A chief financial officer, continuing our example, is especially not involved if he has joined an established firm. This chief financial officer may be a very competent individual with many years of relevant experience. Investors should be cautious, however, when they begin to put the pieces together. A classic example is an inconsistency between what a hedge fund manager's documentation says he is supposed to do and what is actually happening in process.

Let us say we have a hedge fund vehicle in a master–feeder structure. An investor is considering making an investment in an offshore feeder vehicle. As part of the operational due diligence process, the investor conducts a review of both the financial statements and legal documentation of offshore vehicles under consideration. In particular, the investor notes the following section from the private placement memorandum for the offshore vehicle:

> *The management and performance fees shall be collected at the feeder level.*

Attempting to confirm this, the investor looks at the notes of the audited financial statements for the offshore vehicle, which reads as follows:

> *The management and incentive allocation shall be collected by the master fund.*

Clearly, this is a discrepancy. The firm's chief financial officer, especially if he is new to a firm, might not have sat down to review the private placement memorandum and cross-reference this with the financial statements. Ideally, such a discrepancy would be caught by the fund's auditors, but it might not be detected by them. When conducting an operational due diligence review, investors should not take for granted that a firm has reviewed this, or that it evens knows what is contained in this private placement memorandum. This is especially true of firms that do not have in-house legal staff and have not updated their fund's documentation in recent years. Problems can also come about when legal documents, which may have been boilerplate documents to begin with, become stale and no longer reflect the firm's policies or procedures, which may have changed over time.

TIP 7: REFERENCE CHECKING: IMPORTANCE OF IN-SAMPLE AND OUT-OF-SAMPLE REFERENCES

When reviewing references, the most logical place to start with is those references provided directly from hedge fund managers themselves. For purposes of this text, we can refer to these references as *in-sample references*. The problem with these in-sample references is that most hedge fund managers will not provide you with references that have anything remotely critical or negative to say about them. In the normal course of business, there are inevitably certain deals that go awry and certain dealings that lead to misunderstandings and damaged egos. These types of references can prove to be the most insightful to an investor considering an investment in a certain hedge fund. The challenge facing many hedge fund investors is identifying these non-manager-provided or *out-of-sample references*.

Potential hedge fund investors have many sources of out-of-sample references (references not provided directly by the manager) available to them that they might not necessarily be leveraging. These can include such sources as colleagues and other hedge fund investors. For a hedge fund allocator, one of the most valuable sources of reference information is other hedge funds. This is true because, in the close-knit hedge fund industry, investment and operational professionals alike tend to move between hedge funds rather than exit the industry entirely. If a potential investor happens to have a relationship with a hedge fund organization where a certain professional used to work, she can perhaps leverage this relationship as an out-of-sample reference for the hedge fund manager under consideration.

Additionally, out-of-sample references can be identified by analyzing the backgrounds, specifically employment and educational histories, of individuals obtained via hedge fund manager–provided biographies and third-party background investigations. By carefully tracking this information, by both institution and date, a potential investor could identify the fact that a certain hedge fund manager with whom he is considering making an investment had attended university or worked alongside another manager. This other manager could then be contacted to see whether she would provide an independent, out-of-sample reference for the hedge fund manager under consideration.

Several large hedge fund allocators have attempted partially to automate this out-of-sample recognition process by combining branch-mapping software with customer relationship management (CRM) system functionality. Without building out such complex systems, investors should attempt to identify and contact out-of-sample references so as not to have to accept a hedge fund manager's references at face value.

TIP 8: CREDIT ANALYSIS: ARE FUNDS FINANCIALLY VIABLE?

An often-overlooked point in hedge fund investing is the continued financial viability of the firm in terms of revenues and expenses, and not just in terms of NAVs. Put another way, a hedge fund may be realizing profits on its investments; however, if its expenses are greater than its revenues, the firm will eventually go out of business.

This can be monitored on an ongoing basis by reviewing certain trends within an organization over time. These can include overall asset trends, revenue gained from performance and management fees, subscriptions, and redemption flows and expenses.

TIP 9: LONG-TERM PLANNING: KEY STAFF RETENTION, SUCCESSION PLANNING, AND MORE

As with all investments, making a hedge fund investment should be viewed as the beginning of a business relationship. Of course, the primary purpose of this relationship is to make money, both for you and for the hedge fund manager, but there is also something more to this relationship. Elements of trust and friendship are involved. Specifically, in regard to trust, a potential investor is trusting that a hedge fund manager will not lose his money, through either poor investment decisions or fraudulent activity. This trust is not extended merely to a particular person at the hedge fund organization; it is extended to the entire organization that is supporting the key portfolio managers.

This relationship, regardless of how long it actually lasts, should be evaluated at the onset as if it were going to last a long time. That could be long enough for certain key individuals to leave the firm and for others to die off and be replaced by the next generation of up-and-coming hedge fund managers. These are eventual realities of life. As a potential investor in a hedge fund, it is worth considering whether the hedge fund organization and its key principals have given consideration to this via such things as succession planning, key person provisions, equity, and vesting structures to retain key staff over time, and so forth.

TIP 10: GROWTH PLANNING: IS THE MANAGER PROACTIVE OR REACTIVE?

In reviewing the due diligence questionnaires of most hedge funds, or in the course of a due diligence review, investors will invariably inquire about the anticipated capacity of a particular hedge fund's investment strategy. In the early stages of their growth, the typical responses given by funds will be to quote some number that is well above their current assets under management. They may then go on to state that the hedge fund manager has calculated capacity based on some study, or that the manager will continually monitor capacity and investment opportunities over time. Further, responses in relation to capacity inquiries may also include language that indicates that the previous levels quoted will be reevaluated once assets under management approach these levels. This can be interpreted to mean that the hedge fund manager reserves the right to increase capacity levels if investors are willing to allocate more capital in the future.

These responses regarding capacity demonstrate that a hedge fund has put some effort into thinking about and perhaps even planning for the future. However, as part of the operational due diligence process, investors should attempt to gauge whether a hedge fund has devoted any similar effort to planning in anticipation of future demand in noninvestment areas of the firm. *Is the manager reactive to operational challenges or proactive in anticipating them?*

A good example of where operational planning can yield substantial benefits is systems and technology. Depending on the hedge fund strategy under consideration, computing power can be extremely important for the continued growth of a hedge fund. Consider a manager who follows an extremely quantitative investment and research process. Assume that this fund employs a number of very-well-paid PhDs. The time of these individuals is very valuable, and it is to the firm's advantage to allow them to keep working on a continual basis. Further assume that for them effectively to test several research ideas, these PhDs require a great deal of dedicated computing power. Let us say that there is a software problem and several of these computers freeze up at once. We can now compare the responses of a reactive hedge fund and a proactive hedge fund under this simple scenario.

A reactive hedge fund under this scenario is faced with a substantial problem. It has several highly paid PhDs effectively twiddling their thumbs until their computers are repaired or a workaround solution is implemented. A proactive hedge fund, however, may have several spare computers on which these PhDs can continue to run their simulations while the frozen computers are being repaired. Being proactive in this scenario has effectively allowed this second hedge fund's employees to be more productive and made it possible for them to potentially generate additional profits.

Such a scenario can play out in many different areas of a hedge fund's operational landscape. Some of the types of questions investors can ask to determine whether a hedge fund is reactive or proactive include:

- Does the hedge fund develop budgets for future operational expenses? What is the time frame for these budgets (e.g., quarterly or annually)? What is the amount of these budgets?
- Has the firm developed operational milestones or goals?
- When certain milestones are achieved, does the hedge fund anticipate making any organizational changes? (For example, when the firm reaches a certain number of employees, will it hire an employee dedicated to the human resources function?)
- What are the plans to increase operational resources with increased asset growth?
- Who is responsible for generating the strategic direction for the firm's future growth? Are the operational individuals who deal with issues on a daily basis consulted before strategic operational plans are made?
- What assumptions does a hedge fund organization make in regard to its future operational plans? Is the firm overly optimistic or conservative in its assumptions?

Through such inquiries, an investor can attempt to ascertain whether a hedge fund has planned in advance of future demand and anticipated any problems that may arise.

Notes

1. www.urbandictionary.com/define.php?term=phantomware.
2. www.bloomberg.com/apps/news?pid=20601087&sid=aEHnDyK9iIMA&refer =home.

CHAPTER 7

Ongoing Operational Profile Monitoring

Building an initial operational due diligence profile can be viewed as the heavy lifting in the operational due diligence process. This is partially because a hedge fund investor is navigating unfamiliar waters throughout the initial stages of the operational due diligence review. Once this profile has been created and the investor has allocated capital to a hedge fund, she now has an operational roadmap that she can reference on subsequent operational reviews. Unfortunately, many hedge fund investors never make use of this map and simply do not perform ongoing monitoring of non-investment-related factors with any regularity.

There are several reasons why performing ongoing operational due diligence monitoring is a very good idea. First, when performing initial operational due diligence, a potential hedge fund investor eventually comes to the point of making an operational judgment of the firm's operations. By allocating capital to the hedge fund, the investor is essentially drawing an operational line in the sand and stating that this hedge fund is above that line. As organizations change and evolve, it is very likely that the hedge fund will fall below this line, either universally or in certain areas. Without ongoing operational monitoring, an investor is simply hoping that the organization will organically evolve with the pace of the hedge fund's progress.

Second, just as new investment themes emerge within a portfolio, new operational themes develop within organizations. With the breakneck speed at which some successful hedge funds are able to raise assets, a hedge fund organization will likely find itself facing a completely different set of operational challenges than it was facing just a few months earlier. With these challenges come a new set of operational risks that the onus is on the investor to diagnose and monitor.

Third, the process of ongoing operational due diligence monitoring provides hedge fund investors with the opportunity to verify and even learn more detail about the operational data points collected during the initial operational review. This can come about in several ways.

Ongoing operational due diligence also allows a hedge fund investor to monitor what can be referred to as the *seventh theme*—follow-through. The follow-through theme asks: Has a hedge fund followed through on the operational plans and promises it made during the initial operational review? Similar to the five core themes (oversight, controls, connectivity, scalability, and stability) and the sixth theme (consistency), which we have previously discussed, this follow-through theme can be monitored across all the primary, secondary, and blended operational factors. For example, let us say that during an initial operational due diligence review a hedge fund's chief technology officer (CTO) indicates that the firm plans to hire two new software engineers and purchase five new servers. Let us assume that an investor comes back a year later to perform ongoing operational due diligence and again meets with the CTO. There are now a virtually unlimited number of scenarios that the investor can be faced with, including those shown in Exhibit 7.1.

EXHIBIT 7.1   Example of Technology Scenarios Facing the Investor Performing Ongoing Operational Due Diligence

Scenario	Engineers	Servers
A	More than 2 hired	More than four purchased
B	More than 2 hired	Less than four purchased
C	Less than 2 hired	More than four purchased
D	Less than 2 hired	Less than four purchased

Of course, in the real world there are also a number of other related outcome scenarios, such as where the firm has decided to outsource the information technology function and no longer has any in-house software engineers or servers. Alternatively, perhaps the firm purchased one new, large, expensive server that has the capacity of at least four older servers. Similarly, the hedge fund could have hired one senior software engineer who has more knowledge and skill than two junior software engineers.

Considering these scenarios in terms of the follow-through theme, we can now seek to evaluate the fund based on its ability, or inability, to deliver on its previous operational promises. It is important when evaluating a hedge fund's ongoing operational competency on this follow-through scale to remember that the goal is not necessarily to compare the hedge fund's operational promises to the letter of the operational law; rather it is to ensure that the hedge fund has adequately met, or exceeded, its original operational goal of the initial promise. Returning to our example, perhaps the adding of additional software engineers and servers was to facilitate the smooth implementation and continued maintenance of a new third-party accounting system. Regardless of the actions taken to deliver on this promise, in the context of the follow-through theme, we should judge the hedge fund on the *accomplishment* of this goal.

Of course, the methods used to achieve this goal should not be ignored in the overall ongoing operational review of the hedge fund. For example, if the hedge fund decided to work with a third-party consulting firm to implement this new accounting system, rather than hire the software engineers and add the server space, and this ended up costing the firm five times as much, this would seem to be a poor decision and most likely would be negatively reflected in the overall ongoing operational review decision. However, the hedge fund could have had valid reasons for this extra expense and such issues should be vetted.

Another reason to perform ongoing operational due diligence reviews is to provide investors with the opportunity not only to keep tabs on the hedge fund organization itself but to gain insight from those who previously had business relationships with the hedge fund, including former employees, board members, and service providers. Some of this work may be covered during the background investigation process; however, investors should not overlook the importance of taking a proactive approach to monitoring this process. For example, consider a fund that has an employee who departs the firm on bad terms. By reaching out to this employee, as an existing investor, you may be able to gain some extremely valuable insight into any problems that may be already occurring or on the horizon for the hedge fund manager. Many such former employees might be prohibited from talking directly with potential or existing investors; however, if you do not ask, you will not know for sure. Indeed, if a former employee is speaking to you as a hedge fund investor, he is most likely talking to others as well, which may lead to certain unanticipated consequences, such as redemptions.

HOW OFTEN SHOULD ONSITE OPERATIONAL REVIEWS BE CONDUCTED?

How frequently should ongoing monitoring be performed? Those large allocators that perform ongoing operational due diligence typically conduct on-site operational risk reviews approximately every 12 months. The question a hedge fund investor must answer is whether such monitoring is frequent enough. Said differently, How often should I perform an onsite visit to a hedge fund I am invested in so that I will not let a material operational issue slip through the cracks? Before developing an answer to this question, we must first consider what other types of remote monitoring are being performed in the interval between onsite visits.

REMOTE OPERATIONAL DUE DILIGENCE MONITORING

We will define remote operational due diligence monitoring as hedge fund surveillance and intelligence gathering that can be performed outside of the onsite visit. Whereas the basic assumption is that one is performing ongoing remote operational due diligence monitoring on a hedge fund to which he has already allocated, such remote monitoring techniques can also be applied to hedge funds to which an investor is considering making an allocation. The difference is that if the hedge fund under remote monitoring review has already been allocated to, an investor will have already performed initial operational due diligence on the fund and have created an initial operational profile. That said, the extent of risks that can be monitored is generally the same, assuming an equal level of transparency.

We can begin our discussion of remote operational due diligence monitoring in terms of the risks that we can seek to monitor. As alluded to earlier, remote monitoring does not seek to reinvent the operational wheel. The purpose of remote monitoring is not to create an initial operational profile. Indeed, the types of information that can be obtained via remote monitoring often are not complete enough to create such a profile. Rather, the purpose of remote monitoring is to complement an investor's operational knowledge of an existing organization and gain an understanding of any operational developments within an organization. Should any knowledge gained via this remote monitoring cause an investor to believe that the hedge fund organization's operational risk level is in danger of falling or has fallen below the investor's operational threshold, then the investor can take further action, such as direct contact with the fund (i.e., e-mail, conference call), an onsite visit, or even redemption. This process is outlined in Exhibit 7.2.

MEDIA MONITORING

There is a large amount of data generated in the financial media on a daily basis concerning hedge funds. These media include print, online, television,

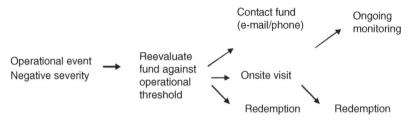

EXHIBIT 7.2 Sample Stages in Remote Monitoring Process

and radio. It is virtually impossible for any one person to sift through it all every day. The purpose of ongoing media monitoring is automate this sifting process to determine whether there is any news, either positive or negative, regarding a hedge fund to which an investor has allocated. This news can relate to wide variety of issues, including a hedge fund's reputation, investments, and future growth plans. In the old days, a company's third-party providers that performed such services were called *clippings services.* The term derived from the act of physically clipping an article of interest out of the newspaper. Today, there are a host of options available to hedge fund investors for efficiently monitoring media of interest.

The most basic of all clipping services is individuals utilizing the Internet to monitor the news themselves. For example, anyone can create a daily news alert for certain keywords via Google. With virtually whatever frequency is desired, one can receive an e-mail containing a listing of all the news articles from news sources that feed into the Google news database. On the upside, this service is completely free and provides individuals with a way to organize and monitor multiple media searches. On the downside, this search does not necessarily cover the types of media that may be relevant to a particular search and does not screen for false positives or relevance. There are a number of more sophisticated and comprehensive tools in the marketplace. Often these services, which charge a fee, offer individuals the ability to query large databases of news media while offering ongoing key word search creation.

Properly utilizing such tools to produce not a mountain of erroneous data but a small subset of useful data that a hedge fund investor may genuinely be interested in is a skill that requires practice and refinement over time. Additionally, as with the traditional clippings services, there are a number of firms in the marketplace today that will monitor news media for any mention of a certain hedge fund. However, as with all outsourced items, investors lose a degree of oversight into this process and often face the problem of having too much irrelevant data delivered as a result of such arrangements.

LITIGATION AND REGULATORY MONITORING

Similar to media monitoring, litigation monitoring refers to the process of scanning the legal system, primarily the courts, for any news that may arise concerning a particular hedge fund. These searches include such things as court docket searches and new case filings. Such monitoring is often more effective in places like the United States, where people tend to sue each other more, as compared with less litigious places such as Japan. Additionally, different jurisdictions have different laws concerning protection of privacy, which may affect what information may be entered into the public record. Furthermore, depending on the nature of the case, certain types of court filings may contain scant, if any, information regarding the actual subject matter of a filing. In certain instances, such filings may not be updated in legal database search engines such as Lexis-Nexis or Westlaw in a timely manner. Subsequently, there may be a delay between the actual filing of a case in court and when it appears in these databases. In such cases, physically visiting a court and searching its records may be the only way effectively to monitor a lawsuit where its progress is of a time-sensitive nature. This is more likely the exception than the rule, and depending on the jurisdiction where the case is being heard and the location of the investor doing such monitoring, considerable expense could be incurred. Investors performing ongoing remote litigation monitoring should be aware that this is an option if such measures are deemed necessary.

Regulatory monitoring focuses on the continuing requirement of certain hedge funds to file reports on an ongoing basis with certain regulators. These requirements may be enforceable regardless of whether a certain hedge fund is registered with the regulatory authority. For example, in the United States, even those funds that are not registered with the Securities and Exchange Commission (SEC) are still required to file Forms 13-D, which require companies to disclose certain details regarding positions that their funds hold in which the funds constitute more than 10% of the outstanding equity of the firm. Such regulatory monitoring can provide hedge fund investors with valuable insights, including confirmation that a certain hedge fund is indeed holding certain positions and whether the fund has competent personnel overseeing the filing process. If there are significant delays or errors in the filings, this may be an early warning sign that someone within the firm, or its legal counsel, is not properly overseeing this process.

HEDGE FUND COMMUNICATION REVIEWS

In addition to monitoring sources external to a hedge fund, such as third-party media and courts, hedge funds themselves generally produce their own documentation, in one form or another, which is distributed to investors on a continual basis. Such documentation can include monthly performance estimates and commentary and reviews of the fund's performance. In addition to useful investment insight and specifics regarding a particular fund's performance, such letters often provide invaluable information as to the operational happenings within a hedge fund, including assets under management, personnel turnover, and the like. Assuming a 12-month revalidation cycle, by monitoring such reviews during the year, investors can keep tabs on what is going on within a fund throughout the year and be better prepared for the following year's onsite revalidation. Additionally, because something might come up in one of these letters that requires immediate action on the part of the investor, it is obviously better to keep up with reading them than to let them pile up and review them once a year before an annual revalidation review.

ASSETS UNDER MANAGEMENT AND PERFORMANCE MONITORING

A few words should be said regarding the remote monitoring of both assets under management (AUM) and performance. A hedge fund's assets under management can serve as a good indicator of a fund's sustainability and growth prospects. AUM levels generally can be monitored from investor letters directly from the funds themselves. Asset figures may also be monitored from third-party databases in the event that a hedge fund reports to such a database.

When reviewing these figures, investors should be conscious of any double counting that may occur between funds. When analyzing assets under management, investors should also be aware of the diversity of the investor base within both a particular fund and the entire firm. Issues can arise when, for example, a firm is overly dependent on a few individual large investors, a certain type of investor, or investors from a particular region. Contagion-type events that may force larger hedge fund allocators, such as funds of hedge funds, to redeem from the underlying hedge funds in which they invest may translate into large redemptions from a hedge fund. If a particular hedge fund had an overly large exposure to funds of hedge funds, it could be overly exposed to the threat of redemptions from this space.

Performance figures may be remotely monitored in much the same manner as AUM levels, via hedge fund newsletters and third-party databases. Many hedge funds also provide midmonth performance estimates as well. Such estimates are often sent informally via e-mail or relayed verbally via the phone. In monitoring the continual performance of their investments in a fund, investors can utilize such information to determine whether a hedge

fund manager is in line both with the fund's peers in whatever space it partic-
ipates, and with the hedge fund's original guidelines. If a certain hedge fund
manager, for example, produces a 58% return for one month, whereas in
the past he has traditionally yielded 15% to 20% returns on an annual basis,
clearly the manager is doing something differently. Is this alone a reason to
redeem? Perhaps not; the hedge fund manager may have had a long-term
theme that recently has come to fruition, or he might have capitalized on
a highly levered bet on a certain opportunity that was within his mandate.
Regardless, such unusual performance would most likely prompt an investor
to reach out to the hedge fund manager to gain further information.

OPERATIONAL EVENTS

Now that we have discussed the basic types of remote operational due
diligence monitoring, we can now discuss what to do with the results of
this monitoring, especially what to do when an operational event occurs.
We will define an *operational event* as an occurrence that causes some
change in the operational profile of an organization. We can broadly classify
the functions required for ongoing operational due diligence as those that
take place during an onsite visit to the hedge fund manager's offices and
those that take place remotely.

Such an event could be related to any single operational factor, such
as the failure of a backup generator, which would be of concern to business continuity planning/disaster recovery (BCP/DR), or cut across multiple
operational factors, such as the departure of the chief compliance officer,
which relates both to personnel turnover and the compliance function.

We can define two different types of operational events: those that
produce a positive change in a hedge fund's operational profile and those
that produce a negative change. It might be argued that an operational event
may occur that could yield *no change* in the operational profile of a hedge
fund. However, since such an event would not yield a fluctuation in a hedge
fund's operational profile, and consequently would not prompt an investor
to take action, such events will not be discussed in detail here.

Operational occurrences that cause a positive change in a hedge fund's
operational profile do not generally prompt much action from existing investors. These could be things such as additional hires, new software system
upgrades, and the tightening of existing compliance policies or internal controls. Certain events, which on the surface may seem positive, such as large
rapid increases in assets, the launching of new funds, or the hiring of a large
amount of personnel, may cause net positive operational gains for an organization; however, the burden that the organization must bear can often result

in increased operational stress throughout the organization. Such growing pains may prompt a hedge fund's investors to increase their monitoring efforts and may even prompt an onsite visit.

EFFECT OF DISCOVERY ON THE MAGNITUDE OF AN OPERATIONAL EVENT

Is the magnitude of an operational event worse if an investor discovers it on his own outside of the fund instead of being informed directly by the fund itself? It is human nature that people like to be told directly from the source. When they are not, especially when the event in question is a negative one, there is a sort of multiplier effect that increases the magnitude of the potential damage done by the negative operational event. Of course, the exact magnitude of such an occurrence cannot be modeled or quantified with any accuracy, but that is not to say that it does not exist. At the end of the day, the operational occurrence might turn out to have minimal impact on the organization, or be of minimal importance to the investor, or both. However, the mere fact that the investor was not told of the occurrence directly by the hedge fund itself might lead to a sense of betrayal and, depending on the circumstances, a deterioration of the trust between the investor and the hedge fund organization as a whole. Where there is doubt and mistrust, despite even positive returns, the relationship may be ruined.

ONSITE VISIT FREQUENCY AND OPERATIONAL EVENTS

As a general rule, most investors feel that the frequency of onsite reviews is positively correlated to the severity of a negative operational event. That is to say, the more severe a negative operational event is the more likely investors are to perform follow-up onsite visits to the hedge fund under review. This relationship is summarized in Exhibit 7.3.

DEVELOPMENTAL OPERATIONAL TRAPS

The vast majority of successful hedge funds that have managed to remain in business over the course of many years have generally done so as a result of some sort of continued evolutionary growth. Whether by increasing levels of assets, or through new strategies and funds, or a combination of the two, such successful hedge fund organizations have changed over time. With

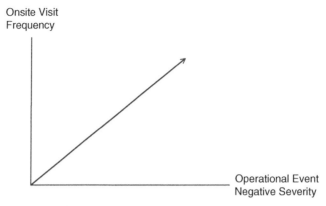

EXHIBIT 7.3 Positive Correlation between Onsite Visit Frequency and Negative Event Severity

growth and change, these evolving organizations have escaped a number of developmental operational traps. Those performing ongoing operational due diligence monitoring sometimes overlook such traps. They focus on the specters of a hedge fund's previous incarnation rather than on how the organization has evolved over time. The following sections will outline some of the key developmental traps faced by hedge funds that investors should be particularly conscious of as they perform their ongoing operational monitoring.

Multijurisdictional and Intrajurisdictional Regulatory Coordination

One issue of increasing importance in recent years has been the focus on the role of one regulator within the traditional jurisdiction of another. An example that highlights this trend came in March 2006, when the United Kingdom's Financial Services Authority signed a Memorandum of Understanding with the U.S. Securities and Exchange Commission (SEC). This memorandum outlines the intention of these organizations to collaborate on a number of issues, including information sharing and onsite regulatory visits. Additionally, this memorandum states that, upon written request, each regulator will provide the "fullest possible cooperation in assisting with the oversight of a Firm, and ensuring compliance with the laws or regulations of the Requesting Authority."[1] Continuing this trend of regulatory coordination, in January 2007, the SEC and the College of Euronext Regulators signed a similar Memorandum of Understanding. The signing of these memoranda by different regulators clearly represents a pattern of increasing international regulatory cooperation and cross-jurisdictional enforcement.

There is also a related trend of intrajurisdictional regulation, that is, collaboration among regulators who operate within the same jurisdiction. A recent example of this came in March 2008, when the SEC and the Commodity Futures Trading Commission announced the signing of a "mutual cooperation agreement to establish a closer working relationship between their agencies."[2] As a result of this new environment, which seems to foster both intrajurisdictional regulation and multijurisdictional regulatory coordination, hedge funds may find it increasingly difficult to isolate the effects of a regulatory violation that occurs in one jurisdiction from the regulator of another.

When analyzing a hedge fund manager, investors should consider the structure a manager has put in place to ensure coordination of the firm's global compliance responsiveness with regulator requests. Specifically, this trend of multijurisdictional coordination presents several unique challenges for hedge fund investors.

Consider an investor who allocates to a hedge fund that has offices only in Stamford, Connecticut and is registered with the SEC. Let us further assume that with time, this hedge fund grows and over the coming year the hedge fund opens a research-and-investment management office in London that is registered with the U.K.'s Financial Services Authority (FSA). When performing ongoing operational due diligence on this hedge fund, an investor must understand how this hedge fund has dealt with the unique implications of being FSA registered. Because of multijurisdictional coordination concerns, this investor must also take care to understand how the hedge fund has coordinated the legal, regulatory, and compliance functions across its offices.

For example, particular challenges may be presented regarding a compliance review of a hedge fund's marketing materials. The FSA may require certain disclosures that the SEC does not. Other concerns relate to such things as electronic communication monitoring, where the SEC and FSA have different standards. Problems can arise when the hedge fund office in each location relies on the advice of compliance consultants and third-party legal counsel in its own jurisdiction (the United States and the United Kingdom in our example), and they are not in communication with each other. Situations arise where each respective office is in full compliance with the local regulator, but it is left up to the firm's internal compliance personnel to oversee the coordination of a global compliance effort. A hedge fund's chief compliance officer (CCO) typically spends the majority of her time in the firm's primary office, in this case, in Stamford, Connecticut. There is generally a bias toward dedicating the majority of the compliance effort to compliance in the home office jurisdiction. Additionally, where the satellite office (in our example, in London) is established after the original CCO is hired, the CCO may not be well versed in the compliance regime in such a far-off jurisdiction and would typically rely on local third-party vendors to assist with the lion's share of regulatory work.

In summary, as a hedge fund grows over time, there may be situations where one regulator penalizes an entire organization for a compliance breach in a far-off jurisdiction. Investors should take care to diagnose not only compliance in each relevant jurisdiction, but how regulatory coordination efforts are being managed across the entire organization.

Silo Creation

Silo creation happens when the way in which information is shared throughout an organization is not optimized. Optimization has to do with the level of transparency, efficiency of communication, and the nature or quality of the information being communicated. In a hedge fund context, evidence of silo creation as an organization grows indicates a decline in communication among the different parts of the firm, which can lead to a number of operational inefficiencies. Silo creation can also serve to multiply the effects of other hedge fund developmental traps, such as the problems associated with different kinds of organizational nesting, which will be discussed in more detail below.

As a hedge fund organization evolves over time, it is not uncommon for it to open satellite offices. These satellite offices are then staffed by existing hedge fund personnel from the home office who are transferred to the satellite office, or local employees who come from the geographical region where the satellite office is located, or a combination of the two. Having employees who work in geographically disparate locations creates a number of challenges that the organization needs to manage. From an operational perspective, there are a number of basic issues, such as how these employees get paid and who is responsible for dealing with the building if something is wrong with the physical office space (e.g., lights go out in the office, sink in the office pantry stops working). Depending on the functions performed in such offices, there are a number of more complex operational issues that need to be addressed as well. For example, if any trades are conducted from this satellite office, how is such information communicated to the home office? Consider the example of a satellite office located in Asia that conducts trades overnight while no one is at the U.S.-based office. If there are any trading issues overnight, or if there are problems with the trading data that is sent over from Asia to the U.S. office, how will such issues be investigated and reconciled if everyone in Asia has already gone home when the errors are noticed in the United States? Developing solutions to such problems may be relatively easy, such as ensuring there is some overlap of employee working hours, or more complex, such as ensuring that all trades carried out in Asia are reconciled in real time to the U.S.-based accounting systems. Developing and implementing successful solutions to such issues boils down to proper operational planning and ongoing communication.

Communication problems do not merely take place among employees in multiple offices. Sometimes people who work in the same office are not effective in optimizing the dissemination of information throughout their organization. For example, if the risk management department daily runs a series of analytics on a portfolio that determine, among other things, net exposures to certain markets and stress testing on the portfolio, it may not share this data with other parts of the firm, such as investor relations, unless there is a problem. Alternatively, the risk management department might simply share a summary report of these analytics with the rest of the firm on a weekly basis. Investor relations might also be daily running its own set of analytics on the portfolio, using a different set of processes and procedures than does the risk management department, for use in its client presentations. In essence, these two different parts of the firm are operating in distinct informational silos.

In performing ongoing operational monitoring on a hedge fund organization, investors should take measures to determine whether there is evidence of silos within a organization. Such silos can create a drag on the efficiency of an organization and in some cases even lead to duplication of efforts. In the event silo creation is detected within a hedge fund, an investor should actively question the existence of such silos and monitor the way in which a hedge fund's senior management attempts to either dissolve the silo or foster its growth.

Organizational Nesting

Continuing the previous example of a hedge fund that has opened multiple offices or launched multiple strategies, we can now address the phenomenon known as organizational nesting. The concepts of silo creation and organization nesting are interrelated. While silo creation focuses on how (or whether) information is shared throughout an organization, organizational nesting relates to the way in which different groups interact with and support each other within an organization. Within a hedge fund, organizational nesting can be applied to two primary scenarios, both of which should cause investors to want to understand the exact way in which different groups interact.

The first scenario focuses on organizational nesting within the hedge fund itself, which we will refer to as *intraorganizational nesting* (ION). ION often develops as a hedge fund grows over time; there are two changes that are likely to occur from an operational perspective. One is the hiring of additional employees. The other is the *formalization of policies and procedures*, and likely their subsequent *codification*, where previously the policies had been simpler and easier to manage and implement with a smaller work staff. With this formalization also typically comes the formalization of departmental roles within an organization. Certain departments interact with and support other departments within the firm, creating an interconnected supportive network. Some departments within the hedge fund organization, such as the compliance function, oversee and support many other departments within the firm, whereas others focus on supporting specific departments or groups. An example of such a specific support arrangement would be the relationship between the back office and the front office.

The second scenario focuses on organizational nesting between the hedge fund and an organization that has a substantial investment in it or acquires it. We will refer to this as *extraorganizational nesting* (EON). The EON phenomenon is the outgrowth of a trend that has emerged in recent years, where financial services firms that have not traditionally participated in the hedge fund arena simply acquire all or part of a successful existing hedge fund organization in order to immediately establish a presence in the space. This has been the approach taken in recent years by a number of investment banks. As a result such an acquisition, the acquired hedge fund can be thought of as being nested under the umbrella of the acquiring organization. This nesting relationship typically provides a certain amount of protection and stability that the original hedge fund organization may not have had on its own. When such an acquisition occurs, the hedge fund's existing investors are typically forced to grapple with the issue of whether such an acquisition, or divestiture of ownership, is a good thing.

Unfortunately, there is not always a clear answer, and the outcome will be dependent on a number of issues. First, an investor should consider whether the acquiring organization will be a hands-on owner. What are its goals in acquiring all of, or a stake in, this hedge fund organization? Is it to leverage the knowledge and expertise of the hedge fund organization to build out an internal hedge fund platform? Perhaps the acquiring organization feels that it can use its institutional capacity to significantly improve on the hedge fund organization and take it to new heights. Some acquirers maintain more of a passive ownership interest and simply seek to capitalize on this new relationship with their newly acquired hedge fund via a white-label arrangement, where the acquiring organization rebrands the hedge fund under its more established institutional name or from a revenue-sharing perspective.

From an operational context, there are generally a number of non-investment-related synergies that seem apparent at face value. Indeed, the acquiring organization typically has vast resources and a number of well-developed systems and internal processes that the hedge fund can leverage. There may, however, be several less apparent non-investment-related challenges that will present themselves over time. Investors should be particularly conscious of the importance of monitoring these often-corrosive developments, which, if not hastily dealt with by senior management within the hedge fund organization itself, as well as by the acquirer, may prove disastrous. One example of such a development relates to employee retention. Typically, when such a total acquisition takes place, senior employees, such as portfolio managers, are provided with a number of financial incentives, such as deferred compensation, to remain with the firm after the acquisition. Such incentives are less common under the scenario where a larger acquiring organization firm acquires only part of a hedge fund organization. Regardless, the acquiring firm, for a number of reasons, may not provide such retention incentives to less-senior employees. For example, the chief financial officer of a hedge fund that is being acquired might have signed a lucrative long-term deferred compensation deal to encourage him to remain with the firm for a period of several years; however, no such offer may be extended to the firm's controller. Consequently, there is a real danger for such individuals either to be poached away by other hedge fund organizations or simply to leave the firm of their own volition as a result of lack of comfort within the newly nested organization. The effect of such a brain drain is that specialized knowledge about the organization will be lost.

Investors should also be conscious of the increased reporting requirements of the hedge fund organization to its internal acquirer counterparties. For example, many large organizations have internal audit departments that sweep through the entire firm. The hedge fund organization may not have had its own internal auditors or ever exposed itself to such a process. While it is likely that a certain amount of due diligence on the firm and its processes was performed by the acquirer before the purchase was made, the ongoing review and implementation of any new recommendations suggested by the internal audit function, particularly with regard to complying with the larger firm-wide policies of the acquiring organization, may put an additional degree of stress on the hedge fund organization. While such recommendations may be made with an eye toward institutionalizing certain practices and improving the overall efficiency with which they are carried out, the hedge fund organization's senior management, who may also be lead portfolio managers and senior operational personnel, may not be receptive to this process. Consequently, this can lead to conflict between the acquirer and the hedge fund, as well as potential distraction of the hedge fund investment managers, which may affect performance for a time.

Another problem investors should be cautious of is the potential for the acquiring organization to institute voluntary turnover of certain employees or departments. An example of such voluntary turnover would be situations in which there is an overlap of functions, often operational, at the hedge fund and the acquiring institution. Within an operational context, such scenarios may include the functions of information technology, legal, compliance, and the back office. For example, when the hedge fund was its own standalone entity, it may have had a need for an individual dedicated to overseeing the reconciliation process. After acquisition, the acquiring organization may have integrated the hedge fund into a centralized internal platform that oversees the reconciliation process overnight for all of the firm's products, including the newly acquired hedge fund. Some hedge fund organizations will negotiate a say in such postacquisition personnel decisions; however, it is unlikely that a hedge fund organization's senior management will stop the acquisition over such minor details.

It could logically be argued that such turnover is not necessarily a bad thing, and that under such a scenario more efficient and cost-effective practices would be employed. If it results in the collateral damage of turnover of certain individuals, so be it. This argument definitely has legs to stand on. However, questions arise when we broaden this turnover argument across multiple operational functions throughout the firm. Indeed, the entire non-investment-related infrastructure previously developed at the hedge fund could already be in place, in a better, more efficient form, at the acquirer's organization. The question then becomes, What is the acquirer actually purchasing, the hedge fund organization or simply its brand name, asset base, and investment personnel? If the answer is the latter, and that is where the acquirer sees the true value of the hedge fund organization, indeed the removal of the previous operational infrastructure, including the personnel, at the underlying hedge fund may be appropriate. Even if this is the case, it is unlikely that such broad changes as laying off all the operational staff will take place in one fell swoop, at the very least so as not to alarm existing investors. Consequently, investors should take a careful look at any such departures to see whether they are emblematic of any trend toward the entire replacement of the operational functions by the acquirer. If so, investors should determine whether they feel the acquirer, which likely has limited hedge fund experience, has the internal operational competency to appropriately support its new hedge fund purchase. If not, investors may begin to consider the hedge fund organization as having an increasing amount of operational risk despite its apparent infrastructural fortitude.

Notes

1. "Memorandum of Understanding Concerning Consultation, Cooperation and the Exchange of Information Related to Market Oversight and the Supervision of Financial Services Firms," March 14, 2006, www.sec.gov/about/offices/oia/ oia_multilateral/ukfsa_mou.pdf.
2. "CFTC, SEC Sign Agreement to Enhance Coordination, Facilitate Review of New Derivative Products," March 11, 2008, www.cftc.gov/newsroom/ generalpressreleases/2008/pr5468-08.html.

CHAPTER 8

Techniques for Modeling Operational Risk

B orrowing from the world of banking, academics and practitioners alike have taken a multitude of approaches to modeling the operational risks of hedge funds. Some of the quantitative approaches have relied on such concepts as *extreme value theory, Kalman filters, chaos theory, Cox processes,* and various *econometric models.* Other approaches have attempted to create infrastructural risk maps against which a hedge fund's organization can be evaluated. The purpose of this chapter is to describe the modeling and graphing approaches most commonly used in the marketplace, and to discuss some of the advantages and caveats of using each model. We will begin with an analysis of *scorecard systems.*

SCORING SYSTEMS

In recent years, a number of scoring methods have been developed for both rating and evaluating the operational risks of hedge funds. The various scorecard approaches have gained popularity in recent years outside of the hedge fund arena for their application to monitoring Sarbanes-Oxley compliance. The following section will discuss how to create a scoring model, providing examples of several different scoring approaches. Once we have discussed how to build such a scorecard system and assign an operational score to a hedge fund, we will then outline the uses of such scores. The entire operational scorecard process is outlined in Exhibit 8.1.

BUILDING A SCORING SYSTEM: CATEGORY DETERMINATION

Each of the scorecard methods generally begins its formation with a predefined series of operational risk categories. These scorecard methodologies

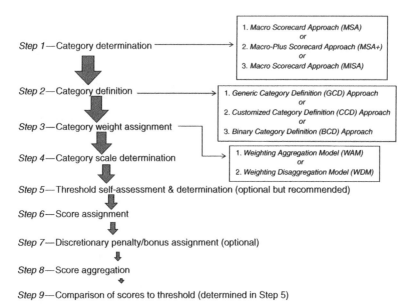

Step 1—Category determination

1. *Macro Scorecard Approach (MSA)*
or
2. *Macro-Plus Scorecard Approach (MSA+)*
or
3. *Macro Scorecard Approach (MISA)*

Step 2—Category definition

1. *Generic Category Definition (GCD) Approach*
or
2. *Customized Category Definition (CCD) Approach*
or
3. *Binary Category Definition (BCD) Approach*

Step 3—Category weight assignment

Step 4—Category scale determination

1. *Weighting Aggregation Model (WAM)*
or
2. *Weighting Disaggregation Model (WDM)*

Step 5—Threshold self-assessment & determination (optional but recommended)

Step 6—Score assignment

Step 7—Discretionary penalty/bonus assignment (optional)

Step 8—Score aggregation

Step 9—Comparison of scores to threshold (determined in Step 5)

EXHIBIT 8.1   Operational Scorecard Process

can be grouped into three general categories:

1. Macro Scorecard Approach (MSA)
2. Macro-Plus Scorecard Approach (MSA+)
3. Micro Scorecard Approach (MISA)

Exhibits 8.2, 8.3, and 8.4 demonstrate examples of each of the scorecard methodologies in their category determination phase. Each of these approaches differs in the number of primary categories utilized, the number

EXHIBIT 8.2   Macro Scorecard Approach (MSA) Methodology Model: Category Determination Phase

Category Number	Primary Category Name
1	Legal/Regulatory/Compliance
2	Trading/Valuation
3	Technology/Business Continuity/Disaster Recovery
4	Assets Under Management/Financial and Organizational Sustainability
5	Quality of Service Providers Utilized
6	Reputation of Employees (including senior mgmt.) and Firm

EXHIBIT 8.3 Macro-Plus Scorecard Approach (MSA+) Methodology Model: Category Determination Phase

Category Number	Primary Category Name	Subcategory Name
1	Legal/Regulatory/Compliance	
1-a		Any previous regulatory violations?
1-b		Nature of compliance control environment
2	Trading/Valuation	
2-a		Trade error frequency and investigation procedures
2-b		Independence of valuation procedures
3	Technology/Business Continuity/Disaster Recovery	
3-a		Frequency of business continuity and disaster recovery testing
3-b		Scalability of technology systems
4	Assets Under Management/Financial and Organizational Sustainability	
4-a		Any recent material subscriptions and redemptions?
4-b		Recent departures of key personnel
5	Quality of Service Providers Utilized	
5-a		Length of relationship with current service providers
5-b		Nature of services provided by service providers
6	Reputation of Employees (including senior mgmt.) and Firm	
6-a		Length and nature of senior principals' capital markets experience
6-b		Any material items uncovered during a background investigation?

EXHIBIT 8.4 Micro Scorecard Approach (MISA) Methodology Model: Category Determination Phase

Category Number	Primary Category Name
1	Assets under management trends (comparison from peak levels)
2	Diversity of investor base
3	Does any single investor constitute larger than 10% of firm-wide assets under management?
4	Business continuity and disaster recovery plan thoroughness
5	Business continuity and disaster recovery plan testing frequency
6	Business continuity and disaster recovery plan scalability
7	Use of offsite data backups
8	Use of tape backups
9	Are tape backups taken offsite?
10	Appropriateness of information security policy
11	Quality of software systems utilized
12	Nature of any employees outside business interests
13	Does the firm have backup power generation facilities?
14	Any previous regulatory violations?
15	Any recent material subscriptions and redemptions?
16	Any material items uncovered during a background investigation?
17	Independence of valuation process
18	Appropriateness of insurance coverage in place and policy limits
19	Have any of the funds ever had to restate the net asset value?
20	Is there any pending litigation against the firm or its principals?

of secondary or subcategories utilized, and the level of detail at which each category attempts to have the scorecard model operator evaluate. Beginning with MSA, this model attempts to evaluate the operational risks of a hedge fund utilizing a top-down approach. Consequently, this method has a small number of high-level operational categories that cover broad operational areas such as compliance and technology.

Let us turn to the MSA+ model. This approach contains all the elements of the MSA model, but adds an additional level of detail via a select number of subcategories. These subcategories fall under the primary categories and seek to add more specificity to the broad areas covered by the primary categories with which they coincide. For example, in Exhibit 8.3, nested under the primary Trading/Valuation category, the subcategories mandate that the scorecard model operator provide an evaluation as to the trade error frequency and investigation procedures as well as the independence of the valuation process.

The conclusion should not be hastily drawn that such factors would not be built into the single primary category score assigned in the MSA model. However, specifically assigning subcategories for these items ensures that they will be addressed directly, rather than being more generally lumped into a single score consideration of the Trading/Valuation functions within a particular hedge fund, and summarized by one score with no underlying subcategory detail. In Exhibit 8.3, each of the subcategories is assigned an equal number of operational data points to be scored. In this example, the number happens to be two. For example, under the Legal/Regulatory/ Compliance primary category, there are two subcategories. Similarly, under Trading/Valuation, there are two subcategories. For purposes of this example, we have constructed the subcategories to contain equal numbers of subcategory items. However, this is by no means an absolute rule. In practice, when designing an MSA+ scorecard model, different numbers of subcategory items certainly can be applied to each primary category, contingent of course on the level of detail sought within each primary category.

The level of detail sought is partly reflective of the model designer's views as to the importance or weight that is to be assigned to each primary category and subcategory. Indeed, there will likely be a positive correlation between the number of subcategory items created under an MSA+ model and the weight assigned to a particular category. The category weighting process will be discussed in more detail in the Category Weight Assignment section. Returning to our discussion regarding equality or lack thereof in subcategories, an MSA+ model could just as easily have been designed with unequal numbers of subcategories, as demonstrated in Exhibit 8.5. The impetus behind creating equal numbers of subcategories is that it may provide the model operator with some sense of coherence throughout the model when comparing the results of different categories' scores. However, forcing a model to adhere to these notions of consistency may lead to the irrational pursuit of detail in certain categories where the model designer may not feel it is appropriate, and should not by any means be viewed as a requirement of MSA+ model design.

Turning to the MISA methodology, this approach seeks to quantify the operational risks of hedge funds with a very minute level of detail by addressing very specific issues through a high number of primary categories. As illustrated in Exhibit 8.4, the issues addressed by the primary categories under the MISA methodology seek to require the scorecard model operator to assign a *quantitative* value to a host of detailed operational factors. In contrast with the MSA model, rather than simply asking the model operator to assign a score to the broad category Technology/Business Continuity/Disaster Recovery, MISA breaks this operational risk area into eight different questions, in category numbers 4 through 13 in Exhibit 8.4.

EXHIBIT 8.5 MSA+: Category Determination Phase with Unequal Numbers of Subcategories

Category Number	Primary Category Name	Subcategory Name
1	Legal/Regulatory/Compliance	
1-a		Any previous regulatory violations?
1-b		Nature of compliance control environment
1-c		Documented compliance policies
2	Trading/Valuation	
2-a		Trade error frequency and investigation procedures
2-b		Independence of valuation procedures
3	Technology/Business Continuity/Disaster Recovery	
3-a		Frequency of business continuity and disaster recovery testing
3-b		Scalability of technology systems
3-c		Dedicated backup power generation facilities
3-d		Offsite tape backup systems utilized
3-e		Quality and nature of any real-time backup capabilities
4	Assets Under Management/Financial and Organizational Sustainability	
4-a		Any recent material subscriptions and redemptions?
4-b		Recent departures of key personnel
5	Quality of Service Providers Utilized	
5-a		Length of relationship with current service providers
5-b		Nature of services provided by service providers
5-c		Significant level of turnover experienced at underlying service providers
6	Reputation of Employees (including senior mgmt.) and Firm	
6-a		Length and nature of senior principals' capital markets experience
6-b		Any material items uncovered during a background investigation?

CATEGORY DEFINITIONS

Once a determination has been made as to which category methodology to utilize, the next step in creating a scoring model is to establish *qualitative definitions* for the different gradations within each category. Not every score-card model creation methodology provides for definitions, and some skip straight to the next step, score assignment. Within the types of models that do omit this step, there is generally less clarity regarding the definition of each of the various different gradations between the numerous levels within a particular scoring scale.

Within models that do provide for category definitions, there are several approaches, each of which allow for different levels of specificity within each definition. The three most common operational risk category definition approaches are:

1. Generic Category Definition (GCD) Approach
2. Customized Category Definition (CCD) Approach
3. Binary Category Definition (BCD) Approach

Exhibits 8.6, 8.7, and 8.8 respectively demonstrate examples of these category definition approaches. Under the GCD approach, generic or non-specific definitions are applied to each category, regardless of the operational subject matter of the category being evaluated. As illustrated in Exhibit 8.6, this approach seeks to equate the quantitative values used to score a particular operational category to a generic qualitative value, such as "extremely robust" for a score of 4 or "robust" for a score of 3. The GCD approach will typically be implemented when a hedge fund investor is interested in assessing the operational competencies of a hedge fund by utilizing the same broad evaluation criteria for each category. The GCD approach is simple to use, and does not necessarily require a great deal of specific operational hedge fund knowledge to be effective. A drawback of this approach is that it lacks the specificity to define unique evaluation criteria for each category.

The CCD approach attempts to compensate for the generalist nature of the GCD approach by providing for specific definitions for each different quantitative score in the ratings scale in each particular category. Exhibit 8.7 demonstrates an example of the CCD approach for the

EXHIBIT 8.6   Generic Category Definition (GCD) Approach

Category Scale	4	3	2	1
Category Definition	Extremely Robust	Robust	Sufficient	Poor

EXHIBIT 8.7 Customized Category Definition (CCD) Approach for the Legal/Regulatory/Compliance Category

Category Scale	4	3	2	1
Category Definition	Dedicated and experienced legal and compliance staff	Dedicated and experienced legal and compliance staff	Legal and compliance staff shared among other parts of the firm	No internal legal and compliance staff
	Use of third-party compliance consultants	Well-documented compliance policies and procedures	Well-documented compliance policies and procedures	No third-party compliance consultants
	Well-documented compliance policies and procedures	Long relationship with high-quality third-party legal counsel	Use of high-quality third-party legal counsel	History of material regulatory sanctions or violations
	Long relationship with high-quality third-party legal counsel	Thorough electronic communication monitoring	History of minor regulatory sanctions or violations	No internal compliance oversight
	Mock audits performed at least once a year	No history of regulatory sanctions or violations	Some level of compliance oversight into general firm issues	
	Quarterly compliance training	Appropriate level of compliance oversight into issues such as personal account dealing and employee gift receipt reporting		
	Thorough electronic communication monitoring			
	No history of regulatory sanctions or violations			
	Appropriate level of compliance oversight into issues such as personal account dealing and employee gift receipt reporting			

EXHIBIT 8.8   Binary Category Definition (BCD) Approach

Category Scale	Pass	Fail
Category Definition	Acceptable level of operational risk established for the category under consideration	Unacceptable level of operational risk established for the category under consideration

Legal/Regulatory/Compliance category, where a specific definition, in this case a different set of criteria, is assigned for each level in the quantitative category ratings scale. So, for example, a score of 3 represents eight different operational criteria, including well-documented compliance policies and procedures and no history of regulatory sanctions or violations, that the hedge fund under consideration must meet in order to receive that score. To receive a score of 2, the hedge fund manager must meet five specific operational criteria.

There are two important points worth noting regarding the CCD model. First, while not a requirement, as one progresses up the operational scale (discussed in the Category Scale Determination and the Meaning of Scores section), in each category the subsequent quantitative scale definitions generally build upon each other while also adding new criteria. To demonstrate, returning to Exhibit 8.7, one of the criteria for a score of 3 is dedicated and experienced legal and compliance staff, which is also one of the criteria required for a score of 4. Constructing the category definitions in this way provides for an iterative construction approach to the score assignment process, and is generally easier for the scorecard model operator to evaluate rather than having disparate criteria for each notch on the category scale. Of course, under such an iterative approach, not every category definition criterion transfers between categories as some are lost while new ones are added.

When following this iterative approach to category definitions, it is worth digressing for a moment to consider which definitions should necessarily transfer or flow among differing categories and which should be relegated to the lower levels of the category scale. Note that we are assuming that we are moving from the lower end of the scale to the higher end of the scale. Indeed, this bottom-up, constructive approach is considered by the majority of operational scorecard model creators as inherently the most intuitive way to approach the construction of iterative category definitions, via an *escalating* constructive methodology, as opposed to starting at the top of the scale and deconstructing or removing criteria as we go. Regardless, both iterative approaches, construction and deconstruction, are equally effective. The category definition process typically begins with the determination of the bookends, or the top and bottom, of both the particular categorical scale as well as the definition parameters. Consequently, constructing the iterative category definitions whether transitioning up the scale or down the scale still accomplishes the same result, the iterative category definitions, and is simply a matter of preference of the model creator.

As the categories aggregate under an iterative construction approach, on top of the addition and subtraction of categories, an existing category can also vary by degree. In Exhibit 8.7, for example, one of the required criteria for score of 2 is "Some level of compliance oversight into general firm issues," while a score of 3 requires an "Appropriate level of compliance oversight into issues such as personal account dealing and employee gift receipt reporting." These two criteria essentially address the same central issue, the level of compliance oversight within an organization; the difference lies in the degree to which such oversight exists within an organization. A higher degree of oversight merits a higher score within the category, and is rewarded by the model.

The second point worth noting regarding the CCD approach is that certain hedge funds may not fit into the specific predetermined category definitions for each quantitative scale within the category. Continuing with the Legal/Regulatory/Compliance category outlined in Exhibit 8.7, how would we evaluate a hedge fund that performs a mock audit once every two years as opposed to the once-every-year criterion established for a score of 4? Clearly, the fund should not be given credit for meeting this criterion with the score of 4, because the frequency of mock compliance audits is less than that mandated, but does that mean the model, according to the category definitions, should not give the hedge fund manager any credit at all? The argument could certainly be made that performing such audits at least once every two years merits a higher operational rating, and subsequently a lower level of operational risk, according to the scale specified in this example, than would be the case for a hedge fund that does not perform audits at all. Based on the category definitions under the CCD approach, however, as outlined in our example, there is no place on the scorecard to reward the manager for this. An investor could redefine the criteria when such a unique scenario comes up, but this can present a host of associated problems. We will discuss the issues that arise as a result of the category redefining process in more detail in the Category Weight Consistency and Reweighting Considerations section. Stated briefly now, examples of the types of issues that can arise include inconsistencies in the scores assigned to the managers under review, and skewed results when comparing managers with redefined categories against other hedge funds scored under the previous CCD approach, which did not contain these additional category definition criteria.

Finally, the BCD approach seeks to evaluate the operational competency of a hedge fund in a particular category in terms of being above or below a certain minimum level, or operational threshold, a related concept we will discuss in more detail in the Threshold Self-Assessment and Determination section. We refer to the BCD approach as being binary in nature because it produces a binary rating. As outlined in Exhibit 8.8, this rating can be qualitative in nature, such as a score of "Pass" or "Fail." Examples of other binary qualitative category scales, depending on the construct of the primary category or subcategory, under the BCD approach include "Yes" or "No," "Success" or "Failure," and "Within Acceptable Guidelines" or "Outside Acceptable Guidelines." The rating scale could also be quantitative in nature, assigning values such as 1 for being above a certain minimum operational level within a particular category and 0 for being below the operational minimum.

The BCD approach is similar to the GCD approach in that both attempt to assign broad or generic definitions to every operational category regardless of the specifics of the category being addressed. Another common characteristic of both approaches is the attractive simplicity of its application; however, as with the GCD approach, a drawback to the BCD approach is lack of precision in category definitions. The primary distinction between the two approaches is that whereas the GCD approach provides for increased flexibility in defining the category scale, the BCD approach limits the range of the category scale to two options, one that meets certain criteria and one that does not.

COMBINATIONS OF CATEGORY DEFINITION APPROACHES

We have just outlined each of the three category definition approaches in isolation. It is important to note that in practice, depending on both the scorecard methodology employed (MSA, MSA+, or MISA) and the construction of the primary categories and subcategories, a combination of category definition methodologies (GCD, CCD, or BCD) can be utilized. Such a combination of multiple category definition methodologies under an MSA+ approach is demonstrated in Exhibit 8.9.

For the purposes of this example, we have four distinct scale *strata*, or *gradations*, for both the CCD approach and the GCD approach. In this case, the examples were constructed in this manner to provide for ease of comparison among the models. There is no strict requirement to have equality with regard to the number of category gradations. In practice, in a scorecard methodology under which the CCD and GCD category definition approaches are combined, the number of category variations could just as easily have been constructed with different numbers of category scale gradations, as illustrated in Exhibit 8.10. The advantage of having the same number of category scale gradations between the two methods is that it provides for some semblance of commonality between the scales of the two methods, notwithstanding the difference in specific category definitions for the primary category and subcategory factors being addressed by each approach.

EXHIBIT 8.9 Combination of Multiple Category Definition Methodologies under MSA+

A. Macro-Plus Scorecard Approach ("MSA+") Methodology Model—Sample Category

Category Number	Primary Category Name	Subcategory Name
1	Legal/Regulatory/Compliance	
1-a		Any previous regulatory violations?
1-b		Nature of compliance control environment

B. Customized Category Definition ("CCD") Approach for Primary Category Scale Definition

Category Number	Primary Category Name	Category Scale	4	3	2	1
1	Legal/Regulatory/Compliance	CCD Approach—Category Definition	Dedicated and experienced legal and compliance staff Use of third-party compliance consultants Well-documented compliance policies and procedures Long relationship with high-quality third-party legal counsel Mock audits performed at least once a year Quarterly compliance training Thorough electronic communication monitoring No history of regulatory sanctions or violations Appropriate level of compliance oversight into issues such as personal account dealing and employee gift receipt reporting	Dedicated and experienced legal and compliance staff Well-documented compliance policies and procedures Long relationship with high-quality third-party legal counsel Thorough electronic communication monitoring No history of regulatory sanctions or violations Appropriate level of compliance oversight into issues such as personal account dealing and employee gift receipt reporting	Legal and compliance staff shared among other parts of the firm Well-documented compliance policies and procedures Use of high-quality third-party legal counsel History of minor regulatory sanctions or violations Some level of compliance oversight into general firm issues	No internal legal and compliance staff No third-party compliance consultants History of material regulatory sanctions or violations No internal compliance oversight

C. Binary Category Definition ("BCD") Approach for Subcategory Scale Definition

Category Number	Subcategory Name		
1-a	Any previous regulatory violations?		
	Category Scale BCD Approach— Category Definition	**Yes** Pre-existing history of violations noted with regulatory authorities with which the hedge fund organization or	**No** No pre-existing history of violations noted with regulatory authorities with which the hedge fund organization or its principals were previously registered with

D. Generic Category Definition ("GCD") Approach for Subcategory Scale Definition

Category Number	Subcategory Name			
1-b	Nature of compliance control environment			
	Category Scale GCD Approach— Category Definition	**Very Robust** Highest level of category competency	**Robust** High level of category competency with room for improvement	**Adequate** Sufficient level of category competency above a minimum threshold of operational risk for the category in question
				Poor Unacceptable level of category competency below a minimum threshold of operational risk

EXHIBIT 8.10 Comparison of CCD and GCD with Different Category Scale Gradations

I. Customized Category Definition (CCD) Approach for Primary Category Scale Definition

Category Number **Primary Category Number**
1   Legal/Regulatory/Compliance

Category Scale	4	3	2	1

II. Generic Category Definition (GCD) Approach for Subcategory Scale Definition

Category Number **Subcategory Number**
1-b   Nature of compliance control environment

Category Scale	Robust	Adequate	Poor

Within models that do provide for category definitions, this process typically begins with the determination of qualitative definitions for the top and bottom bookends of the rating scale, after which variations in between these extremes are generally filled in. Consider the compliance category within an MSA model. The determination of the top of the scale may be something along the lines of, "Thoroughly documented compliance policies and procedures, and staff sufficient to support a high level of compliance oversight and control within the firm." The definition for the score at the bottom of the scale may read, "Poor level of internal controls, not documented; lack of dedicated compliance staff; questions concerning the compliance controls and oversight in place." Possible definitions for a score that lies between the top and bottom of the scale could be, "Partially documented compliance policies overseen by shared compliance personnel who also have other duties within the firm; sufficient compliance oversight in place." Once the bookends have been qualitatively defined, the remaining variations in between the extremes can then be determined, using either a constructive or a deconstructive process.

CATEGORY WEIGHT ASSIGNMENT

Once the category selection method has been made and the individual primary categories and subcategories have been determined, the next step is to assign weights to each of the categories. The purpose of this exercise is to consider the question of whether certain categories should be given more or less importance. For example, investors may consider valuation to be more important than compliance. Consequently, they would assign more weight to this particular category. However, investors may have no particular opinion as to whether any one individual category should be given more or less weight than any other category. In this case, all categories would receive equal weighting. Exhibits 8.11, 8.12, and 8.13 respectively demonstrate

EXHIBIT 8.11   Sample Category Weights under the MSA Category Determination Model

Category Number	Primary Category Name	Weight
1	Legal/Regulatory/Compliance	10%
2	Trading/Valuation	20%
3	Technology/Business Continuity/Disaster Recovery	15%
4	Assets Under Management/Financial and Organizational Sustainability	20%
5	Quality of Service Providers Utilized	20%
6	Reputation of Employees (including senior mgmt.) and Firm	15%
	Total	100%

EXHIBIT 8.12 Sample Category Weights under the MSA+ Category Determination Model

Category Number	Primary Category Name	Subcategory Name	Subcategory Weight	Primary Category Weight*
1	Legal/Regulatory/Compliance			10%
1-a		Any previous regulatory violations?	7%	
1-b		Nature of compliance control environment	3%	
2	Trading/Valuation			20%
2-a		Trade error frequency and investigation procedures	10%	
2-b		Independence of valuation procedures	10%	
3	Technology/Business Continuity/Disaster Recovery			15%
3-a		Frequency of business continuity and disaster recovery testing	5%	
3-b		Scalability of technology systems	10%	
4	Assets Under Management/Financial and Organizational Sustainability			20%
4-a		Any recent material subscriptions and redemptions?	5%	
4-b		Recent departures of key personnel	15%	
5	Quality of Service Providers Utilized			20%
5-a		Length of relationship with current service providers	12%	
5-b		Nature of services provided by service providers	8%	
6	Reputation of Employees (including senior mgmt.) and Firm			15%
6-a		Length and nature of senior principals' capital markets experience	8%	
6-b		Any material items uncovered during a background investigation?	7%	
			Total	100%

*Sum of Subcategory Weights.

EXHIBIT 8.13   Sample Category Weights under the MISA Category
Determination Model (Equal Weighting Example)

Category Number	Primary Category Name	Weights
1	Assets under management trends (comparison from peak levels)	5%
2	Diversity of investor base	5%
3	Does any single investor constitute larger than 10% of firm-wide assets under management?	5%
4	Business continuity and disaster recovery plan thoroughness	5%
5	Business continuity and disaster recovery plan testing frequency	5%
6	Business continuity and disaster recovery plan scalability	5%
7	Use of offsite data backups	5%
8	Use of tape backups	5%
9	Are tape backups taken offsite?	5%
10	Nature of any employees outside business interests	5%
11	Does the firm have backup power generation facilities?	5%
12	Appropriateness of information security policy	5%
13	Quality of software systems utilized	5%
14	Any previous regulatory violations?	5%
15	Any recent material subscriptions and redemptions?	5%
16	Any material items uncovered during a background investigation?	5%
17	Independence of valuation process	5%
18	Appropriateness of insurance coverage in place and policy limits	5%
19	Have any of the funds ever had to restate the net asset value?	5%
20	Is there any pending litigation against the firm or its principals?	5%
	Total	100%

examples of the assignment of different sample weights to the different
primary categories and subcategories under the MSA, MSA+, and MISA
category determination models.

WEIGHTING AGGREGATION MODEL

The example in Exhibit 8.14 provides that the overall primary category
weightings are the sum of the individual underlying subcategory weights

EXHIBIT 8.14 Weighting Aggregation Model (WAM)

Category Number	Primary Category Name	Subcategory Name	Total Weight Assigned to Category (i.e., sum of Primary Category and Subcategory Weights)	Subcategory Weights	(Primary Category Weights)— (Subcategory Sub-Total)
1	Legal/Regulatory/Compliance		10%		4% = 10% − 6%
1-a		Any previous regulatory violations?		4%	
1-b		Nature of compliance control environment		2%	
			Subcategory Subtotal	6%	
2	Trading/Valuation		20%		10% = 20% − 10%
2-a		Trade error frequency and investigation procedures		6%	
2-b		Independence of valuation procedures		4%	
			Subcategory Subtotal	10%	
3	Technology/Business Continuity/Disaster Recovery		15%		8% = 15% − 7%
3-a		Frequency of business continuity and disaster recovery testing		3%	
3-b		Scalability of technology systems		4%	
			Subcategory Subtotal	7%	
4	Assets Under Management/Financial and Organizational Sustainability		20%		14% = 20% − 6%
4-a		Any recent material subscriptions and redemptions?		2%	
4-b		Recent departures of key personnel		4%	
			Subcategory Subtotal	6%	
5	Quality of Service Providers Utilized		20%		9% = 20% − 11%
5-a		Length of relationship with current service providers		9%	
5-b		Nature of services provided by service providers		2%	
			Subcategory Subtotal	11%	
6	Reputation of Employees (including senior mgmt.) and Firm		15%		5% = 15% − 10%
6-a		Length and nature of senior principals' capital markets experience		6%	
6-b		Any material items uncovered during a background investigation?		4%	
			Subcategory Subtotal	10%	
			*Totals	50%	50%

*Note: Equals 100%.

for each particular primary category. We refer to this as the Weighting Aggregation Model (WAM). For example, looking at the primary category of Technology/Business Continuity/Disaster Recovery, the aggregate weight of this category in the overall primary category weighting is 15%. This 15% is divided between two underlying subcategories, Frequency of business continuity and disaster recovery testing and Scalability of technology systems, with weights of 3 and 4%, respectively, and the remaining 8% is allocated to the primary category.

WEIGHTING DISAGGREGATION MODEL

A different approach toward weighting is demonstrated in Exhibit 8.15. Here, the primary category is assigned a weighting separate from the subcategories. We will refer to this as the Weighting Disaggregation Model (WDM). The weight assigned to the primary category does not represent the sum total of the underlying subcategory weights, but rather something else entirely. The percentage assigned to the primary category weighting under this model reflects the operational remainder of the specific items under the primary category umbrella not covered by the subcategories. For example, let us review the Technology/Business Continuity/Disaster Recovery primary category. In our example, this primary category has two subcategories. The total weight assigned to both the primary category and the subcategories

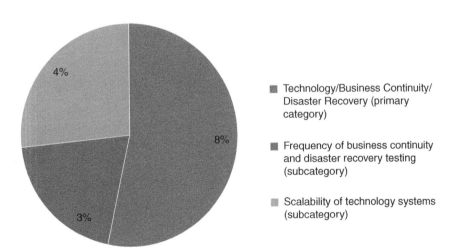

EXHIBIT 8.15 Weighting Disaggregation Model (WDM) Allocation of Primary and Subcategory Weights

equals 15%. So far, this is the same as the example we had previously examined in Exhibit 8.14. The difference under WDM, as compared to WAM, is the way in which this 15% is allocated. Rather than allocating weights to the two subcategories, Frequency of business continuity and disaster recovery testing and Scalability of technology systems, with weights of 5% and 10% respectively, we have instead, in Exhibit 8.15, allocated to these subcategories weights of 3% and 4%, respectively. This now accounts for 7% of the total 15% we have decided to allocate to the Technology/Business Continuity/Disaster Recovery primary category. The approach outlined in Exhibit 8.15 allocates the remaining 8% to the primary category. This relationship is summarized in Exhibit 8.16. A comparison of the WAM and WDM weighting approaches for the Technology/Business Continuity/Disaster Recovery primary category is summarized in Exhibit 8.16.

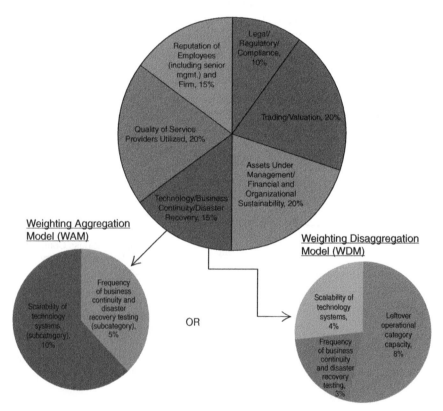

EXHIBIT 8.16   Comparison of the WAM and WDM Weighting for the "Technology/Business Continuity/Disaster Recovery" Primary Category

There are two questions we must now address in comparing the weighting approaches in Exhibits 8.14 and 8.15:

1. What exactly does this 8% represent?
2. What is the difference if we allocate the percentages in different amounts, if the net percentage represented by the primary category and related underlying subcategories still amounts to 15% in aggregate?

Let us address these questions in order. First, the outstanding 8% under WDM represents the leftover operational competencies that are yet to be evaluated and have not been addressed by the subcategories. Leftover competencies should not be thought of as a free bonus in the weighting scheme or weighting capacity that is given to boost the hedge fund manager's score. On the contrary, this 8% merely represents the amount of importance given by the scorecard model to the items not covered by the subcategories. The hedge fund manager must earn a certain score, based on the category definitions, in order to capitalize on the full potential of this weighting category. In our example, within the Technology/Business Continuity/Disaster Recovery primary category, leftover operational competency factors that could be lumped into this 8% figure include considerations such as the presence of dedicated information technology personnel on staff at the hedge fund, whether the hedge fund works with any third-party firms to conduct an audit of the technology platforms in place to determine their appropriateness for meeting the firm's needs, and the amount of excess storage space maintained on the firm's network.

One attractive feature of WDM is that it gives the scorecard model operator flexibility in the decision-making process in terms of exactly what factors this 8% represents. When comparing different types of hedge funds across different categories, such flexibility may be sought after. One disadvantage of WDM is that the definition of this 8% essentially lies in the mind of the model scorer. Most scorers following WDM do not take the time to spell out the specific criteria that earn a hedge fund manager a certain category score within this 8% category. This relates to a second primary drawback of WDM. The use of this nebulous catchall 8% category does not necessarily facilitate easy comparison among multiple operational categories for a single hedge fund or similar categories across multiple hedge funds.

In regard to the second question listed earlier, it is surely logically valid to question what point there is to any of this specific percentage allocation, when the net weighting results for a particular primary category and related underlying subcategories still amount to the same aggregate weight, in this case 15%. A similar, related question would be, in the grand scheme of the entire scorecard model, in any subsequent aggregate single score that may be the result of each of the individual scores, does it really matter whether we allocate 10% or 4% to the category weighting for the scalability of technology?

From a qualitative perspective, it is plausible that by allocating these different weights, the model creator is expressing different views as to the operational risks, or importance, represented by the scalability of technology of a particular hedge fund under the different allocation percentages. From a quantitative perspective, consider a hedge fund that does not build or buy new technology in anticipation of new demand but rather only when the demand already exists. A 10%, or overweight, rating to this category, versus 4%, or underweighting, in this example, would penalize such a manager. However, a hedge fund that makes a large investment in technology and infrastructure well in advance of any potential demand would be rewarded by a 10% weighting in this category versus a lower 4% rating. Is the 10% weighting in this category versus a 4% weighting necessarily the more correct weighting scheme? There is no one clear answer to such a question, and the quality of the scorecard model result would clearly vary based on a number of factors, including how the other 5%, using our 15% for the total category in our example, is allocated. In summary, the way in which the 15% weighting is allocated can make a significant difference both from a qualitative and quantitative perspective in terms of the result produced by the scorecard model in use.

WAM VERSUS WDM

How does a hedge fund investor decide whether to select WAM or WDM? The answer has to do with a host of issues, including the preferences of the model creator and the degree to which the model creator desires specifically to define certain issues within a subcategory context. Similar to the CCD approach toward category definition, WAM places very specific constraints on the way in which weights can be allocated for a particular category.

In comparison, WDM provides for greater flexibility in allocating any remaining weighting percentage not allocated to the subcategories to the primary category. WDM's increased flexibility does come at the sacrifice of the increased standardization of WAM, which may provide for ease of comparison among different categories and different hedge funds across similar categories. In summary, both approaches should be considered when addressing the issues of weighting in scorecard design, and the appropriate approach should be selected based on a particular hedge fund investor's operational risk management goals and constraints.

CATEGORY WEIGHT CONSISTENCY AND REWEIGHTING CONSIDERATIONS

Questions arise as to whether the weights should be consistent across all hedge funds, by either strategy, region, or other considerations. For example, for a manager who trades in high volumes exclusively in highly liquid instruments, such as managed futures, an investor may not consider the issue of valuation to be as important as issues of business continuity and information technology (IT). The reason for this may be that without a large, continued investment in IT and business continuity, issues of slow technology connectivity with certain exchanges may lead to lost profits, or even actual slippage losses for the fund. Consequently, for such a strategy it would then be appropriate for an investor to adjust the weights accordingly.

Such reweighting for hedge fund managers can lead to potentially misleading results when we are trying to compare managers across different strategies as we are no longer comparing consistent weightings. To avoid an apples-to-oranges comparison, it is advisable to leave the weighting the same for each hedge fund manager being scored. However, this presents the problem that the score may not accurately reflect the true concerns or importance a manager may place on each category. One solution to this problem is the use of discretionary scores outside of predefined discretionary categories. This allows investors to re-jig models (i.e., penalize or reward a manager where the predefined scorecard methodology would not have); however, this type of adjustment is highly subjective and also can lead to skewed results.

Another question worth considering is how certain weighting schemes may change over time depending on the evolution of certain market risks. For example, before the events of September 11, 2001, exogenous risks from such events as terrorism were not necessarily at the forefront of operational due diligence reviews. Now, as we have discussed, contingency planning for business continuity and disaster recovery is a crucial part of every operational due diligence review. If a hedge fund allocator had been using a model that either did not consider business continuity and disaster recovery at all or had assigned it a very low weighting, after September 11, 2001, the weighting of this category would have had to be reevaluated and most likely increased to reflect the new risks in the marketplace.

Of course, categories such as valuation will hold a permanent place in the scorecard category matrix, but over time we may witness the creation of new categories and the possible merger of existing categories, such as systems and technology, or the possible deletion of categories, such as regulatory oversight for certain jurisdictions. The way in which models should account for such changes is a point worth considering. It is important for those utilizing hedge fund scorecard approaches to model operational risk to understand that if a change is made to the scoring methodology, scoring categories, or weightings, each existing manager in the portfolio must be rescored to facilitate comparison among scores.

FACTOR MARGINALIZATION

Often, for one reason or another, certain factors, either during the course of an operational review or because of overly rigid design of the particular operational due diligence framework being utilized, are given more importance than others. The particular import each individual investor assigns to certain categories is reflective, in a scorecard model, of the weight assigned to each category in calculating the final operational score. As compared to equal weighting for each category, there is nothing necessarily wrong with giving certain categories more or less importance or weight.

These weights, being representative of an investor's particular views toward the importance of the operational categories, can be typically correlated to the amount of time and resources an investor will allocate to reviewing that particular area of a hedge fund's operations. Additionally, in order not to produce an overly voluminous operational due diligence report that is too steeped in minutiae to be useful, emphasis is typically added to historically large areas of non-investment-related exposure or to exposures as they are discovered in the course of the due diligence process.

One potential pitfall that is the downfall of many an investor and operational due diligence professional alike is that inevitably these seemingly "less important" operational risk factors run the risk of becoming marginalized in the final analysis of the firm's noninvestment competencies. This is not to say that they are often not covered as part of the operational due diligence process; rather it is simply that the due diligence magnifying glass is applied with greater scrutiny to the areas traditionally viewed as having more risk. A typical example of this is the juxtaposition between valuation and IT.

As it should be, valuation is typically at the forefront of most investors' scale of factors that should be given more operational weight. For example, if a hedge fund has questionable valuation procedures, albeit excellent IT infrastructure, most investors would typically shy away from investment. However, a hedge fund with stellar valuation policies coupled with a poor IT infrastructure will pass muster more often than not.

Another reason not to overly discount one category over another is that, when viewed in the entire scope of a firm's operational landscape, IT and valuation are often closely integrated. If the IT function is not adequate, it can lead to miscommunication between systems, such as between a hedge fund's internal accounting system and its administrator, or perhaps the loss of support data should the firm need to produce documentation as to how it valued certain positions either for a regulator or for the firm's auditor.

In summary, while the evaluation of a firm's valuation procedures is generally more important than IT in the majority of circumstances, this is not to say that the importance or weight of IT considerations should be sacrificed for the sake of traditionally more important factors, such as valuation.

CATEGORY SCALE DETERMINATION AND THE MEANING OF SCORES

Another variation applies in the meaning that certain assigned values hold. In one model, which for the sake of example may range from 0 to 10, a value of 10 may mean that a hedge fund manager has reached the highest level of competency within a certain aspect of his operations. In another hedge fund operational risk scorecard methodology, a score of 0 may mean there are no outstanding operational risk concerns with regard to a certain aspect of a hedge fund manager's operations, and consequently a score of 0 would be the best attainable score for a certain category. Regardless of the particular scale utilized, scale consistency throughout the rating of different hedge funds' operational risks is a key characteristic that should be present to facilitate comparison among different operational rating scores. As demonstrated in Exhibit 8.17, if an investor rates one particular category utilizing a scale of 1 to 3 (Hedge Fund A, in our example), and then for a different hedge fund evaluates the same factor utilizing a scale of 1 to 6 (Hedge Fund B), or to be even more extreme, a binary rating evaluation of Yes or No (Hedge Fund C), comparison of the same category among the different funds becomes a difficult task as we are no longer comparing apples to apples.

EXHIBIT 8.17   How Differing Category Scales for the Same Category Can Make Comparisons among Hedge Funds Difficult

Hedge Fund A							
	Category Scale	3	2	1			
Primary Category Name	Legal/Regulatory/Compliance						
Hedge Fund B							
	Category Scale	6	5	4	3	2	1
Primary Category Name	Legal/Regulatory/Compliance						
Hedge Fund C							
	Category Scale	Pass	Fail				
Primary Category Name	Legal/Regulatory/Compliance						

THRESHOLD SELF-ASSESSMENT AND DETERMINATION

Once the particular category methodology and definitions have been determined, hedge fund investors must next determine their own individual operational threshold levels within each category. This operational threshold can be determined holistically, in regard to a final single aggregate operational score, or for each individual category in the particular scorecard model being utilized. Performing this threshold self-assessment process, before being presented with the particulars of any one hedge fund's operations, allows investors to make determinations as to the degree of their individual operational risk aversion in a more independent setting. Often, when no threshold is defined, investors find themselves, for one reason or another, accepting certain operational practices where, had they been presented with the questions of such risks in a generic sense (i.e., not applicable to any one hedge fund), they might have come to a different conclusion. This not to say that an investor should not accept an operational practice that may be below a particular threshold, but that such a breach should be a conscious one.

Another point regarding the operational threshold self-assessment process that is worth considering is the relationship between threshold determination and reputational risk. As we have noted, reputational risk is often one of the most challenging operational risk issues for investors to reconcile. In the course of performing an operational due diligence review, in particular the background investigation component, issues relating to the reputation of a hedge fund or its employees may be uncovered. Determining where these issues lie in relation to a particular operational threshold must often be done on a case-by-case basis due to the uniqueness of the issues uncovered.

Of course, investors establish general guidelines as to certain issues that may come up, regardless of the particulars involved, that will simply eliminate a hedge fund from the investor's investable universe. An example of a general rule would be a hedge fund that employs anyone who has committed a felony or had been convicted of any crime related to the financial services industry. In regard to other issues, though, the answer as to which side of the operational threshold they lie on may be less clear to certain investors.

Consider a hedge fund manager who was convicted of driving while under the influence. Assuming all else is equal, would this one conviction cause most investors to decide not to invest with this manager? How would the answer change if it were a conviction for shoplifting instead? What if the shoplifting conviction had occurred 20 years ago? Would the answer change if it were a conviction for possession of narcotics? What about the distribution of narcotics instead? If there were no conviction, but a hedge fund manager undergoing divorce proceedings is being accused of infidelity, would this change an investor's answer? Perhaps the issue relates not to a particular employee at a hedge fund, but to his family. What if a certain employee's child is convicted of underage drinking? Would the investor's answer change if it is instead a conviction for murder? When such unique reputational issues arise, investors are often best served by applying any penalties or discounts for such risks via the use of discretionary penalties, which will be discussed in more detail later. That said, performing a self-assessment as to where one's threshold lies in regard to such reputational issues *before* they arise, for the reasons cited, is often preferred.

The term *operational threshold* has been used in this text in several instances without really being defined. This lack of formal definition is partly due to the fact that it may have slightly different implications depending on context. Within the context of this discussion regarding operational scorecard methodologies, we can define the operational threshold as the minimum level of operational risk below which an investor is not willing to make an allocation to a particular fund. It can be thought of as a particular investor's *floor* for operational risk.

It should be reiterated that this operational threshold is specific to each investor. Certain investors may have higher or lower thresholds for different investment-related issues depending on a number of factors unique to them and their organizations. Operational thresholds can be applied to final aggregate scores of models in their entirety, or to individual operational scorecard model subcategories, or both. See Exhibit 8.18 for samples of multiple operational thresholds of different investors.

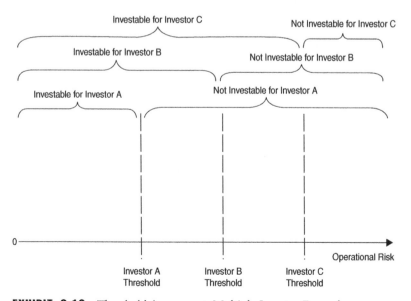

EXHIBIT 8.18 Threshold Assessment: Multiple-Investor Example

The use of operational thresholds can create difficult-to-reconcile situations for hedge fund investors. One question would be whether multiple thresholds should be created in order to evaluate different types or groups of hedge fund managers who may each have similar commonalities. For example, should a different threshold be established for Asian-based hedge fund managers where a different regional operational best practice standard is in place compared with that of the United States? Or, continuing our example, should a universal operational threshold be applied to all hedge funds regardless of regional considerations? If such is the case, then Asian hedge fund managers would most likely be penalized universally. Even if a penalty does not cause these Asian managers to fall below the operational threshold, and consequently an investor would still, according to our definition of the operational threshold, be willing to allocate to them, should they be considered to be of a lower operational quality even if they are on the high end of the operational quality scale for the region? Should an investor allocate less capital to them because they have less of an operational conviction about them?

SCORE ASSIGNMENT

Regardless of which category methodology is utilized, once the categories on which a hedge fund manager will be evaluated have been determined, the next step in the scoring process is to assign a score to each category. Once again, there is a wide variety in the way scores are assigned and the scale over which such scores are applied. For example, certain methodologies may use only an integer scale. Others may allow the scorer to apply non-integers, either on a certain percentage basis (e.g., 1.5 to 2 to 2.5) or across a more stepped scale (e.g., 1 to 1.2 to 1.4 to 1.6 to 1.8 to 2). Still other methods may not use numerical values, instead applying stars, diamonds, or other nonnumeric metrics in order to evaluate a hedge fund manager's operational risks. Finally, some methods do not seek to assign a particular score at all, instead relying on a binary evaluation of either Pass or Fail. One variation of such a binary scoring approach is to add a third, Needs Improvement rating in between Pass and Fail. In such a case, Needs Improvement would indicate that the hedge fund in question poses an acceptable level of operational risk in a certain operational evaluation category; however, in the opinion of the model scorer, there is room for improvement. It is important to note that some scorecard methodologies combine several of these different approaches. Exhibits 8.19, 8.20, and 8.21 demonstrate examples of

EXHIBIT 8.19 Example of Score Assignment under the Macro Scorecard Approach (MSA) Methodology Model

Category Number	Primary Category Name	Score
1	Legal/Regulatory/Compliance	3
2	Trading/Valuation	2
3	Technology/Business Continuity/Disaster Recovery	4
4	Assets Under Management/Financial and Organizational Sustainability	4
5	Quality of Service Providers Utilized	1
6	Reputation of Employees (including senior mgmt.) and Firm	2

score assignment under the MSA, MSA+, and MISA scorecard methodology models.

Concerning the MAS+ model, similar to the variations available within the category weighting determinations under both WAM and WDA, we can investigate similar variations in regard to decisions related to score assignment. In Exhibit 8.20, only the subcategories received scores. An alternative method would have been to provide both the primary categories and subcategories with scores. This, of course, would be possible only under WDM, where the category weighting scheme provides for a weight to be given to the primary category score. This is shown in Exhibit 8.22. In this example, the score of 4 assigned to the primary category Assets Under Management/Financial and Organizational Sustainability represents an evaluation of the leftover operational competency for this primary category, which was not addressed by the two subcategory factors.

Yet another variation exists within the primary category scoring assignment that can be considered an offshoot of WAM. This approach is shown in Exhibit 8.23. For demonstration purposes, we have altered the scores assigned to be only quantitative in nature, as opposed to also containing qualitative responses, such as "Yes" or "No," for which we could assign discretionary scores, to be discussed in more detail in the section on Discretionary Penalties and Bonuses. Additionally, to facilitate this quantitative reassignment, we have slightly altered some of the subcategory headings as well, when compared to Exhibit 8.22. Returning to our example, in Exhibit 8.23, the primary score category weighting represents the average of the two related subcategory scores.

EXHIBIT 8.20 Example of Score Assignment under the Macro-Plus Scorecard Approach (MSA+) Methodology Model

Category Number	Primary Category Name	Subcategory Name	Subcategory Score
1	Legal/Regulatory/Compliance		
1-a		Any previous regulatory violations?	No
1-b		Nature of compliance control environment	3
2	Trading/Valuation		
2-a		Trade error frequency and investigation procedures	4
2-b		Independence of valuation procedures	2
3	Technology/Business Continuity/Disaster Recovery		
3-a		Frequency of business continuity and disaster recovery testing	3
3-b		Scalability of technology systems	4
4	Assets Under Management/Financial and Organizational Sustainability		
4-a		Any recent material subscriptions and redemptions?	Yes
4-b		Recent departures of key personnel	3
5	Quality of Service Providers Utilized		
5-a		Length of relationship with current service providers	4
5-b		Nature of services provided by service providers	2
6	Reputation of Employees (including senior mgmt.) and Firm		
6-a		Length and nature of senior principals' capital markets experience	3
6-b		Any material items uncovered during a background investigation?	4

EXHIBIT 8.21 Example of Score Assignment under the Macro Scorecard Approach (MSA) Methodology Model

Category Number	Primary Category Name	Score
1	Assets under management trends (comparison from peak levels)	3
2	Diversity of investor base	Pass
3	Does any single investor constitute larger than 10% of firm-wide assets under management?	No
4	Business continuity and disaster recovery plan thoroughness	2
5	Business continuity and disaster recovery plan testing frequency	3
6	Business continuity and disaster recovery plan scalability	4
7	Use of offsite data backups	No
8	Use of tape backups	Yes
9	Are tape backups taken offsite?	No
10	Appropriateness of information security policy	3
11	Quality of software systems utilized	Yes
12	Nature of any employees outside business interests	2
13	Does the firm have backup power generation facilities?	3
14	Any previous regulatory violations?	No
15	Any recent material subscriptions and redemptions?	No
16	Any material items uncovered during a background investigation?	Yes
17	Independence of valuation process	3
18	Appropriateness of insurance coverage in place and policy limits	2
19	Have any of the funds ever had to restate the net asset value?	No
20	Is there any pending litigation against the firm or its principals?	No

EXHIBIT 8.22 Example of Score Assignment under WDM

Category Number	Primary Category Name	Subcategory Name	Subcategory Score	Primary Category Score
1	Legal/Regulatory/Compliance			3.5
1-a		Any previous regulatory violations?	No	
1-b		Nature of compliance control environment	5	
2	Trading/Valuation			4
2-a		Trade error frequency and investigation procedures	4	
2-b		Independence of valuation procedures	2	
3	Technology/Business Continuity/Disaster Recovery			3
3-a		Frequency of business continuity and disaster recovery testing	3	
3-b		Scalability of technology systems	4	
4	Assets Under Management/Financial and Organizational Sustainability			4
4-a		Any recent material subscriptions and redemptions?	Yes	
4-b		Recent departures of key personnel	3	
5	Quality of Service Providers Utilized			2
5-a		Length of relationship with current service providers	4	
5-b		Nature of services provided by service providers	2	
6	Reputation of Employees (including senior mgmt.) and Firm			3
6-a		Length and nature of senior principals' capital markets experience	3	
6-b		Any material items uncovered during a background investigation?	4	

EXHIBIT 8.23 Example of the Macro-Plus Scorecard Approach (MSA+) Methodology Model: Subcategory and Primary Category Scores with Weighted Average

Category Number	Primary Category Name	Subcategory Name	Subcategory Score	Primary Category Score
1	Legal/Regulatory/Compliance			3.5 = (4 + 3)/2
1-a		Nature of previous regulatory violations?	4	
1-b		Nature of compliance control environment	3	
2	Trading/Valuation			3 = (4 + 2)/2
2-a		Trade error frequency and investigation procedures	4	
2-b		Independence of valuation procedures	2	
3	Technology/Business Continuity/Disaster Recovery			3.5 = (3 + 4)/2
3-a		Frequency of business continuity and disaster recovery testing	3	
3-b		Scalability of Technology Systems	4	
4	Assets Under Management/Financial and Organizational Sustainability			3 = (3 + 3)/2
4-a		Nature of recent subscriptions and redemptions	3	
4-b		Recent departures of toy personnel	3	
5	Quality of Service Providers Utilized			3 = (4 + 2)/2
5-a		Length of relationship with current service providers	4	
5-b		Nature of services provided by service providers	2	
6	Reputation of Employees (including senior mgmt.) and Firm			3.5 = (3 + 4)/2
6-a		Length and nature of senior principals' capital markets experience	3	
6-b		Any material items uncovered during a background investigation?	4	

DISCRETIONARY PENALTIES AND BONUSES

Once scores have been assigned to each category, many scoring models allow the model operator to apply discretionary penalties or bonuses based on a number of factors. These discretionary factors can be thought of as overarching concerns that the particular scoring model methodology in question considers to be outside of the particulars of a certain category, but important enough to influence a hedge fund manager's score. Discretionary bonuses or penalties can be focused within a specific category or applied universally to a total final score. Additionally, these discretionary bonuses and penalties can be either multiplicative or additive factors, and either positive or negative.

Discretionary penalties are generally applied to things such as an unusually short length of track record, assets under management below a certain minimum, questionable issues raised from a background investigation, concerns about the regulation of a certain jurisdiction in which a particular hedge fund is domiciled, previous drawdowns that may have lasted longer than a predefined time period or been of a certain percentage magnitude, high personnel turnover, or a fund's lack of a certain percentage of independent board members. Similarly, discretionary bonuses may be applied to situations where a certain hedge fund is above a certain asset level or has a track record longer than a certain predefined period.

Exhibit 8.24 is based on Exhibit 8.21. One difference between these two exhibits is that in Exhibit 8.24 the score assigned to the primary category is the weighted average of the related underlying subcategories, whereas in Exhibit 8.21 the primary category score represents the leftover operational competency in the primary category. A second difference between the two exhibits is that Exhibit 8.24 seeks to quantify, via a discretionary penalty, those subcategories that have binary category scales. So, for example, the subcategory "Any previous regulatory violations?" under the Legal/Regulatory/Compliance primary category was scored with a value of "No." Let us assume that the category definitions for this subcategory were constructed under the BCD approach, and that the only two category scale options were "Yes" or "No." Let us further assume that the hedge fund under review in our example did not have any previous regulatory violations and subsequently received a score of "No" for this subcategory. As referenced earlier, certain scoring methodologies seek to convert qualitative scores, such as "Yes" or "No" in our example, to a quantitative discretionary bonus or penalty depending on their value. In this case, the model does not award a discretionary penalty for a "No" answer and no action is taken that influences the weighted average subcategory score. Turning to the "Any recent material subscriptions and redemptions?" subcategory under the Assets Under Management/Financial and Organizational Sustainability

EXHIBIT 8.24 Macro-Plus Scorecard Approach (MSA+) Methodology Model: Comparison of Subcategory and Primary Category Scores with and without Discretionary Scores Applied

Category Number	Primary Category Name	Subcategory Name	Subcategory Score	Primary Category Score with Discretionary Penalty Applied	Primary Category Score without Discretionary Penalty Applied
1	Legal/Regulatory/Compliance			3 = (3) + (0 discretionary penalty bonus)	3 = (3) + (0 discretionary penalty bonus)
1-a		Any previous regulatory violations?	No*		
1-b		Nature of compliance control environment	3		
2	Trading/Valuation			3 = (4 + 2)/2	3 = (4 + 2)/2
2-a		Trade error frequency and investigation procedures	4		
2-b		Independence of valuation procedures	2		
3	Technology/Business Continuity/ Disaster Recovery			3 = (3 + 4)/2	3 = (3 + 4)/2
3-a		Frequency of business continuity and disaster recovery testing	3		
3-b		Scalability of technology systems	4		
4	Assets Under Management/Financial and Organizational Sustainability			3 = (3)	3 = (3)
4-a		Any recent material subscriptions and redemptions?	Yes**	2	3
4-b		Recent departures of key personnel	3		
5	Quality of Service Providers Utilized			2 = (4 + 2)/2	2 = (4 + 2)/2
5-a		Length of relationship with current service providers	4		
5-b		Nature of services provided by service providers	2		
6	Reputation of Employees (including senior mgmt.) and Firm			3 = (3 + 4)/2	3 = (3 + 4)/2
6-a		Length and nature of senior principals' capital markets experience	3		
6-b		Any material items uncovered during a background investigation?	4		
			Weighted Average Single Total Score	1.8 = [(3 + 3 + 3 + 2 + 2 + 3)/6] – (1.0 discretionar penalty for 'Yes' value for subcategory 4-a)	2.8 = (3 + 3 + 3 + 3 + 2 + 3)/6

*Note: Value of 'No' does not merit a discretionary penalty or bonus.

**Note: Value of 'Yes' merits a discretionary penalty of +1.0.

primary category, we see that this subcategory has been scored with a value of "Yes."

Let us further assume that the model views this as a negative feature (i.e., one that creates more operational risk for the hedge fund under review), and assigns a discretionary penalty of 1 for such an answer. This would have the effect of subtracting a value of 1 from the final weighted average score calculated for the hedge fund manager. To see the effect of the application of this discretionary penalty, we can compare the values of the final weighted average single total operational risk score with the penalty and without. As demonstrated in Exhibit 8.24, with the discretionary penalty the manager received an overall operational risk rating of 1.8, versus a nondiscretionary penalty score of 2.8. Clearly, the model severely penalizes a hedge fund for having previous regulatory violations.

Depending on the category scale, a discretionary penalty of 1 need not be as severe in one model as it would be in another model scale. For example, on a quantitative scale ranging from 1 to 4, a discretionary penalty of 1 would have a much greater impact than if the scale were much broader in range, say from 1 to 20. This brings up a final point that we will discuss in relation to discretionary penalties and bonuses—the determining of the magnitude of the values of such factors.

Discretionary Magnitudes

As with the determination of the categories themselves and subsequent category scale, category definitions, and category weights, the values assessed for certain discretionary penalties or bonuses are reflective of the personal opinions of the model creator as to the operational risks prevalent in hedge funds. One attractive feature of discretionary questions is that they can be added to a scorecard model without necessarily affecting existing primary and subcategory scores. The reason for this is that discretionary scores are generally applied to the overall final operational score of a hedge fund. So for example, if a new discretionary factor were added to the scorecard model, each of the previously scored funds would have to be rescored and a proper bonus or penalty added for this new discretionary factor but, each underlying subcategory would not have to be rescored.

SCORE AGGREGATION: SUM TOTALING AND WEIGHTED AVERAGES

Once the scores for each category have been assigned, the next step under the majority of scorecard methodologies is to aggregate the scores in some manner. This provides us with one figure or metric that can be used to summarize the operational competency of a hedge fund. That is not to say that the individual category scores are unimportant and should not be considered. On the contrary, such individual category scores can provide valuable insight into where the operational competencies and weaknesses of a particular manager lie, whereas an aggregation of such figures attempts to summarize these individual scores.

One method of individual category score aggregation is to simply sum up each of the scores. A more common method is to take a weighted average of the individual category scores. The use of a weighted average allows the aggregate score to be equated to the same scale as the individual category scores. For example, if each individual category is evaluated on a scale of 1 to 4, the final aggregated weighted average score would also be somewhere on the 1-to-4 scale.

Returning to Exhibit 8.23, which depicted the MSA+ model with both subcategory and primary category scores with weighted averages applied to the primary category, we can now extend this example to discuss score aggregation of the entire weighted average score. In Exhibit 8.23 we can see that each of the primary category scores, which you will remember are the averages of the related subcategories, have been added up and divided by the total number of primary categories, in this case six, to produce a single weighted average operational risk score for the hedge fund in question of 3.25.

CRITICISMS OF SCORECARD MODELS

There are several criticisms of the operational scorecard modeling systems. One argument is that when applying such scores situations will arise that may not fit neatly into a predefined scoring category. For example, when evaluating the length of a hedge fund manager's track record, consider a hedge fund manager who has spun out on his own from a larger shop where he previously managed a similar fund for seven years. Also assume that the threshold level with which a certain model evaluates length of track records is three years. Any less, and a discretionary penalty is applied. However, track records greater than six years are awarded a discretionary bonus by the model. On one hand, the argument could be made for a discretionary penalty, since technically this manager's new fund does not have an established track record. On the other hand, since the new strategy is materially similar to the previously managed strategy, just at a different firm, the argument could be made to validate the previously established seven-year track record via the awarding of a discretionary bonus. In such a case, there is no one correct answer. Rather, when evaluating a final score, the interpreter of such a score needs to be conscious of the amount of discretion involved in assigning such a score.

A second criticism of scorecard models is that a manager who may meet a hedge fund investor's qualitative operational threshold may fall below the score determined by following the rules of a certain model. When such a case arises, the question becomes whether the hedge fund investor should not invest because the model has instructed him not to, or whether he should rely on his qualitative assessment. Of course, the point could be made that such situations will arise only if this investor's qualitative threshold and quantitative threshold are not aligned. Just as the determination of a particular investor's operational threshold is not an exact science, neither is this alignment process. Regardless, for the sake of argument, let us assume that even if such a realignment occurs, the hedge fund investor may find himself in the converse situation, where after a qualitative assessment he determines that he should not allocate to a certain hedge fund manager. However, the quantitative scoring model indicates that the operational risks of a particular hedge fund are above this particular investor's operational threshold. Once again, the investor is faced with the question of whether he should follow the guidance of the scorecard model or his qualitative assessment.

Another criticism of scorecard models is the tendency of the scorer to *backfit* the model. The model operator assigns the scores with a predetermined conclusion in mind. As a result, the score produced by the model is not entirely independent. Even before a potential investor has any direct contact with a hedge fund, there are often a number of indirect contact points of influence. Whether manufactured in the rumor mills or even inspired by the recommendations of fellow investors, these first impressions of hedge funds are often effected from a distance. Just as positive rumors can boost a reputation, so, too, can negative ones be damning. As a precaution, such preconceived notions should serve as guideposts and not as conclusively determinative.

While the collective consciousness of the hedge fund community may be able to condemn a fund, often (though not always) performance speaks louder than words and potential hedge fund investors might find themselves performing operational due diligence on a hedge fund that they already have preconceived notions about before a page of documentation has been read. It is, of course, naïve to assume that such preconceived ideas will be discarded and a hedge fund's operational risks will be evaluated in isolation. On the contrary, the insight of others, be it true fact or manufactured rumor, can serve to fuel understanding of the often latent operational risks that may be buried within a fund's operational folds. However, such preconceived notions should not persuade investors to draw hasty conclusions, and this is particularly true when it comes to score assignments.

An example of the influence of such preconceived notions is in regard to those operational issues that may be on the borderline of a particular operational threshold. The scorecard model operator with a predisposition to approve a certain hedge fund may err on the side of being above the threshold as opposed to below it, despite the category definitions. Such predetermined conclusions can often be drawn because the scoring process is generally at the very end of the operational due diligence process, almost as an afterthought.

It would be difficult for the scoring to occur earlier in the process, as the information acquired throughout the operational due diligence process is necessary to determine the score to assign based on the strategy definitions. Consequently, it is the responsibility of the scorer to exercise a certain degree of independence by removing any foregone conclusions and predispositions when evaluating a fund based on the model definitions. As one can imagine, this is sometimes difficult to do and can lead to biased model results.

BENEFITS OF SCORECARD MODELS

Among the primary benefits of scorecard models is that they provide for a quick and intuitive way to analyze the particular operational competences of a particular hedge fund, as well as to compare the operational risks of different hedge funds. As outlined earlier, such scores are generally highly subjective and open to interpretation, but they nonetheless hold value as, at the very least, a basic benchmark upon which further analysis of a hedge fund's operational risks can be built.

VISUALIZATION TECHNIQUES

As the modeling of hedge fund operational risks has developed over time, and the amount, types, and complexity of operational data being collected have increased, there are a host of visualization techniques to help both investors and operational risk professionals better synthesize this data in a timely and efficient manner. Two such related visualization techniques, which are already widely used in a host of different situations throughout the world of finance, are *heat mapping* and *tree mapping*.

Heat Mapping

"A heat map is any data visualization which uses color to represent data values in a two-dimensional image."[1] Typically, those items that are of greater importance or riskiness are given a higher heat rating, signified by a brighter (typically red) color. Items of less importance or risk have cooler hues, such as blue or green. An example of a heat map is shown in Exhibit 8.25.

As a cautionary note, when going through the process of assigning colors in a heat map, colors cannot be assigned universally based on the values assigned. A good example of this is under the BCP approach, utilizing a "Yes" or "No" rating. If an investor is evaluating the primary category

EXHIBIT 8.25 Example of Heat Map Construction Data

Category Number	Primary Category Name	Score
1	Assets under management trends (comparison from peak levels)	3
2	Diversity of investor base	Pass
3	Does any single investor constitute larger than 10% of firm-wide assets under management?	No
4	Business continuity and disaster recovery plan thoroughness	2
5	Business continuity and disaster recovery plan testing frequency	3
6	Business continuity and disaster recovery plan scalability	4
7	Use of offsite data backups	No
8	Use of tape backups	Yes
9	Are tape backups taken offsite?	No
10	Nature of any employees outside business interests	3
11	Does the firm have backup power generation facilities?	Yes
12	Appropriateness of information security policy	2
13	Quality of software systems utilized	3
14	Any previous regulatory violations?	No
15	Any recent material subscriptions and redemptions?	No
16	Any material items uncovered during a background investigation?	Yes
17	Independence of valuation process	3
18	Appropriateness of insurance coverage in place and policy limits	1
19	Have any of the funds ever had to restate the net asset value?	No
20	Is there any pending litigation against the firm or its principals?	No

of Use of Offsite Data Backups, a "No" score for this particular primary category may be viewed negatively and receive a red color. A "No" score, however, for a different category may conversely be viewed in a positive light by the model, and therefore will not necessarily be red. Consider the category, "Any previous regulatory violations?" Most scorecard models and investors alike would consider the lack of any previous regulatory violations in a positive light and would reward a "No" response with a lighter-hue color. In summary, the color difference is the result of the *meaning* of the "No" rating in that category, as opposed to evaluating it solely on the value of "Yes" or "No."

There are many color variations within the heat mapping context. One approach is to utilize a stoplight color system, where red indicates a stop signal, or an unacceptable level of risk, yellow indicates a level of risk to be undertaken with caution, and green indicates an acceptable level of risk. An example of a stoplight heat map is given in Exhibit 8.26.

Tree Mapping

"Treemaps are a family of algorithms that are space-filling partitions of a two-dimensional area. Treemaps take as input a list of *n* numbers and a rectangle. They partition the area into *n* rectangles, one per input number. The rectangles are guaranteed to fill the input rectangle, and the rectangles

EXHIBIT 8.26   Example of Stoplight Heat Map Construction Data

Category Number	Primary Category Name	Score	Color
1	Legal/Regulatory/Compliance	3	Yellow
2	Trading/Valuation	2	Red
3	Technology/Business Continuity/Disaster Recovery	4	Greeen
4	Assets Under Management/Financial and Organizational Sustainability	4	Green
5	Quality of Service Providers Utilized	1	Red
6	Reputation of Employees (including senior mgmt.) and Firm	2	Red

Legend

Operational Score Range	Color
From 0 up to and including 2	Red
From 2 up to and including 3	Yellow
From 2 up to and including 4	Green

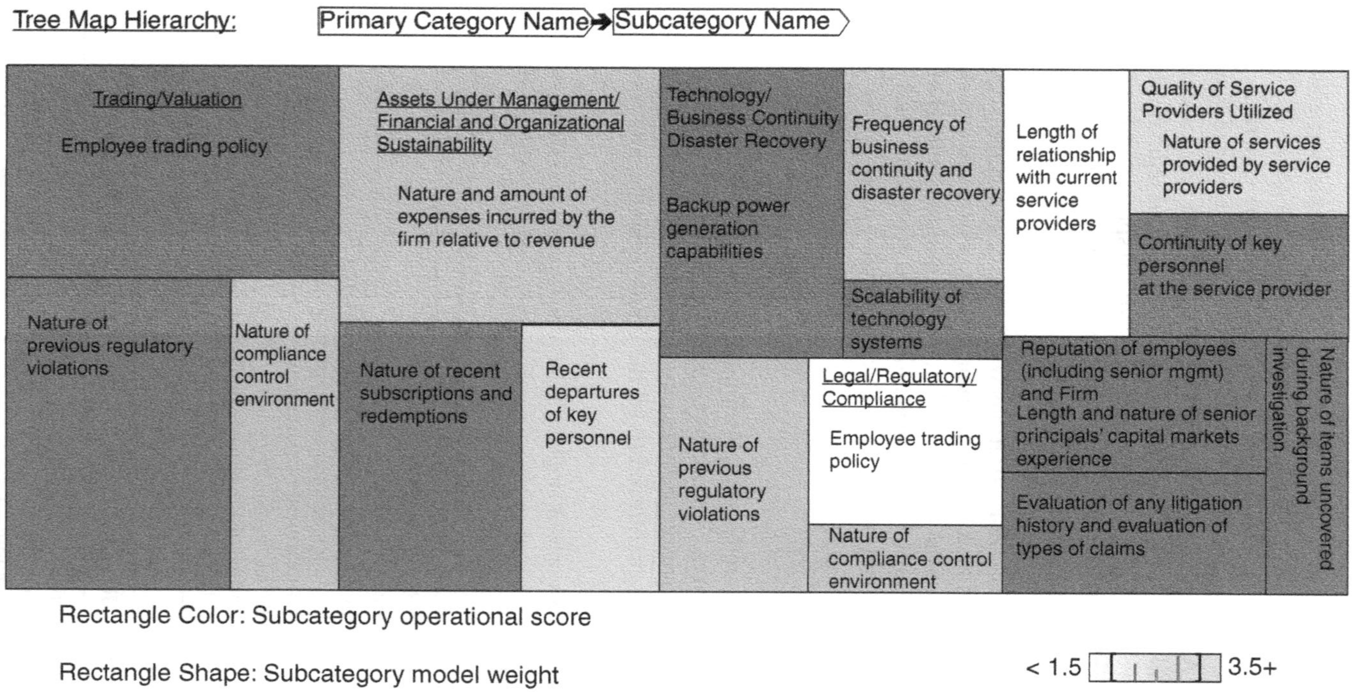

Tree Map Hierarchy: Primary Category Name → Subcategory Name

Trading/Valuation

Employee trading policy

Nature of previous regulatory violations

Nature of compliance control environment

Assets Under Management/ Financial and Organizational Sustainability

Nature and amount of expenses incurred by the firm relative to revenue

Nature of recent subscriptions and redemptions

Recent departures of key personnel

Technology/ Business Continuity Disaster Recovery

Backup power generation capabilities

Frequency of business continuity and disaster recovery

Scalability of technology systems

Nature of previous regulatory violations

Legal/Regulatory/ Compliance

Employee trading policy

Nature of compliance control environment

Length of relationship with current service providers

Quality of Service Providers Utilized

Nature of services provided by service providers

Continuity of key personnel at the service provider

Nature of items uncovered during background investigation

Reputation of employees (including senior mgmt) and Firm

Length and nature of senior principals' capital markets experience

Evaluation of any litigation history and evaluation of types of claims

Rectangle Color: Subcategory operational score

Rectangle Shape: Subcategory model weight

< 1.5   3.5+

EXHIBIT 8.27 Combination of a Heat Map and a Tree Map with Respect to Score (Color) and Weight (Shape)

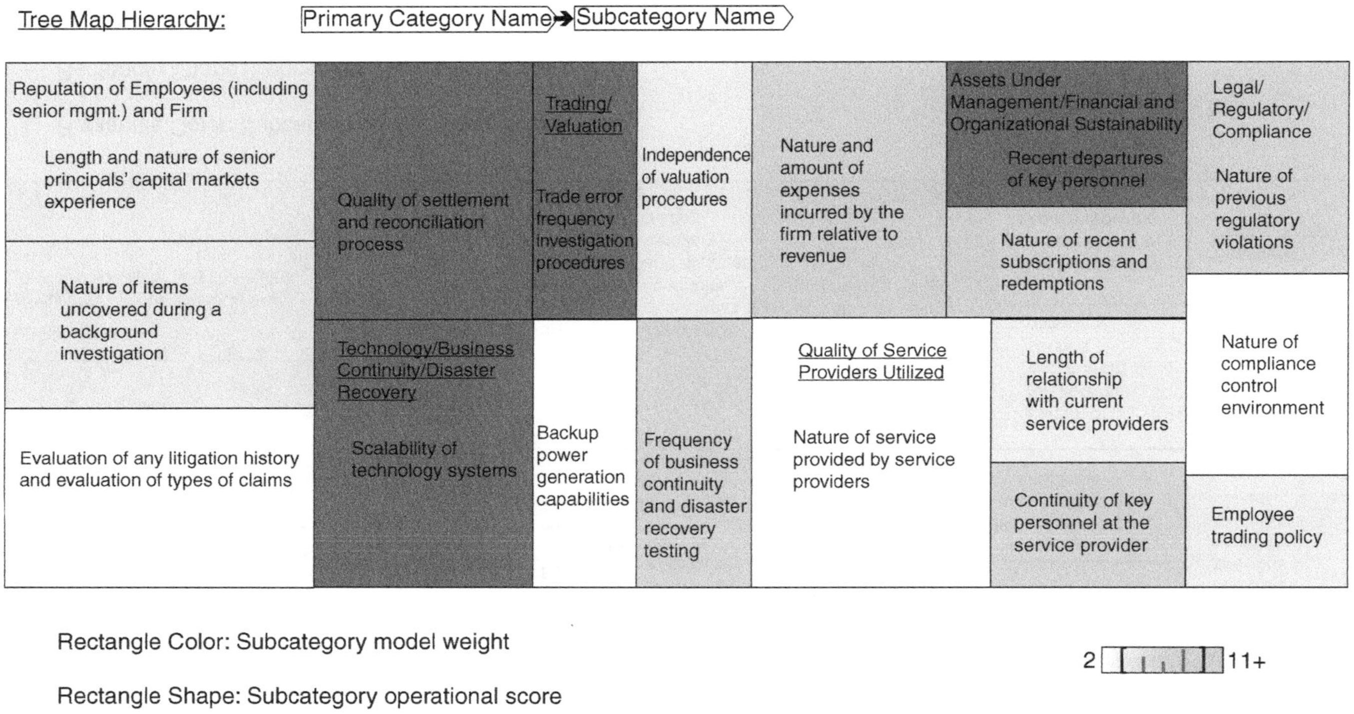

Tree Map Hierarchy: | Primary Category Name → Subcategory Name |

Reputation of Employees (including senior mgmt.) and Firm

Length and nature of senior principals' capital markets experience

Nature of items uncovered during a background investigation

Evaluation of any litigation history and evaluation of types of claims

Trading/Valuation

Quality of settlement and reconciliation process

Trade error frequency investigation procedures

Independence of valuation procedures

Nature and amount of expenses incurred by the firm relative to revenue

Technology/Business Continuity/Disaster Recovery

Scalability of technology systems

Backup power generation capabilities

Frequency of business continuity and disaster recovery testing

Quality of Service Providers Utilized

Nature of service provided by service providers

Assets Under Management/Financial and Organizational Sustainability

Recent departures of key personnel

Nature of recent subscriptions and redemptions

Length of relationship with current service providers

Continuity of key personnel at the service provider

Legal/Regulatory/Compliance

Nature of previous regulatory violations

Nature of compliance control environment

Employee trading policy

Rectangle Color: Subcategory model weight

Rectangle Shape: Subcategory operational score

2 [ ] 11+

EXHIBIT 8.28 Combination of a Heat Map and a Tree Map with Respect to Score (Shape) and Weight (Color)

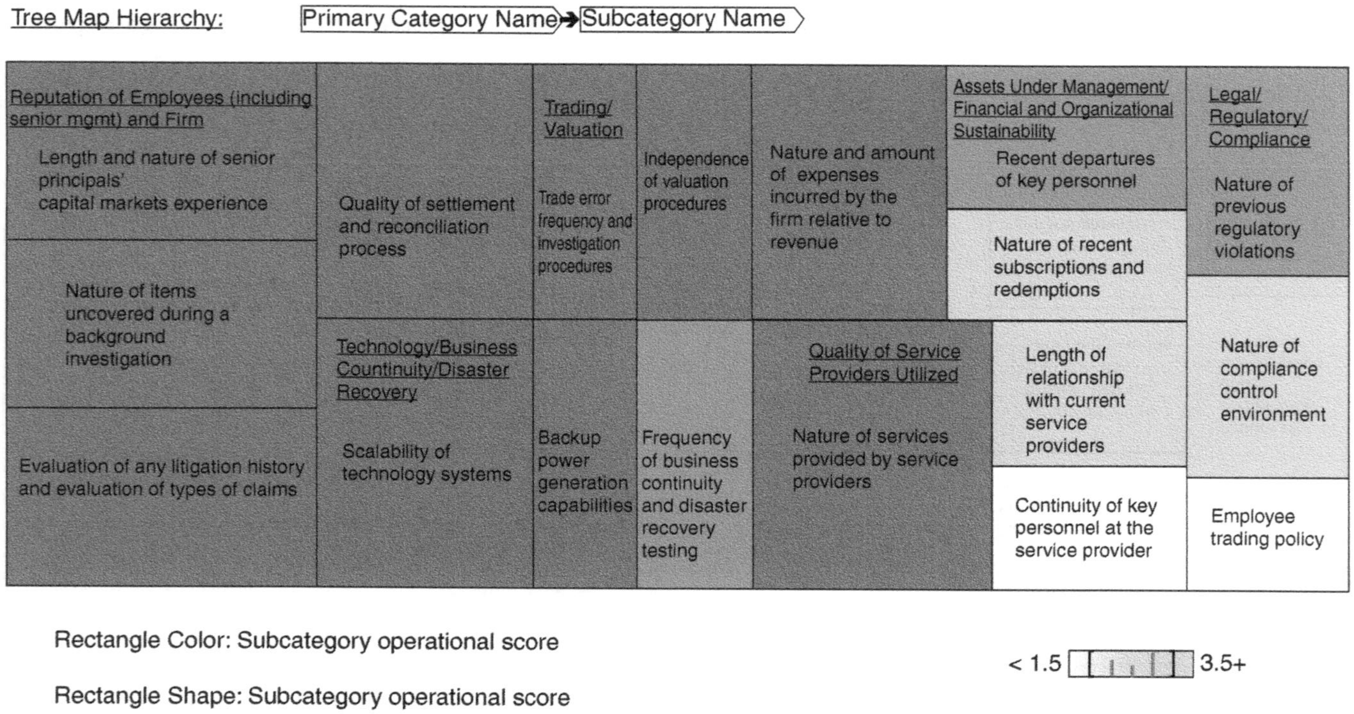

Tree Map Hierarchy: Primary Category Name → Subcategory Name

Reputation of Employees (including senior mgmt) and Firm

Length and nature of senior principals' capital markets experience

Nature of items uncovered during a background investigation

Evaluation of any litigation history and evaluation of types of claims

Technology/Business Continuity/Disaster Recovery

Scalability of technology systems

Quality of settlement and reconciliation process

Trading/Valuation

Trade error frequency and investigation procedures

Independence of valuation procedures

Nature and amount of expenses incurred by the firm relative to revenue

Backup power generation capabilities

Frequency of business continuity and disaster recovery testing

Quality of Service Providers Utilized

Nature of services provided by service providers

Assets Under Management/Financial and Organizational Sustainability

Recent departures of key personnel

Nature of recent subscriptions and redemptions

Length of relationship with current service providers

Continuity of key personnel at the service provider

Legal/Regulatory/Compliance

Nature of previous regulatory violations

Nature of compliance control environment

Employee trading policy

Rectangle Color: Subcategory operational score

Rectangle Shape: Subcategory operational score

< 1.5   3.5+

EXHIBIT 8.29 Combination of a Heat Map and a Tree Map with Respect to Score (Color) and Score (Shape)

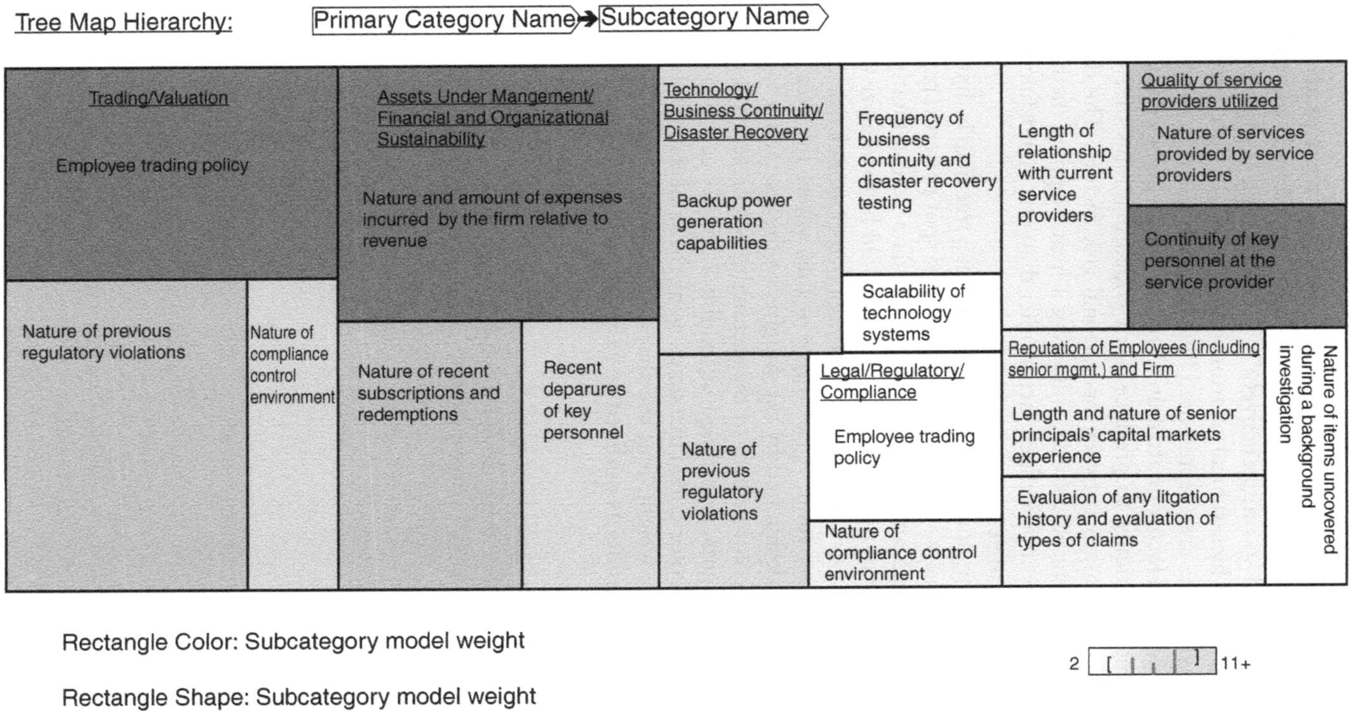

Tree Map Hierarchy: Primary Category Name ➔ Subcategory Name

Trading/Valuation

Employee trading policy

Nature of previous regulatory violations

Nature of compliance control environment

Assets Under Mangement/ Financial and Organizational Sustainability

Nature and amount of expenses incurred by the firm relative to revenue

Nature of recent subscriptions and redemptions

Recent deparures of key personnel

Technology/ Business Continuity/ Disaster Recovery

Backup power generation capabilities

Nature of previous regulatory violations

Frequency of business continuity and disaster recovery testing

Scalability of technology systems

Legal/Regulatory/ Compliance

Employee trading policy

Nature of compliance control environment

Quality of service providers utilized

Nature of services provided by service providers

Continuity of key personnel at the service provider

Length of relationship with current service providers

Nature of items uncovered during a background investigation

Reputation of Employees (including senior mgmt.) and Firm

Length and nature of senior principals' capital markets experience

Evaluation of any litigation history and evaluation of types of claims

Rectangle Color: Subcategory model weight

Rectangle Shape: Subcategory model weight

2 [ ] 11+

EXHIBIT 8.30 Combination of a Heat Map and a Tree Map with Respect to Weight (Color) and Weight (Shape)

223

are proportional in area to the list of input numbers. Treemaps are designed to be applied hierarchically, so any given resulting rectangle can itself contain a treemap, and so on, recursively"[2] Tree mapping is most commonly utilized to diagram hierarchical relationships. There are differently shaped rectangles, where the area represented by each rectangle is in proportion to a specific predefined factor or attribute. Tree mapping can be combined with heat mapping techniques to produce color-coded diagrams that detail the hierarchical relationship between operational risk factors. The differently shaped rectangles can be colored, following a heat mapping methodology, to represent a different predefined factor other than one that defines the area or shape of the rectangles.

One benefit of organizing operational data in a tree map is that it allows investors to more easily recognize exceptions and spot patterns, particularly when analyzing large amounts of operational data across multiple hedge funds. One example of the use of a tree map would be to analyze the scores and weights for a series of different secondary operational risk categories for a particular hedge fund. An example of this, where the area or shape of the rectangles is designated by the weights of the secondary factors and the intensity of the color or heat of the rectangles is represented by the sub-category model weights, is outlined in Exhibit 8.27. We can also construct three other similar, color-coded tree maps using the same data set by varying the factors, score or weight, and the shape and colors of the rectangles to produce different results as outlined in Exhibits 8.28, 8.29, and 8.30.

Notes

1. www.labescape.com/info/articles/what-is-a-heat-map.html.
2. http://iv.slis.indiana.edu/sw/treemap.html.

CHAPTER 9

Bridging the Gap: Incorporating Operational Risk Considerations into the Portfolio Construction and Asset Allocation Process

U p to now, this text has discussed the definitions of operational risk and described the operational due diligence process, that is, the techniques for collecting operational data regarding a hedge fund, as well as the process of making an ultimate determination as to the operational competencies and risks of a hedge fund. In Chapter 8, techniques for modeling the collected operational data were discussed. As important as the *operational* due diligence process is, it is only half of the due diligence equation. The other half is *investment* due diligence. This relationship is summarized in Exhibit 9.1. Different hedge fund allocators may put different importance on the operational due diligence process versus the investment due diligence process. It does not have to be a perfect 50–50 split of efforts or weight, as suggested by Exhibit 9.1. This is an organizational decision that each investor will have to make on his or her own, contingent on a number of factors, including the due diligence resources available to the investor and the particular due diligence challenges presented by each hedge fund under consideration. No investor can say in all honesty that he or she has performed complete hedge fund due diligence while ignoring one side of the equation entirely. Only with both parts of the hedge fund due diligence equation complete can an investor focus on the asset allocation decision.

As intimated throughout this book, the vast majority of hedge fund investors treat the operational due diligence process as a filter for the operational downside risk, or *operational beta*. This approach should not be criticized. On the contrary, any logical hedge fund investor would seek to minimize exposure to the often outlier, blowup-type events that have littered

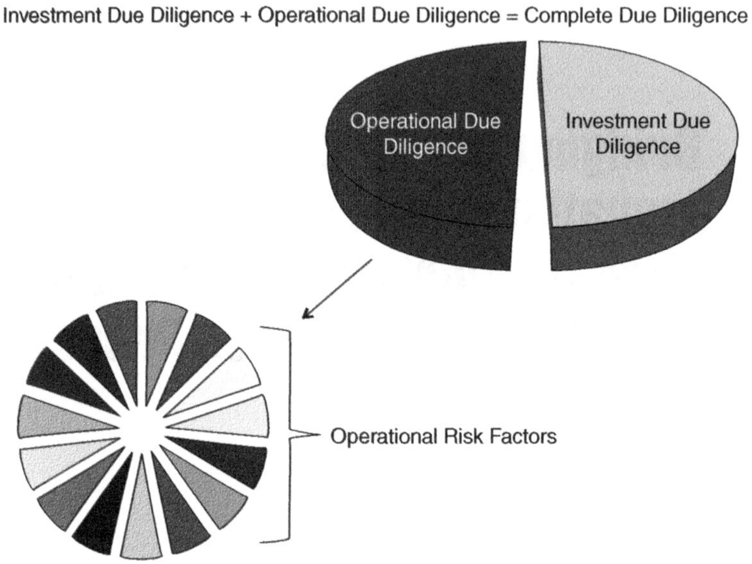

Investment Due Diligence + Operational Due Diligence = Complete Due Diligence

Operational Due Diligence

Investment Due Diligence

Operational Risk Factors

EXHIBIT 9.1 Hedge Fund Due Diligence Equation

the headlines of late. This, however, should be only the first phase of the operational risk management process. Often a substantial amount of effort is put into collecting operational data in order to diagnose operational risk; yet most investors utilize this data to evaluate the operational risk of hedge funds only in relation to a particular threshold. This chapter espouses four viewpoints with respect to the way in which operational risk data can be used to add value in the portfolio construction and asset allocation processes:

1. Investors should proactively monitor and manage their exposures to operational risks by incorporating directional operational views into the hedge fund portfolio construction process.
2. The conglomeration effects of operational risk exposures should be an initial consideration when constructing a portfolio of hedge funds. Such conglomeration effects should be continuously monitored once the portfolio has been constructed.
3. Calculations of the total risk present in a hedge fund should include factors for operational risk. The inclusion of such factors, with one exception, an operationally riskless hedge fund, necessarily increases the overall riskiness of a hedge fund and presents a more accurate picture of the total risk of hedge fund investing.
4. The expected returns of hedge funds should be discounted for operational risk considerations present at these funds.

More generally, the goal of this chapter is to outline techniques for integrating the results of an initial operational due diligence review into the asset allocation process. Such integration of operational considerations into an asset allocation framework allows investors, in either a customized portfolio of hedge funds or a pooled fund of hedge funds environment, to make conscious choices about the types and amounts of operational risks to which they are exposing themselves. By proactively owning these risks, rather than turning a blind eye toward them or, even worse, being in complete denial of their existence beyond a certain minimum threshold, hedge fund allocators have significant opportunity to either partially hedge against certain operational risks or factor global operational directional bets into the overall allocation and portfolio construction process.

PROACTIVE MONITORING: GRAPHICAL UNIVERSE CREATION

We will begin our discussion of the extension of operational risk decisions into the asset allocation process with an examination of the results of an operational risk scorecard analysis. Once a series of operational scores have been assigned to a variety of individual hedge fund managers, we can then begin to discuss the analysis of these scores individually, as well as the comparison of these scores among multiple hedge funds. One comparison technique, which we will discuss in this section, is the process of graphing each of the final operational scores for a group of hedge funds on a single set of axes in order to create an initial operational risk universe. These scores could represent either hedge funds that are in a portfolio of hedge funds, hedge funds under consideration for investment, or both. Exhibit 9.2 demonstrates an example of the creation of such a universe.

Once a universe has been created, we have a benchmark from which to compare the addition of the final operational score that will be calculated for a subsequent hedge fund. Such comparisons on certain levels are intuitive; for example, if a manager does not meet certain basic minimum operational criteria, then she would not be considered investable. Above that minimum threshold, the operational competencies of other managers can sometimes become lost in the shuffle. Graphical universe creation, similar to tree mapping, provides a quick and easy way to contrast a new hedge fund's operational risk score information against previously scored hedge funds. After an initial universe has been created, we can begin to add other graphical analysis techniques to analyze any trends or patterns that may run through these operational scores. For example, we can run a linear regression through the data, as demonstrated in Exhibit 9.3, or track the moving average of the operational scores over time, as shown in Exhibit 9.4.

Hedge Fund	Final Operational Score
A	3
B	2.5
C	4
D	3
E	2.5
F	2.5
G	2
H	3
I	2.5
J	3
K	3.5

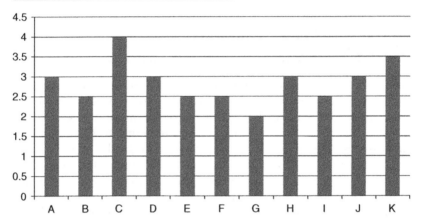

EXHIBIT 9.2 Example of a Graphical Universe Creation with Final Operational Scores

The previously described techniques, such as linear regression and moving average tracking, were based on an existing set of operational data. We can also use such techniques to aid in forecasting future operational scores. That is not to say that a linear regression model of an existing universe will allow an investor to predict with any accuracy the operational score of the next hedge fund on which he performs operational due diligence. Instead, by using a linear regression forecast based on the existing scores of hedge funds reviewed, contingent on whatever data we are graphing at the time, an investor can make a guess as to the general range of values the operational score of the next fund (assuming that fund would be investable based on a particular investor's criteria) under review should have. If the score of the next fund varies greatly from the regression line, an investor should review

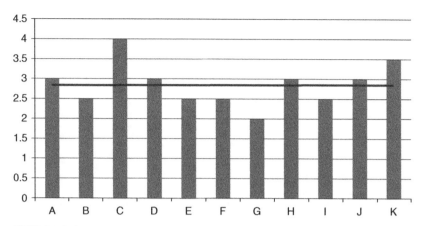

EXHIBIT 9.3 Example of Linear Regression Analysis on Sample Universe

why a certain fund has received a much higher, or lower, operational score than the linear regression analysis of the existing universe would have predicted. An example of using a linear regression line to predict a future score is given in Exhibit 9.5.

When a new manager is added to the universe, the shift in the linear regression line from the one constructed for the previous universe should also be examined for any materiality. An example of the analysis of such a shift in the linear regression line is shown in Exhibit 9.6. The purpose of these types of analyses is that where a new hedge fund is added to the

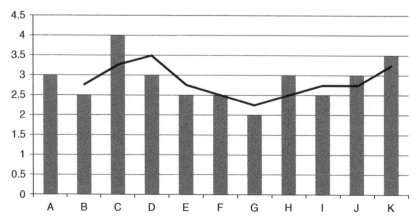

EXHIBIT 9.4 Example of Moving Average Tracking on Sample Universe

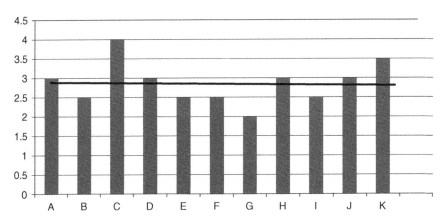

EXHIBIT 9.5 Example of Linear Regression Forecasting on Sample Universe

universe that has a substantially higher or lower operational score than the rest of the investable universe, investors should consider whether they have adequately vetted and considered such risks relative to the rest of the hedge funds that sit alongside it in a portfolio of hedge funds.

Graphical universe analysis techniques can also be utilized to look at subsections of hedge fund managers within the larger total operational score universe. Assume that a large hedge fund allocator, such as a fund of hedge funds, wants to analyze the results of all of the final operational scores for each of the hedge fund managers held in a certain portfolio. For purposes of this example, we can refer to these managers as the *portfolio universe*. This fund of hedge funds may then wish to analyze subsets of this universe. These subsets could include regional subsets of hedge fund managers (e.g., all managers domiciled in Asia), strategy subsets (e.g., all global macro hedge fund managers), or assets under management subsets (e.g., all managers who have over $1 billion under management). Subset analysis can be useful when considering the addition of new hedge fund managers within a certain sector or the replacement of existing portfolio managers with new managers.

Now that we have discussed several techniques for analyzing the data produced as the result of a scorecard approach, we can now discuss the process for utilizing such scores to both screen hedge funds for certain operational risks and construct portfolios that can assist investors in implementing directional operational objectives. Before we continue our discussion regarding directional operational views and their implementation when constructing a portfolio of hedge funds, it is important to clarify a

Before Addition of New Manager:

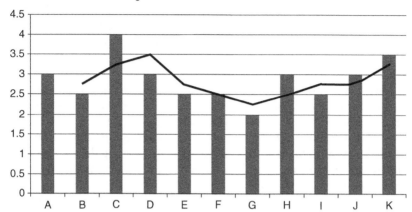

After Addition of New Manager:

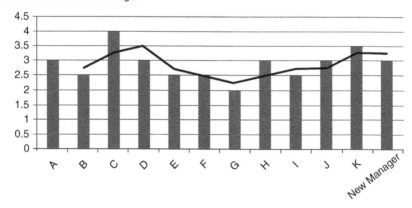

EXHIBIT 9.6 Example of Shift in Moving Average with Addition of New Manager to Sample Universe

basic assumption we are making. We assume that when investors invest in an underlying hedge fund, they are gaining exposure to the operational risks of that hedge fund. This statement is nothing revolutionary or even new to the discussion of operational risk in this text. It is nonetheless noteworthy, as it directly relates to how investors accept such risks. For example, if a hedge fund has a certain amount of operational risk with respect to valuation issues, by allocating to this fund investors are proactively voting with their wallet, and stating that these valuation risks are above their minimum operational threshold. Additionally, by making an allocation to this hedge fund, investors are actively deciding to accept such risks. The problem is that most investors internalize this dialogue and do not proactively make such choices or actively manage the operational risk exposures they have taken, whether consciously or unknowingly.

Furthermore, the additive effects of such operational risks within portfolios of hedge funds, beyond certain minimum thresholds, are often not considered as part of the portfolio construction process. It is during this portfolio construction process where problems of the conglomeration of operational exposures to certain risks first arise. By ignoring these conglomeration effects, investors may combine several funds with common operational weaknesses or exposures in the same portfolio without ever realizing it. Consequently, the resulting portfolio may have larger operational exposures to certain risks and be overall more risky than originally intended.

PROACTIVE MANAGEMENT OF OPERATIONAL RISKS

As we will demonstrate, the proactive management of directional operational views does not need to be based solely, or even at all, on the results of the scorecard approach. The yardstick by which operational views are measured could be qualitative in nature. Indeed, it could be argued that the scores assigned by an investor when completing an operational scorecard for a hedge fund already contain reflections of the investor's qualitative evaluation and biases toward certain operational factors. Consider a hedge fund investor who has a high-level operational bias for avoiding managers who are based in a certain jurisdiction, because she feels the financial regulatory regime lacks certain oversight or enforcement capabilities, as compared to other jurisdictions that she believes are more stringent. We can assume that as part of the scoring process this investor will assign a lower score to a hedge fund that operates in such an emerging jurisdiction than to an already established one. Consequently, it could also be argued that hedge fund investors who take an active role in designing the categories and rating scales of the scorecard model inherently, by design, run the risk of building in certain model design biases reflective of their preexisting operational views. Such biases may result in model error, which would skew the results of an operational review via biased category design. There is nothing inherently wrong with this on face value, as the purpose is to evaluate operational risks based on comparison to a preexisting investor threshold. Therefore, having the investor, either by intention or subconsciously, build this threshold into the category design is not necessarily something to be frowned upon;

however, as referenced in Chapter 8, too much of such a practice can lead to foregone conclusions before the scores are assigned.

Before introducing the process by which such directional operational views can be implemented, we should stress that the screening process by which we go about implementing such views need not relate in any way to the scorecard process. It is true that attempting to quantify the results of an operational due diligence review facilitates certain types of analysis. It is often easier to manipulate numbers as opposed to qualitative concepts. That is not to say that such a qualitative review is impossible. On the contrary, the benefit of the approach we will discuss is that both quantitative operational scores and qualitative operational notions can be analyzed in order to construct a portfolio of hedge funds that best coincides with a particular series of operational goals. We call the process for doing this *Multivariate Commonality Analysis*.

PROTECTING AGAINST CONGLOMERATION RISKS: MULTIVARIATE COMMONALITY ANALYSIS

Once the operational due diligence process for a particular hedge fund is complete, investors are left with a number of different operational data points concerning the hedge fund manager under consideration. Investors can then attempt to quantify this data via a modeling technique such as an operational scorecard. By analyzing this data, investors can come to a determination as to the operational riskiness of the hedge fund. The process of Multivariate Commonality Analysis picks up where the scorecard process leaves off to build a bridge linking the asset allocation and operational due diligence processes.

As investors perform the operational due diligence process, they will begin to gather certain operational data that is not necessarily specific to any one hedge fund but rather reflective of operational trends in the space. These trends could relate to a number of different factors. For example, an investor may be told by a number of different hedge funds that they have had an increasing amount of trouble from a particular software vendor in obtaining support for an existing accounting system. Another example may be that an investor may hear from a number of U.K.-based hedge funds that the Financial Services Authority has ramped up monitoring efforts in regard to activities in certain types of instruments or participation in a certain group of publicly listed companies. Such data may cause an investor to develop particular views with respect to certain high-level operational trends over time. These view may not necessarily be the outgrowth of rumors heard during the due diligence process. On the contrary, investors could develop these views from their own individual research on operational issues, perhaps under an *operational mosaic theory* approach.

Such macroeconomic or global operational views on certain operational subjects could be the outgrowth of beliefs about the future of certain investment themes. An example of such a correlated outgrowth would be an investor who believes that due to the current world social climate there will be an increasing demand for security products that assist in the prevention of identity theft through increased data security. The investor begins to research the different technologies in this space, including several information security products utilized by financial services firms, including hedge funds. This could translate into a specific operational view that any hedge fund this investor allocates to must meet a certain high threshold with regard to its information security policies. Perhaps this investor feels that a certain information security product is head-and-shoulders above all others and, all things being equal, wants to overweight his exposure to hedge funds that utilize this product.

Additionally, investors could simply be in search of diversity and not wish to overexpose themselves to any one vendor or counterparty. With the recent events in the credit markets, the monitoring of such counterparty exposures of the underlying hedge funds to which investors have allocated has been especially important. This has been of specific importance recently for such hedge fund counterparties as prime brokers and cash management organizations. In addition to understanding how a hedge fund monitors its counterparty exposures as part of the operational due diligence process, once investors are comfortable with this process it is important to understand that when a hedge fund has counterparty risk to a certain organization, investors are taking on part of the risk to this counterparty via their investment in the hedge fund. Similarly, it is of paramount importance for investors to monitor such counterparty exposures within portfolios of hedge funds.

One example that highlights the importance of monitoring such counterparty exposures took place in August 2007, when Sentinel Management Group, a third-party cash management firm utilized by many hedge funds, froze withdrawals by its clients, some of which included hedge funds. This led to a flurry of media surrounding Sentinel and the hedge funds that had exposure to it, potential losses for the funds that had exposures, and an increased focus on the cash management processes of hedge funds in general. As an aside, in a subsequent lawsuit, the Securities and Exchange Commission (SEC) accused the company of misappropriation of money from client accounts. More recently, the bankruptcy trustee for Sentinel Management Group has sued its former auditor, McGladrey & Pullen, for, among other claims, malpractice. In terms of portfolio construction, if an investor had proactively decided to diversify exposure to hedge funds that utilized

Sentinel, he most likely would not have realized as significant losses due to the failure of Sentinel compared with an investor who had constructed a portfolio of several hedge funds that utilized Sentinel. Managing operational risks toward a goal of diversity could lead to benefits under such a scenario. Regardless of how such opinions are formed or change over time, prudent investors will seek to actively manage the operational risks to which they are exposed because of underlying hedge fund investments. The process of managing such risks can be implemented by careful selection during the initial hedge fund allocation process as well as the ongoing rebalancing process.

OPERATIONAL DIRECTIONAL VIEWS

The purposes of developing viewpoints with respect to certain operational risks could be to protect against these risks, either actual or anticipated, create an operational hedge, or make a directional bet to overweight or underweight a certain operational exposure. When constructing a portfolio of hedge funds, either for an individual investor or in a larger fund-of-hedge-funds context, there are significant latent risks present due to the aggregation of operational exposures that may not be appropriately monitored by the vast majority of conventional risk management departments. These departments tend to focus instead on the aggregation of investment-related exposures or macroeconomic considerations.

In particular, with regard to systematic operational exposures, an investor may have a particular macroeconomic investment view or theme that runs throughout his portfolio, such as an opinion as to the nature of inflation in the United States, the direction of the price of oil, or the impact of Chinese demand on the price of steel. Operational risk considerations are a type of macro-operational overlay to the investment allocation decision-making process. It should be noted that in the process of Multivariate Commonality Analysis, the operational views that are being screened for are of a generalist nature.

Said another way, the operational goals that Multivariate Commonality Analysis seeks to optimize around must be of a global as opposed to a local nature. In the operational hedge fund context, local items can be thought of as idiosyncratic risks specific to a certain hedge fund. Examples of such idiosyncratic operational risks could be the risks associated with a specific employee of the hedge fund or a proprietary accounting system. Such operational factors are specific to a certain hedge fund, and so, by definition, because of their uniqueness, an investor cannot optimize around these idiosyncratic operational factors. For example, an investor seeking to avoid exposure to a certain individual employed by a hedge fund will simply not invest with the specific hedge fund that employs this individual. There is nothing to diversify, or overweight, or underweight, since the factor exists only in the individual operational landscape of a single hedge fund.

However, global or macro-operational factors can be thought of as operational factors that are common to or shared among several hedge funds. Examples include counterparty exposures, regulatory registrations, use of nonproprietary software and hardware, and so on.

EXAMPLE OF MULTIVARIATE COMMONALITY ANALYSIS

Consider an example where an investor is seeking to construct a portfolio of hedge funds. Via the investment due diligence process, this investor has found seven different investable funds from each of four different hedge fund style categories. The investor wants to construct a portfolio with eight hedge funds in total by selecting two funds from each category. As a result of her investment analysis, this investor has a preference for two funds in each category over the others, but considers all investable for her portfolio. Now the investor seeks to screen these 28 funds (seven funds from each category times four categories) through an operational due diligence process. During her operational due diligence, the investor scores the funds' operational risk using a Macro-Plus scorecard approach. For this example, we will consider the seven funds in one particular hedge fund style category, Global Macro. The scores the investor has assigned to the Legal/Regulatory/Compliance category are shown in Exhibit 9.7. The investor then decides to set her operational risk threshold for each primary operational category at 2. Any hedge funds with an operational score in a particular primary category above

EXHIBIT 9.7 Scores for Primary Compliance Category for Ten Global Macro Funds

	Overall Compliance Score (1 to 5)
Fund 1	1
Fund 2	2
Fund 3	2.5
Fund 4	4
Fund 5	1.5
Fund 6	4.5
Fund 7	3

EXHIBIT 9.8 Threshold Screening and Resulting Portfolio for Primary
Compliance Category for Seven Global Macro Funds

	Overall Compliance Score (1 to 5)	Below Threshold Level (Less Than or Equal to 2)	Above Threshold Level (>2)
Fund 1	1	1	
Fund 2	2	2	
Fund 3	2.5		2.5
Fund 4	4		4
Fund 5	1.5	1.5	
Fund 6	4.5		4.5
Fund 7	3		3

Resulting Hedge Fund Portfolio:

Fund 3	2.5
Fund 4	4
Fund 6	4.5
Fund 7	3

a 2 are considered investable, and those with a score of 2 or lower are not
investable. The results of this operational threshold screening process are
shown in Exhibit 9.8.

To illustrate the process of implementing these views under a Multivariate Commonality Analysis approach, we will consider three different
objectives (scenarios) with respect to two operational global data points
under the Legal/Regulatory/Compliance primary category. The first global
operational data point will be a list of regulators with whom the underlying
hedge fund is registered. This data point is inclusive of both compulsory
registrations and any that may be voluntary. The second macro-operational
data point will be the names of the compliance consulting firms utilized, if
any. In this example, we will consider these factors among four different
hedge funds. The raw data for each of the two operational data points for
each fund is outlined in Exhibit 9.9.

FIRST OBJECTIVE: TOTAL DIVERSITY GOAL

Under the first scenario, we will consider a goal of total diversity with
respect to each of the two abovementioned operational factors. This goal

EXHIBIT 9.9   Raw Sample Data for Two Factors

Fund A		
	Factor 1—Regulatory Registration	SEC, FSA registered
	Factor 2—Compliance Consultant	Compliance Consultant A used
Fund B		
	Factor 1—Regulatory Registration	FSA registered
	Factor 2—Compliance Consultant	Compliance Consultant A used
Fund C		
	Factor 1—Regulatory Registration	HK SFC, FSA registered
	Factor 2—Compliance Consultant	Compliance Consultant B used
Fund D		
	Factor 1—Regulatory Registration	SEC registered
	Factor 2—Compliance Consultant	N/A—No compliance Consultant utilized

could be the result of several different investor motivations. In regard to the first global operational data point, the list of regulatory regimes in which the hedge fund is registered, an investor may not have a strong conviction about the regulatory regimes of any jurisdiction in which a certain fund is registered; she wants to diversify her exposure to such regulators via the underlying hedge funds in which they invest. A second motivation for diversity in regulatory regime exposure could be that an investor does not want to overweight any single regulator in particular, instead preferring to diversify the regulatory risk present in her portfolio.

Similarly, with respect to the second global operational data point, the list of compliance consulting firms utilized by the hedge funds, an investor might not have strong conviction about any one compliance consulting firm, and subsequently would not want to overweight his exposure to any single firm. Another motivation for wanting to diversify compliance consulting risk is that an investor might not have enough knowledge about compliance consulting firms to make a directional operational bet with regard to these firms (i.e., overweight or underweight). Therefore, total diversity with respect to this factor may be a desirable goal.

The first step in the Multivariate Commonality Analysis process is to construct a *Commonality Matrix* for each global operational data point or factor under consideration. In this case, we will construct two Commonality

Matrixes, one for each factor. The purpose of the Commonality Matrix construction is to cross-reference each of the hedge fund managers' global operational data points. Additionally, the Commonality Matrix will allow us to outline which factors each fund has in common with the other funds under comparison. The Commonality Matrixes with respect to each operational data category are shown in Exhibit 9.10. The results of the constructed Commonality Matrix will allow an investor to determine which funds have certain factors in common. For example, in relation to the first factor of regulatory registration, Fund A and Fund B are both registered with the Financial Services Authority (FSA), as indicated in the Commonality Matrix. Fund D and Fund C, however, have no common registrations and as such the Commonality Matrix has been labeled with *no commonality* of registration between the two hedge funds for the regulatory registration factor. Similarly, concerning the second global operational data point, the list of compliance consultants registered with, only Fund A and Fund B share a common compliance consultant, Compliance Consultant A. All the other funds share no commonality among compliance consultants.

The next step in the Multivariate Commonality Analysis process is to analyze the results of the Commonality Matrixes. This is outlined in Exhibit 9.11. We can then cross-reference these results, as outlined in Exhibit 9.12. The conclusion drawn from this Multivariate Commonality Analysis is to select Fund A and Fund D.

SECOND OBJECTIVE: FSA OVERWEIGHT GOAL

Our second scenario relates to a situation where an investor sets outs with the global operational objective of overweighting his exposure to the FSA. The motivation for this operational view could be that the investor feels that hedge funds that are FSA registered are subject to higher scrutiny than in other jurisdictions; perhaps the recent implementation of the MiFid initiative is a factor in shaping his views, and this increased scrutiny is viewed in a positive light by this investor. For this scenario, let us assume that the investor wishes to maintain total diversity of compliance consultants. Using the same raw data from Exhibit 9.9, we can review the results of the Commonality Matrix of the first factor with respect to its adherence to the FSA overweight goal. The results of this analysis are summarized in Exhibit 9.13. We can then cross-reference these results as outlined in Exhibit 9.14. The conclusion drawn from this Multivariate Commonality Analysis is two different fund combinations: Fund A and Fund C or Fund B and Fund C.

EXHIBIT 9.10 Two Commonality Matrixes for Two Different Operational Categories

Factor 1—Regulatory Registration

	Fund A	Fund B	Fund C	Fund D
Fund A		FSA	FSA	SEC
Fund B	FSA		FSA	NO COMMONALITY
Fund C	FSA	FSA		NO COMMONALITY
Fund D	SEC	NO COMMONALITY	NO COMMONALITY	

Factor 2—Compliance Consultant

	Fund A	Fund B	Fund C	Fund D
Fund A		Compliance Consultant A used	NO COMMONALITY	NO COMMONALITY
Fund B	Compliance Consultant A used		NO COMMONALITY	NO COMMONALITY
Fund C	NO COMMONALITY	NO COMMONALITY		NO COMMONALITY
Fund D	NO COMMONALITY	NO COMMONALITY	NO COMMONALITY	

EXHIBIT 9.11 Analysis of Common Factor Results from Commonality Matrixes with Total Diversity Goal

Factor 1—Regulatory Registration

Goal—Total diversity of regulators

An investor would not want the following portfolio combinations:
Fund A + Fund B
Fund A + Fund C
Fund A + Fund D
Fund B + Fund C

Any other combinations would yield diversified regulator risk:
Fund A + Fund D
Fund D + Fund C

Factor 2—Compliance Consultant

Goal—Total diversity of compliance consultants

An investor would not want the following portfolio combinations:
Fund A + Fund B
Fund C + Fund D

Any other combinations would yield diversified compliance consultant risk:
Fund A + Fund D
Fund A + Fund C
Fund B + Fund C
Fund B + Fund D

EXHIBIT 9.12 Summary Analysis of Common Factor Results from Commonality Matrixes

Goal—Total Diversity of Regulators	*Goal—Total Diversity of Compliance Consultants*	*Comments*
	Fund A + Fund C	No Match
	Fund B + Fund C	No Match
	Fund B + Fund D	No Match
Fund D + Fund C		No Match
Fund A + Fund D	Fund A + Fund D	Match

EXHIBIT 9.13　　Analysis of Common Factor Results from Commonality Matrixes with FSA Overweight Goal

---

Factor 1—Regulatory Registration

Goal—FSA overweight

An investor would not want the following portfolio combinations:
Fund A + Fund D
Fund B + Fund D
Fund C + Fund D

Any other combinations would yield FSA overweight goal:
Fund A + Fund B
Fund A + Fund C
Fund B + Fund C

Factor 2—Compliance Consultant

Goal—Total diversity of compliance consultants

An investor would not want the following portfolio combinations:
Fund A + Fund B
Fund C + Fund D

Any other combinations would yield diversified compliance consultant risk:
Fund A + Fund D
Fund A + Fund C
Fund B + Fund C
Fund B + Fund D

EXHIBIT 9.14　　Summary Analysis of Common Factor Results from Commonality Matrixes with FSA Overweight Goal

Goal—FSA Overweight	Goal—Total Diversity of Compliance Consultants	Comments
Fund A + Fund C	Fund A + Fund C	Match
Fund B + Fund C	Fund B + Fund C	Match
	Fund B + Fund D	No Match
		No Match
	Fund A + Fund D	No Match
Fund A + Fund B		No Match

THIRD OBJECTIVE: FSA UNDERWEIGHT GOAL

The third and final scenario is a situation where an investor sets outs with the operational objective of underweighting his exposure to the FSA. The investor's motivation for underweighting the FSA could be the converse of the reasoning of another investor wanting to overweight the FSA, such as the belief that hedge funds that are registered with the FSA may be subject to a lower level of regulatory scrutiny than those that are SEC registered. Perhaps a particular investor feels that the obligations of FSA registration are too onerous for hedge funds, and consequently wants to underweight his exposure to FSA-registered managers. It should be made clear at the outset of this discussion that the notion of underweighting a particular factor, such as the FSA, does not necessarily imply the overweighting of other factors.

Once again, using the same raw data from Exhibit 9.9, we can review the results of the Commonality Matrix for the first factor with respect to its adherence to the FSA underweight goal. The results of this analysis are summarized in Exhibit 9.15. We can then cross-reference these results as outlined in Exhibit 9.16. The conclusion drawn from this Multivariate Commonality Analysis is two different fund combinations: Fund B and Fund D or Fund A and Fund D.

CONCLUSIONS OF SCENARIO ANALYSIS

As we have just seen, the benefit of Multivariate Commonality Analysis is to allow investors to add another degree of customization to the portfolio construction process. This customization can help investors to be more proactive in monitoring their operational risk exposures and even make directional bets regarding certain global operational factors. As just demonstrated, such customization techniques do make a difference when it comes to fund selection. Contingent on the operational goals specified, the Multivariate Commonality Analysis in each of the three scenarios described earlier produced different results as to which two hedge funds should be selected. While all four funds, out of the original seven, in the Global Macro category were above the minimum operational threshold, and therefore considered investable, such analysis allows investors to be proactive in managing operational bets rather than simply selecting any two out of the four based solely on investment considerations.

EXHIBIT 9.15 Analysis of Common Factor Results from Commonality Matrixes with FSA Underweight Goal

Factor 1—Regulatory Registration

Goal—FSA underweight

> **An investor would not want the following portfolio combinations:**
> Fund A + Fund B
> Fund A + Fund C
> Fund B + Fund C
>
> **Any other combinations would yield FSA underweight goal:**
> Fund B + Fund D
> Fund C + Fund D
> Fund A + Fund D

Factor 2—Compliance Consultant

Goal—Total diversity of compliance consultants

> **An investor would not want the following portfolio combinations:**
> Fund A + Fund B
> Fund C + Fund D
>
> **Any other combinations would yield diversified compliance consultant risk:**
> Fund A + Fund D
> Fund A + Fund C
> Fund B + Fund C
> Fund B + Fund D

EXHIBIT 9.16 Summary Analysis of Common Factor Results from Commonality Matrixes for FSA Underweight Goal

Goal—FSA Underweight	*Goal—Total Diversity of Compliance Consultants*	*Comments*
Fund B + Fund D	Fund B + Fund D	Match
Fund C + Fund D		No Match
Fund A + Fund D	Fund A + Fund D	Match
	Fund A + Fund C	No Match
	Fund B + Fund C	No Match

CONSIDERING OPERATIONAL REVIEWS IN THE HEDGE FUND PORTFOLIO REBALANCING PROCESS

The process of portfolio construction should be a dynamic one. Indeed, existing hedge fund portfolio allocations are often rebalanced with some frequency. To clarify, rebalancing refers to the process of reevaluating the weights of each manager in the portfolio as a percentage of the total hedge fund allocation, as well as possibly adding new managers and/or removing certain existing managers. The results of the rebalancing process are generally reflective of a number of factors, including the shifting financial climate, certain macroeconomic views, and investors changing opinions about these macroeconomic factors.

A common caveat in regard to the rebalancing of hedge fund portfolios is that investors should avoid a process of just optimizing historical data. For example, historically positive-performing managers may tend to revert back to poor performance over time as eventually cycles change and these managers realize negative returns. When rebalancing portfolios of hedge funds, it is important for investors to consider the same operational conglomeration risks that were originally reviewed at the time the initial hedge fund portfolio was constructed. Additionally, the rebalancing process provides investors with the opportunity to incorporate any new directional operational views they may have developed since the time of the last rebalancing.

OPERATIONAL DRAG

We can define *operational drag* as the negative effects of operational risk on the efficiency of an organization. This concept can be analogized to the theory of drag in aviation. The NASA website defines drag as "the aerodynamic force that opposes an aircraft's motion through the air."[1] In a hedge fund operational risk context, operational drag is the forces within an organization that oppose the forces of operational efficiency and competency. The higher the operational riskiness of an organization, the higher the operational drag. This positive correlation is summarized in Exhibit 9.17. Translating this concept into an expected-return framework, we can see the negative correlation between expected return and operational drag, as summarized in Exhibit 9.18. By lowering the operational drag throughout the organization, a hedge fund can increase its operating efficiency and subsequently lower its total operational risk.

Operational drag is positively correlated with operational risk, but this correlation is not necessarily linear. This statement requires a bit of clarification. Consider the operational risks associated with business continuity

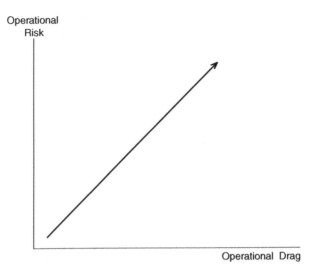

EXHIBIT 9.17 Positive Correlation between Operational Risk and Operational Drag

planning and disaster recovery (BCP/DR). While a hedge fund may have exposure to the risks associated with a less-than-perfect BCP/DR plan, this risk exposure does not necessarily impact the operating efficiency of a hedge fund unless a business disruption event occurs. On days where everything runs smoothly, the risk has not manifested itself as an actual drag on the

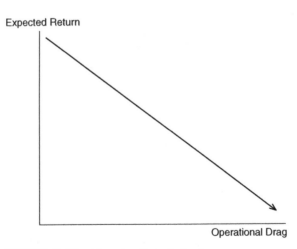

EXHIBIT 9.18 Negative Correlation between Expected Return and Operational Drag

EXHIBIT 9.19   Sample Analysis of the Operational Drag versus the Operational Score

	Operational Competency	Operational Drag
Category 1	2.5	1.5
Category 2	3.5	0.5
Category 3	2	2
Category 4	1	3
Category 5	2.5	1.5
Category 6	2.5	1.5
Total	*14*	*10*

operations of the organization. The question worth considering now is, Does this lack of realization mean that an investor should not account, plan, discount, or hedge for the operational risks associated with this BCP/DR imperfection? A prudent, risk-averse investor would most likely reply in the negative.

There is no one agreed-upon way by which the operational drag on an organization should be calculated. We can expand the definition of operational drag to think of it not only in terms of the negative implications it has for the operational efficiency of an organization, but also as an indicator of where there is room for operational improvement. Within a scorecard context, this operational room for improvement is the difference between the perfect operational score within a particular category scale and the operational score given to the hedge fund under consideration. A sample analysis of the operational drag (i.e., room for improvement) as compared to the operational competency (i.e., earned operational score) for six different operational categories is outlined in Exhibit 9.19.

One way we propose to utilize the individual operational drag for each operational risk category for purposes of applying operational risk considerations toward analysis of hedge fund risks and expected returns is via the creation of a metric that we call the *Operational Factor*. Returning to Exhibit 9.19, we can assign values to the operational drag in each category. This value assignment is summarized in Exhibit 9.20. Reviewing this data, we see that the value of overall operational drag of this particular hedge fund in relation to the six categories under review is 10. Interpreting this data, we can further state that out of a total operational competency possible of 24 (i.e., a maximum score of four for each of the six categories), this fund has demonstrated it is approximately 58.3% operationally competent with an operational drag of 41.7%. Despite the fact that these two percentages sum up to a total of 100%, it is important to remember exactly what this 100% represents.

	Operational Competency	Operational Drag
Category 1	2.5	1.5
Category 2	3.5	0.5
Category 3	2	2
Category 4	1	3
Category 5	2.5	1.5
Category 6	2.5	1.5
Totals	*14*	*10*

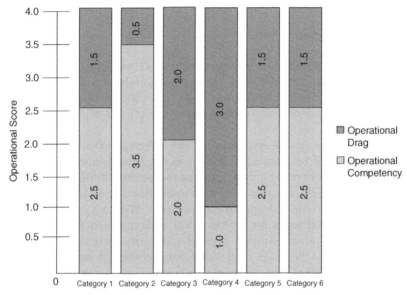

EXHIBIT 9.20   Operational Drag versus Operational Competency

It does *not* represent the total non-investment-related risk landscape of a hedge fund. Rather, it represents only the entire operational risk diagnosed by the categories that the scorecard model has designated. Therefore, if certain operational risk considerations were omitted from the category creation process, then these category scores could not represent those risks. It could be argued that the purpose of discretionary scorecard bonuses or penalties is to account for those risks unaccounted for within the primary scorecard categories. Generally, these discretionary scores are based on certain predefined criteria. A weakness of the use of such discretionary scores, and in a broader context, scorecard models in general, is that there is no way to address unique operational risks for operational issues specific to one hedge fund, or reflect the changing nature of an investor's global operational views, as mentioned earlier. So the question remains, How do we go about accounting for the remaining operational risks present in a hedge fund that are unaccounted for by the scorecard model?

META RISKS

The April 15, 2008, report of the Investors' Committee of the President's Working Group on Financial Markets issued a report titled, "Principles and Best Practices for Hedge Fund Investors." This report references the notion of *meta risks,* which it defines as "the qualitative risks beyond explicit measurable financial risks. They include human and organizational behavior, moral hazard, excessive reliance on and misuse of quantitative tools, complexity and lack of understanding of market interactions, and the very nature of capital markets in which extreme events happen with far greater regularity than standard models suggest."

The concept of meta risks is nothing new. It has been focused on in regulatory and tax regimes in an attempt to provide regulatory guidance toward the administration of certain social policies. It is sometimes referred to as "the risk management of risk management."[2] In a hedge fund operational risk context, we can think of meta risks as the catchall category used to account for all non-investment-related risks not covered by the particular scorecard model in use.

Questions could be raised about the value of adding such a discretionary, black-box factor to our analysis. In response, we could argue that while there is a high degree of subjectivity in assigning a value to these meta risks, that does not mean that they should be simply ignored. Further, the assignment of such a value by an investor will necessarily be reflective of that investor's operational views. Therefore, the meta risk value assigned will generally take into account the particularities of any one investor's views toward to riskiness of a certain operational factor relative to his threshold.

Finally, the assignment of a value to meta risks is an area where a highly skilled operational risk professional, who has a deep understanding of operational trends in the marketplace, can add direct value to the risk management and portfolio construction process. This is similar to the way in which other risk management professionals and portfolio hedge fund managers can add value by being correct on the nature and degree of bets they make in selecting investments. In summary, the process of assigning values to meta risks is inherently subjective and can vary from investor to investor; however, the subjective way in which these values are applied does not imply that the process of accounting for such risks should be ignored.

OPERATIONAL FACTOR

Now that we have established a procedure for calculating the operational drag for each different hedge fund category, as well as defined the concept of meta risks, we can discuss a new concept we are proposing in this text, called the *Operational Factor*. The formula is as follows:

$$\text{Operational Factor} = (X) \times [\Sigma(\text{Operational Drag for Each Category})]$$
$$+ (Y) \times (\text{Meta Risk Factor})$$

The Meta Risk Factor represents the quantitative value assigned to represent the value of the meta risks present in a particular hedge fund manager. X represents the weight assigned to the operational drag risks and Y represents the weight assigned to the Meta Risk Factor. The sum of X and Y should equal 100%.

The Operational Factor represents the total operational risk that is unaccounted for in the scorecard plus any other risks that are included in the Meta Risk Factor. Therefore, the sum of these factors, regardless of how they are weighted, should equal 100%, which represents the total amount of operational riskiness of a hedge fund. This is demonstrated in Exhibit 9.21. It should be noted that the assignment of the weights of X and Y is entirely discretionary. Some investors may feel that a 50–50 split is warranted. Others may feel that the scorecard methodology they are employing is very comprehensive and therefore they want to give X a much higher weighting than Y. Different weighting methodologies for X and Y each have their benefits and drawbacks; however, it is important to note that both X and Y should be given some degree of weight. That is, X and Y should both be greater than zero. This is because even if an investor uses a million-category scorecard, there will still be other meta risks unaccounted for that should be represented with a positive weight given to Y.

The inclusion of the meta risks in the equation for the operational factors merits clarification. If we think of the operational scorecard as an attempt to quantify those risk areas that are of particular importance to an investor, and these have traditionally been key areas of particularly high operational risk exposures, and we further think of the discretionary penalties and bonuses in relation to key areas of sensitivity that an investor universally wants to reward or penalize, then the apparent question becomes, what other operational risks are we not accounting for? The answer lies in the fact that the scorecard, by its very nature, is self-limiting in the number and types of operational risk areas reviewed. In an attempt to acknowledge this, many operational due diligence professionals seek to accompany a scorecard

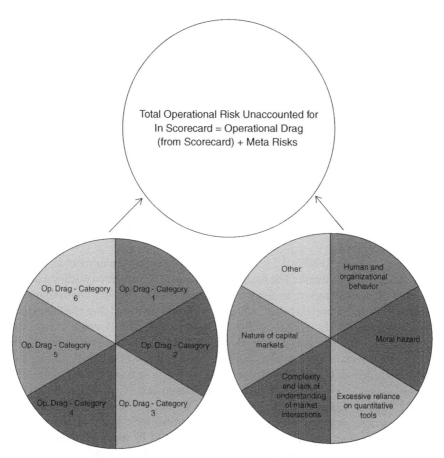

EXHIBIT 9.21 Example of Operational Factor Weighting Components

with a verbal summary of the highlights of their review of the different operational areas of a firm. This practice is certainly advisable, as most users of an operational due diligence report, be they investors or investment professionals on an investment committee, want more detail as to how certain category scores were arrived at. The question we are raising in this text is, even with the multitude of free text fields and areas for the filling in of all the descriptive areas of a firm, why should the entire operational due diligence process be so limiting as to not include these other meta risk categories?

For example, consider a hedge fund that employs relatives. Most modern scorecard category methodologies, inclusive of discretionary categories, do not contain a way to score a hedge fund based on such a criterion. Yet, most operational risk professionals, and likely investors as well, would agree that having relatives work in the same firm is generally frowned upon. This is especially true when one employee works, for example, as a trader, while his brother works in the back office. Such arrangements are fraught with inherent conflicts of interest that many investors and hedge funds alike seek to avoid. There is nothing wrong with the practice of employing relatives on face value, and if the appropriate system of checks and balances is in place, such conflicts may be partially mitigated. That said, most would still agree that there is an increased element of operational riskiness inherent in such a situation; yet most operational risk reviews either would not include such a fact, or would relegate it to deep within the textual descriptions of a firm. The purpose of including a Meta Risk Factor in the calculation of the Operational Factor is to help those reviewing the operational risks of a hedge fund to account for, and seek to quantify, such risks that do not fit on the scorecard.

Returning to Exhibit 9.21, we have included six different meta factors in the meta-factor universe. The first five are those that have been outlined in the above-mentioned report to the President's Working Group. The remaining factor has simply been labeled "Other." It should be stated that the examples of meta risks in the report to the President's Working Group are by no means the only categories that should be utilized when evaluating meta risks. However, assuming that these are the categories we will utilize, we have included an Other category to account for those meta risks that are not included in any of the other five meta risk categories. These other meta risks could be such vague things as an investor's reflection that she felt a hedge fund manager was not being completely truthful with her, but she cannot put her finger on why that would be. They could be more concrete items, such as when a hedge fund investor notices that a hedge fund under review has lavish offices and branded coffee mugs. Do any of these things make the hedge fund more operationally risky? The answer to such a question will vary from investor to investor. If the answer is yes, an investor should openly account for such risks rather than refer to them in passing or not actively mention them at all.

Another question could be raised in regard to the Meta Risk Factor: Why not simply add new discretionary categories every time a new risk, which the scorecard had not previously accounted for, comes up? There are several reasons why utilizing the Meta Risk Factor is preferable. First, if new discretionary categories are added each time a new risk comes across an investor's plate, then each of the existing managers under review need to be rescored with this additional discretionary factor in mind. Second, the risk included in the meta risk category may be unique to the particular hedge fund under review. As such, adding the discretionary category covering such risks would have no effect on the other hedge funds previously reviewed.

Additionally, the process of making such additions would invariably lead to an overly cumbersome scorecard full of discretionary one-off categories.

OPERATIONAL SCENARIO ANALYSIS

Hedge fund risk managers as well as those that manage portfolios of hedge funds perform all kinds of scenario analysis on their underlying investments. Generally, one of these scenarios is a total shock case where the capital markets as a whole, or whichever relevant section of the markets the manager is concerned with, experience a contagion-type, large-scale drawdown event. For both groups, hedge fund managers and those who oversee investment in portfolios of hedge funds, the results of these hypothetical scenarios generally factor into their allocation decisions. Via this approach, these managers seek to determine the absolute limits of the losses to which they may be exposed from these market dislocations as a result of the allocations in their portfolios.

Returning to our original thesis, we could logically pose the question as to why a risk manager would not create similar shock-type scenarios for the failure of a certain counterparty, manager fraud, a net asset value (NAV) restatement, a run on the bank in the form of mass redemptions at a hedge fund, or a host of other operational factors? To hazard a guess, I would say that this, in part, has to do not with the most patently intuitive knee-jerk reaction of notions of unwarranted manager optimism, but rather with two common points of view held by investors and hedge fund managers alike when posed with certain aspects of operational risk:

1. The ever-cynical, "If something bad (on the scale of a market-wide, contagion-type operational event) happens, everyone will be in the same boat."
2. "If I ignore operational risk, it will go away."

To argue the first point, we could simply point to the reaction of certain market participants directly after the events of September 11, 2001. Many of those investors, including hedge funds, that were able to continue trading and participate in markets when others were not, made a great deal of money. Clearly, when large-scale operational market events occur, there are multiple dinghies in the water, not all of which are sinking.

In regard to the second point, most investors are not born contrarians. Most people simply do not like to believe that established institutions, which manage hundreds of millions of dollars, or may have been in business for over 150 years, could ever experience crushingly large investment losses or even fail as a result of operational issues. This is like the 800-pound operational gorilla sitting in the corner of the room that no one wants to talk about. Certain investors, particularly those with short-term memory loss regarding the latest hedge fund blowup due to operational failure, are in a state of denial and subsequently do not properly account, or discount, for these risks when modeling the expected returns of their hedge fund investments. Others, however, meet these risks head on, account for them, and perform scenario analyses of them.

CAN OPERATIONAL RISK BE ENTIRELY ELIMINATED?

When discussing the concepts of operational drag and operational efficiency, a question worth considering is whether operational risk can ever be entirely eliminated. Said another way, is it possible for an investor to perform operational due diligence on a hedge fund and come to a determination that the fund has zero operational risk? Is operational risk, by its very nature, a symbiotic concept coexisting with its hedge fund host? After all, operational risk for a particular hedge fund could not exist without the hedge fund itself—but can the hedge fund exist without operational risk? Such theoretical questions may approach the borders of existentialism and are perhaps better left to philosophers rather than hedge fund investors, but we will do our best to frame a response to these questions in a practical context.

A generally accepted tenet of operational risk management is that the operational risk exposures of a hedge fund can certainly be mitigated by that hedge fund via thoughtful planning and execution of operational best practices. The question of whether such mitigation procedures in and of themselves can entirely eliminate operational risk necessarily relates first to how an investor defines operational risk. As we saw in Chapter 1, this is a difficult task, as there is no one commonly accepted definition. As a general rule, the broader the definition utilized, the more difficultly an investor will have in verifying the elimination of operational risk.

For example, if an investor defines operational risk solely in the context of the primary and secondary factors we have discussed throughout this text, then it is theoretically possible, by implementing operational best practices appropriate to the hedge fund under consideration, that a hedge fund could eliminate, to the satisfaction of a particular investor, all of the operational risks in each of the chosen operational categories. If, however, an investor defines operational risk as all the non-investment-related risk factors associated with a hedge fund, then it could certainly be argued that operational risk can never be fully eliminated. Why is this so? A good first attempt to answer this question relates to the following observation about human behavior in relation to the operational risks it poses for hedge funds:

> *An organization that is made up of people does not exhibit equilibrium because it is a living entity. It is always in the process of becoming something new and always in transition. As opposed to a machine, an organization of people is emergent in that it evolves over time and it is adaptive in that it reacts to feedback.*[3]

A hedge fund organization is not a sentient machine, but rather an organization primarily consisting of human knowledge workers who are prone to error. Additionally, as the above observation suggests, this organization is changing and adapting over time to its environment. Such changes include operational factors.

Up to now, we have considered operational risk mitigation in the context of actions taken by the hedge fund itself to minimize internal operational risk. There is a recent trend among hedge fund investors to seek external hedges to operational risk, such as insurance policies, against failures of hedge funds due to certain operational factors such as fraud. This trend will be further discussed in Chapter 10; however, for purposes of this discussion, we should consider whether even a combination of such external operational hedges, combined with operational best practices internal to the hedge fund, can completely eliminate the operational risk of a hedge fund. Once again, this relates to the broadness of the definition of operational risk utilized by the investor. Based on the available market data, and the evolving nature of the hedge fund organization, it would seem that even with application of such external hedges operational risk cannot be totally eliminated.

The final consideration concerning the possibility of totally eliminating operational risk will be the time frame over which we are considering the hedge fund. The longer the time under consideration, the more difficult the proof of elimination becomes. Consider the following two statements:

1. On Tuesday, April 14, 2009, between 2:34 A.M. and 2:35 A.M. Eastern Standard time, a particular hedge fund will have no operational drag as a result of zero operational risk at that point in time.
2. During 2009, the same hedge fund referenced above will have zero operational drag or failures as a result of zero operational risk exposures during this year.

Which of these two statements can be made with a higher degree of certainty? Due to the shorter length of time covered by the first statement, it is intuitive that this statement has a higher probability of being realized. Of course, the answer might change if we add to the hypothesis that the firm's chief technology officer decided to sabotage the firm and erased all its files and relevant backups at 2:33 A.M. The point is that while there is a higher likelihood of statement 1 being correct over statement 2, it is simply a prediction and cannot be asserted with 100% certainty. There is a chance, despite any internal operational best practices and controls, as well as the overlay of external hedges, that an unpredicted and unplanned for non-investment-related failure will damage the efficiency of the organization. Exactly how much damage is where the application of a discount factor to expected return comes into play.

FACTORING OPERATIONAL RISK INTO TOTAL RISK CALCULATIONS

The inclusion of such factors necessarily, with the one exception a riskless operational hedge fund, increases the overall riskiness of a hedge fund and presents a more accurate picture of the total risk of hedge fund investing. Calculations of the total risk present in a hedge fund should include factors for operational risk.

When considering the riskiness of a hedge fund, among the more commonly used terms are two interrelated concepts: *volatility* and *beta*. Within a hedge fund operational risk context, empirical evidence suggests that there is not necessarily a correlation between market volatility and operational risk. That is not to say that there is no correlation at all, but rather that such correlations cannot be generalized. For example, let us consider the operational risks related to counterparty exposures of a hedge fund. If events in the market cause the stability of a particular counterparty to come into question, then a hedge fund that has a large exposure to this counterparty, such as a prime broker, would generally be considered as having more operational risk than a hedge fund that did not have such exposure. If, however, we consider the operational risks concerning a less-market-facing area of a hedge fund's operational risk framework, such as its own internal accounting system, volatility of the financial markets would likely not have any material effect on the operational risk associated with the use of this system. Consequently, when considering the relationship between volatility and operational risk, only certain operational categories are generally affected and the impact of such market volatility can vary greatly among hedge funds.

Similarly, we cannot establish any conclusive rules for the relationship between a hedge fund's beta and its operational risk. The fact that a particular hedge fund is either more highly correlated or uncorrelated with the rest of the market or its hedge fund peers does not translate directly to notions of its operational riskiness. Other hedge fund evaluation techniques, such as the Sharpe Ratio and the Information Ratio, attempt to provide a framework for comparing hedge funds, in part, on the basis of return expectations. While we will later address the approach to discounting expected returns for operational risks, which would, all else being equal, reduce certain measurements such as the Sharpe Ratio, in this section we are discussing other risk calculations. Due to this lack of correlation, for the most part, among operational risk, volatility, and beta, we cannot simply increase the beta or volatility expectations of a hedge fund to account for increased operational risk. Rather, we are suggesting that when evaluating a hedge fund's total risk, we should not only consider such traditional measurements as beta, but also expand the discussion to the operational risk levels present in the hedge fund. This is summarized in the following formula:

$$\text{Total Hedge Fund Risk} = (\text{Investment Risk}) + W(\text{Operational Factor})$$

where W represents the discretionary multiplier. The purpose of the multiplier is to account for the magnitude by which an investor seeks to account for operational risk regarding investment-related risks. This multiplier could be based on a host of particular global operational views. One way to quantitatively monitor such risks is via measurements such as operational drag, a concept we introduced earlier in this chapter.

BEYOND SCORECARD APPROACHES: DISCOUNTING EXPECTED RETURN

As alluded to earlier in this text, the traditional mantra regarding hedge fund operational risk is that it is *risk without reward*. This statement should be examined in more detail before being accepted as fact. It has at its root the individual concepts of risk and reward. We can begin our discussion of this topic with Dr. Harry Markowitz, one of the seminal founders of modern portfolio theory.

A revolutionary area of Dr. Markowitz's studies included research in extending concepts of risk measurement and diversification toward the modern notions of *present value theory* held at the time. This research eventually led to the development of the *efficient frontier* and its integration into the *Capital Asset Pricing Model* (CAPM). There are a number of assumptions underlying the Markowitz portfolio theory. These assumptions include:

- Investors seek to maximize the expected return of total wealth.
- All investors have the same expected single-period investment horizon.
- All rational investors are risk-adverse; that is, they will accept greater risk only if they are compensated with a higher expected return.
- Investors base their investment decisions on the expected return and risk of an investment.

Dr. Markowitz analyzed these assumptions in the context of expected return versus risk, defined as standard deviation, in order to prove the benefits of diversity in security selection. This relationship is summarized in Exhibit 9.22.

The third assumption is the one that we will focus on for the purposes of our discussion. When considering the relationship between expected return and operational risk, we should first define what we mean by *expected return*. In this context, and for purposes of extending the Markowitz portfolio theory with some degree of common framework, we can think of expected

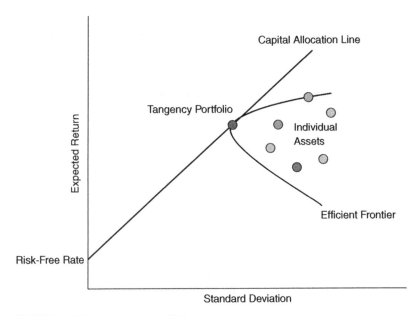

EXHIBIT 9.22 Markowitz Efficient Frontier

return as expected investment return. This could be contrasted with notions of expected operational return, a concept that is a bit more abstract. Said another way, if an investor is looking at possibly investing in a hedge fund, she has return expectation for that fund. From the hedge fund's perspective, there is a certain return, which may or may not coincide with the hedge fund investor's expected return, that the fund itself will generally espouse. These are investment-related performance expectations, and this is what is meant by *expected return* in this text.

Now let us turn to the next element, risk. Dr. Markowitz used the concept of standard deviation as a proxy for risk. According to Merriam-Webster, *standard deviation* can be defined as "a parameter that indicates the way in which a probability function or a probability density function is centered around its mean and that is equal to the square root of the moment in which the deviation from the mean is squared."[4] To clarify, regarding hedge fund operational risk, we will be continuing our discussion under the assumption that the standard deviation concept used by Dr. Markowitz does not refer to all risk, but simply investment-related risk. It could be argued that this investment expected return automatically includes any potential discount for operational considerations. This may be true when calculating the expected return for a portfolio of stocks; however, when the vast majority of hedge fund investors evaluate the return expectations of hedge funds, these forecasts are based almost exclusively on investment considerations and do not formally apply expected return discounts for operational risk. Consequently, as this is the common practice in the market, this is the logical framework under which our argument will progress. Dr. Markowitz's expected-return-versus-standard-deviation framework, as applied to our discussion of hedge fund operational risk, applies solely to investment-related risks.

As discussed earlier in the chapter, many hedge fund investors view the operational due diligence process as a safety net that will protect them from a certain level of operational risk. When discussing the notion that investors should apply discounts to the expected returns of either individual hedge funds or portfolios of hedge funds, many investors and portfolio construction professionals alike would argue that this process is already being implemented. Their reasoning goes something like this:

> *Our operational due diligence process screens for the operational risks of hedge funds. If a hedge fund has a certain level of operational risk beyond our organization's threshold, however it is defined, we will not consider this fund as investable. As such, we apply a 100% discount for funds that possess a level of operational riskiness beyond our threshold and no discount for funds that possess a level of operational riskiness with which we are comfortable.*

Also, they will typically state, for funds with which they are comfortable, they qualitatively have more operational convictions about some managers over others and factor these convictions into the asset allocation and portfolio construction weighting processes.

What we are suggesting here is a new approach. An all-or-nothing discount approach, such as previously described, is representative of a lack of process refinement. This binary threshold analysis extracts utility out of only the most basic level of the operational data acquired during the operational due diligence process. Once this initial threshold analysis is run, investors should both seek to implement particular operational goals in portfolio construction, via a methodology such as Multivariate Commonality Analysis, and factor in discounts for the operational riskiness evident in these portfolios. While it could be argued that they skew expected returns toward the area of conservatism or have an overall dampening effect, such discounts are simply practical. The logic behind this argument is as follows.

First, investors acknowledge and validate the notion that the potential for operational risk does indeed exist in hedge funds by the mere fact that they conduct operational due diligence. If not, what would they hope to achieve or screen for with this process? Now that we have established that operational risk is indeed a real concern, we can turn to the threshold portion of this argument. As part of an operational due diligence review, it is virtually impossible for an investor to give a review of a hedge fund's non-investment-related risk factors a perfectly clean bill of operational health. Indeed, we will concede that if the perfect operational hedge fund does exist, then an investor should not apply any sort of discount for operational risk to the expected return forecasts. I will add that if there is a perfect operational hedge fund out there, I have not come across it yet. Aside from the extreme of the perfect operational hedge fund, as part of the operational due diligence process an investor will invariably note some operational areas for improvement. This necessarily implies that there is an element of operational risk present in the hedge fund. The party line, as outlined earlier in the logic of the classical reasoning, is that as long as this operational risk is above the threshold, it is bearable and should not necessarily be factored into expected return analysis. To the contrary, we argue that such an approach is implicitly hypocritical.

On the one hand, operational traditionalists acknowledge operational risk, but on the other hand, they refuse, other than in vague, qualitative ways, to give these risks any weight as long as they are within acceptable guidelines. It could be because there is a lack of research or understanding as to how to accurately calculate the discount factors that should be applied to expected returns, as well as a lack of publicly available operational data regarding hedge funds. Also, a lack of understanding generally exists as to how to properly overlay these discount factors onto expected investment returns. Another stumbling block in regard to implementing this process is that there is a lack of consensus concerning which operational factors and global operational views should be considered more or less important. Perhaps it is because of a general lack of conviction about expected returns of hedge fund managers; however, if this were the case, then the importance of style drift considerations would be minimalized as well.

DISCOUNTED EXPECTED RETURNS WITH THE OPERATIONAL FACTOR

We can now take into account the Operational Factor previously calculated, and include this in our discussion of expected returns and operational risk. As discussed throughout this chapter, the expected returns of hedge funds should be discounted by some factor to account for their operational risks. One way in which we propose to adjust this operational risk utilizing the Operational Factor would be:

$$E(R)_{New} = E(R)_{Old} - [(Z) \times \text{Operational Factor}]$$

where Z represents the discretionary multiplier. The purpose of the multiplier is to account for the magnitude by which an investor seeks to discount the expected return. This multiplier could be based on particular operational views at the time, the degree to which an investor feels such operational risks are relevant, and so on.

The notion of discounting expected returns based on the magnitude and types of operational risk present at a particular hedge fund may at first seem contradictory to the idea we have expressed in this text—that a risk-averse investor would logically seek to be compensated for a taking on a higher degree of operational risk. These two ideas are not opposites, but rather complements.

As a hedge fund is more operationally risky, a risk-averse hedge fund investor necessarily demands higher returns. The concept of discounting expected returns for the operational risk present at a particular hedge fund is similarly representative of the higher returns expectation. With the one exception of a theoretical operationally riskless hedge fund, we will generally assume that all hedge funds have some degree of operational risk. As such, discounting quoted hedge fund expected returns to account for this risk seeks to bring an investor's return expectations back in line with the amount of return one would expect for the operational risk present at a fund.

For example, based on our knowledge of the relationship between expected return and operational risk, if we would expect a certain hedge fund to post annual returns in the range of 14% to 18%, and the manager espouses in marketing materials expected annual returns of 25% to 30%, then, using the Operational Factor analysis, we can discount this 25% to 30% range accordingly until perhaps it is more in line with our 14% to 18% range.

The challenges in implementing discount factors with precision for those diagnosed extant operational risks should be viewed as exactly that—challenges that need to be met by investors and academicians. Lack of knowledge or understanding as to how exactly to implement this discounting process does not invalidate the concept.

OPERATIONAL HAIRCUTS

Expected hedge fund returns are typically provided in annual terms (e.g., "this hedge fund expects to generate 12 to 15% annually"). We have just demonstrated one approach for utilizing the Operational Factor to discount these quoted expected returns to include operational risk considerations. Such expected returns, however, are discounting returns on an annual basis, as well. Being able to discount such expected returns on a more frequent basis (e.g., monthly) would generally be of more use to investors. One method we propose to do this is via the use of a monthly operational haircut for performance estimates. Many hedge funds, when quoting estimated monthly return, will build a haircut into the returns. This haircut in essence serves to lower expectations so that when a higher actual performance number for the month is eventually provided, investors will be pleasantly surprised. We are proposing that investors apply their own operational haircuts to hedge fund return estimates.

Consider a hedge fund that purports to make 20% per year. For a particular month, the estimate is that they are up 2%. Let us assume that an investor discounts the annual expected return via the Operational Factor and Z multipliers outlined earlier, and determines that the 20% expected return should be reduced to 19% for operational risk concerns. This 1% discount would not need to be applied evenly throughout the year. Furthermore, it is simply an estimated discount factor. The hedge fund may in practice experience losses of greater than 1% due to operational drag concerns. Subsequently, the investor could discount this 2% monthly estimate with an operational haircut of greater than 1/12 of 1% (i.e., 12 months in a year) based on a number of different factors, including the particular global operational views and the magnitude at which an investor feels a certain hedge fund is operationally exposed to things such as counterparties. In summary, the application of monthly operational haircuts by investors allows for a more manageable way to discount return estimates so they are more reflective of a particular investor's shifting operational views.

EXPECTED RETURN AND OPERATIONAL RISK

There is an inherently negative correlation between expected return and operational risk. As an investor invests in a hedge fund with a higher degree of operational risk, there is an expectation of a lower return. Intuitively this relationship is not necessarily linear (i.e., there is not a one-to-one correlation between a decrease in one unit of expected return for each additional unit of operational risk), regardless of how we choose to define such units. Rather, based on analysis of the expectations of logical, risk-averse Markowitz investors, we could expect this relationship to be curvilinear, as represented in Exhibit 9.23. In practice, of course, this relationship and the subsequent expectations of return per additional unit of operational risk differ for each investor. Before we can construct specific models on an investor-by-investor basis, we must first develop a generalized graphical model.

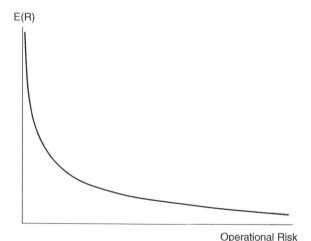

EXHIBIT 9.23 Relationship between Expected Return and Operational Risk

SHAPE OF THE EXPECTED RETURN VERSUS OPERATIONAL RISK CURVE

The approximate slope of this curve and its shape are areas that require further research by academicians and practitioners alike. Such research will be facilitated only as more operational risk data becomes publicly available. Assuming that for the risk-averse hedge fund investor we have represented the shape of the relationship between expected return and operational risk approximately accurately, we can now overlay a hypothetical operational risk threshold somewhere on this axis. Everything to the left of the sample threshold would be considered investable by our hypothetical investor. Everything to the right of the sample threshold is below the minimum operational risk competency level, and is too operationally risky to be considered for an allocation from an investor. This is presented in Exhibit 9.24.

There are situations in which a hedge fund investor would be willing to venture past his predetermined operational threshold to invest in a certain hedge fund. When breaching this operational threshold, the risk-averse investor will necessarily expect a higher level of return for bearing this

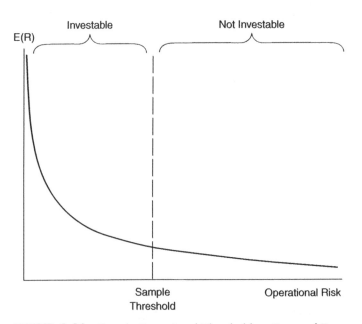

EXHIBIT 9.24 Sample Operational Threshold on Expected Return and Operational Risk Graph

extraordinary risk. This is not, however, what the graph in Exhibit 9.24 demonstrates. If we continue to follow the graph of expected return versus operational risk in that exhibit, it would appear that despite the increased operational riskiness of this manager we would have a lower expected return, that is, when compared to a manager with a lower degree of operational risk. In practice, however, if investors are willing to invest past their unique initial operational threshold, they should be compensated for breaching this barrier.

The question could be logically posed as to why anyone would venture past this threshold when he could achieve the same expected return by accepting lower levels of operational risk. The motivations for venturing past this threshold are numerous. In practice, the most common incentive for breaching this barrier is due to a scarcity of hedge funds in certain sectors of the hedge fund industry that may have lower levels of operational risk. This is particularly true of certain investments in emerging markets.

For example, a hedge fund could be based in an emerging market where certain operational practices are not common or relevant. A good example of this would be in the compliance and regulatory arena. Consider an investor who is strongly contemplating allocating capital to a hedge fund based in Xanadu, which has identified very promising investments in taking activist positions with traditional, family-run xylophone manufacturing firms that have recently become publicly traded. Let us assume that in Xanadu, training on sexual harassment may not be commonplace. There may not be laws that require sexual harassment training. Let us assume that the theoretical threshold being applied is considered to be an absolute one (i.e., the same operational best practice threshold is applied to every hedge fund regardless of investment strategy, geographical location, assets under management, length of track record, or a whole host of factors).

When looking at our risk-averse investor's absolute threshold, in this scenario, training in non-investment-related issues, such as sexual harassment training, is a requirement to be above the threshold. Therefore, in this case, the hedge fund manager would fall below the minimum operational threshold to be considered for investment. Consequently, if an investor is willing to allocate to this Xanaduian manager, then a higher degree of expected return would be anticipated as a result of the increased operational risk present.

SECOND OPERATIONAL THRESHOLD

In practice, as we move further along the operational risk spectrum and past the first operational risk threshold, there is an ultimate practical limit to the

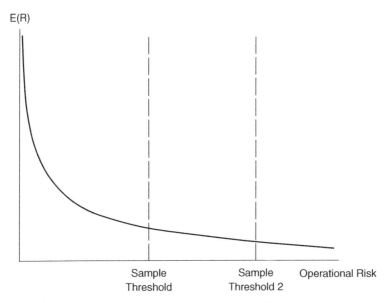

E(R)

Sample
Threshold

Sample
Threshold 2

Operational Risk

EXHIBIT 9.25 Two Sample Operational Thresholds on Expected Return and Operational Risk Graph

absolute maximum amount of operational risk that an investor would be willing to accept regardless of the potential for return. This maximum level of operational risk is represented by sample threshold 2 in Exhibit 9.25. In regard to the second operational threshold, our risk-averse investor would still consider everything between the first sample threshold and the second sample threshold investable, but would demand a much higher premium for bearing this extraordinary level of operational risk. This is demonstrated in Exhibit 9.26.

Here is an interesting question: What does the shape of our curve look like in between the first threshold and the second threshold? Whatever the shape, one common factor is that once the original curve touches the first operational threshold, the expected return must increase at a positive rate as the curve moves toward the second operational threshold. Why is this so? A risk-averse investor would breach the threshold only with the implicit assumption of receiving an increasing return. If not, the investor could receive a higher expected return by investing to the left of the first threshold.

One guess as to the shape of the curve past the first operational threshold for our generic risk-averse investor could be that the expected return jumps up by an exponential amount, as demonstrated in Exhibit 9.26. It is

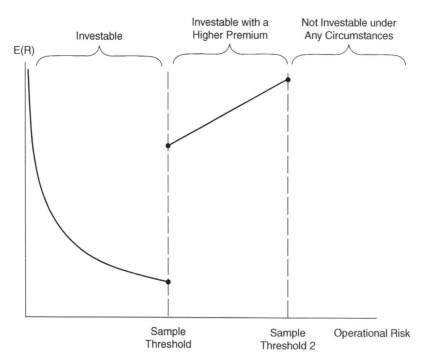

EXHIBIT 9.26 Example of Expected Return Jump Followed by Linear Progression of Expected Return versus Operational Risk

not necessarily the case that after an initial jump the expected return will continue to increase in a linear manner. Rather, the expected return could be curved, or perhaps the point where the expected return curve hits the first operational threshold is an inflection point and the curve would begin to mirror itself, as demonstrated in Exhibit 9.27.

FINAL THOUGHTS

As noted in both Chapter 8 and this chapter, assigning quantitative values to operational risk considerations is a tricky and inherently subjective process. However, that does not mean that it should not be done. At the end of the day, the purpose of evaluating such operational risks is to allow investors to make a determination as to how comfortable they are writing a check to a hedge fund, how large that check should be, and when the hedge fund becomes so operationally risky that they need to cash out. Assigning

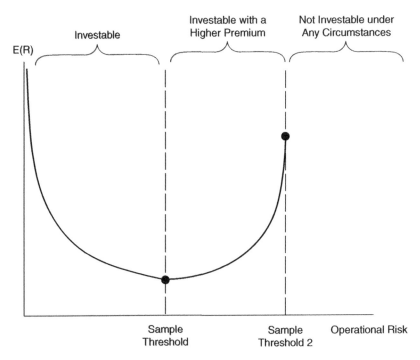

EXHIBIT 9.27 Example of First Threshold as a Mirrored Inflection Point

quantitative values to operational risks allows investors to better perform such initial and ongoing analysis. More publicly available hedge fund operational data and research is required by both market practitioners and academics to aid in refining the calculation of a number of topics introduced in this chapter, including the appropriate discount factors, multipliers, and meta risk factors.

Notes

1. www.grc.nasa.gov/WWW/K-12/airplane/drag1.html.
2. John Braithwaite, "Meta Risk Management and Responsive Governance," paper for *Risk Regulation, Accountability and Development Conference*, University of Manchester, June 26–27, 2003.
3. Charles Tapia, "Low Frequency, High Impact Operational Risk Events," July 2003, www.garp.com/documents/Articles/LFHIRiskEvent.pdf.
4. http://mw4.m-w.com/dictionary/standard%20deviation.

CHAPTER 10

Looking Ahead: Trends in the Space

If there were one constant in the hedge fund industry, it would be continual change. Perhaps the mercurial nature of this space has been a core element of its success. Indeed, in the search for continued alpha, more than ever it seems that, at least from an investment perspective, traditional style category definitions no longer apply universally. As new *hybrid* managers have evolved, that is, those who trade in multiple sectors (e.g., an event-driven manager who trades distressed debt and makes private equity side-pocket investments), it is increasingly unclear where to draw the line between a single-strategy manager and a multistrategy manager. The same can be said of the operational risk environment in which these hedge funds operate. The purpose of this chapter is to discuss several recent trends, both realized and emerging, that have begun to affect the hedge fund operational risk due diligence landscape. Understanding and anticipating such operational trends will be of essential importance to investors as they continue to make larger hedge fund allocations in this increasingly complex and changing operational environment.

INCREASED USE OF CONSULTANTS

As discussed throughout this text, it is now common for most hedge funds to seek advice from those outside the hedge fund organization on myriad operational issues. This trend has led to the creation of entire industries dedicated to serving the different operational needs related to each operational category. One of the more popular areas where third-party consultants are used is that of compliance.

During the early stages of the modern hedge fund resurgence, most hedge fund organizations utilized a combination of in-house general counsel (if they were large enough to have a general counsel on staff) and third-party law firms to oversee the compliance function. With developments such as the brief period of required Securities and Exchange Commission (SEC) registration of hedge funds, as well as the general realization of the importance of properly overseeing the compliance function, and an overall increase in the operational minimums most investors were willing to accept in regard to oversight of the compliance function, more hedge funds began to bolster their compliance efforts. This led to the birth of new compliance consulting firms that specifically service the hedge fund industry. These firms typically work in conjunction with a hedge fund's internal chief compliance officer and general counsel and to a lesser extent with third-party legal counsel, to assist the hedge fund in overseeing the compliance and legal functions.

Another area of increased use of consultants among hedge funds has been in that of valuation. Valuation consulting firms were in existence well before the recent popularity of the hedge fund industry. These firms traditionally provided investment banking–type opinions regarding valuations for merger and acquisition (M&A) transactions. As investors have placed greater importance on transparency in pricing policies as well as the independent verification of the hedge fund's internal fair-value pricing of thinly traded or illiquid positions, these traditional bulge-bracket firms have expanded their valuation services to cater to the hedge fund community.

The use of such valuation consultants has recently been of particular importance as more hedge fund portfolios increasingly have ventured into less liquid securities, where multiple independent quotes are more difficult to obtain. More specifically, examples of positions that valuation consultants are typically brought in to value include leveraged loans, real estate investments, certain types of asset-backed securities, private investments in public equity (PIPEs), trade and bankruptcy claims, convertible securities, and various types of derivative instruments, including mortgage derivatives, interest rate derivatives, and equity derivatives.

For hedge funds investors, the trend toward the increased use of consultants has both positive aspects and drawbacks. The use of third-party valuation consultants can provide investors with an additional sense of comfort knowing that an independent third party is evaluating and providing guidance on certain operational issues.

One caveat investors should consider regarding such valuation firms is that the hedge funds themselves are the clients of these third parties, not the hedge fund investors. That is not to suggest that the opinions of any third-party consultant would be tainted by this affiliation, but rather that hedge funds control what to do with such information. A situation could arise where a hedge fund engages a third-party valuation consultant to value an illiquid position it is holding. If the hedge fund substantially disagrees with the determination of the third-party consultant, it can simply choose not to utilize the valuation provided by the consultant in reviewing its portfolio, and further, not to share information of this disagreement and other valuations with investors. Of course, this situation is the exception rather than the norm, but it is certainly not outside the realm of possibility.

Another point of consideration for hedge fund investors is that the frequency with which certain consultants are engaged is generally left to the discretion of the hedge fund manager. For example, consider a hedge fund that engages a compliance consultant to perform a mock audit. The hedge fund might tout the fact that it has used a third-party firm to independently review its compliance policies and procedures, but leave the frequency, if any, with which the third-party firm returns to conduct more such mock audits up in the air. The firm will generally not establish a firm policy of having such audits performed with any sort of regularity.

However, some hedge funds may have internal pricing policies that outline scenarios under which the use of third-party valuation consultants is mandatory in the event a certain number of independent verifications, such as broker quotes, cannot be obtained. Examples of such scenarios include positions over a certain dollar amount, positions that become a certain percentage of a portfolio, or positions where firms own more than a certain percentage of the shares outstanding in a security. Where a firm plainly outlines the situations in which third-party consultants will be utilized, investors can take an additional level of comfort in knowing that the firm has tied itself to the use of consultants and there will be a certain minimum level of continued independent oversight. Of course, the firm could decide to alter its policies and procedures to discontinue the use of consultants. That said, frequent firm-wide policy changes are generally frowned on and would be easier for investors to detect than changes in policies that are not spelled out to begin with.

A final note on the trend of increasing use of consultants is the rising cost bases of the hedge funds that use consultants. The more a hedge fund uses different types of consultants, the more financial resources it must expend on the use of such consultants. While this may or may not have a direct impact on the net asset value (NAV) of a fund in which a particular investor is invested, contingent on whether the hedge fund manager charges these expenses directly to the fund, it will increase the overall expenses of the hedge fund. A hedge fund investor's gut reaction to this scenario might be, "Why should I care, as long as I am making money and it doesn't affect the value of my investments?" Such thinking may be short-sighted. If we instead take a long-term view of hedge fund investing and the investor views his hedge fund allocation as a strategic partnership, then this reaction is questionable. With an increasing cost base, a hedge fund may have less discretionary capital to put toward such things as new talent acquisitions and the upgrading of existing operational infrastructural support staff and technology. This may cause the eventual deterioration of a hedge fund's edge, be it an investment edge, an operational edge, or both, relative to its peers. Of course, increasing expenses could be offset by increasing revenues from management and incentive fees, but there is no guarantee that the rate of these revenue increases, if any, would necessarily offset increasing consulting expenses. Such issues of revenue versus expense comparison are ultimately the decision of senior management of the hedge fund. However, investors should be conscious of the actual costs associated with the number and frequency of use of consultants, especially in hedge funds that are in the early stages of their development.

COMMODITIZATION OF BACKGROUND INVESTIGATIONS AND CANNED OPERATIONAL DUE DILIGENCE REPORTS

With the continued growth of the hedge fund industry, there has been a proliferation in recent years of background investigation firms that specialize in catering to the needs of hedge fund investors who perform background investigations as part of the hedge fund due diligence process. As previously discussed, the majority of the information in these reports comes from searching publicly available records and databases, all of which are in the public domain. Often the value of such reports lies not in the sleuthing performed in unearthing secrets hidden deep in someone's past, but rather in distilling the results database and record queries into an easily digestible format for investors. The format of these reports varies greatly among background investigation vendors and often the more successful ones are better at presenting this data. This has become especially true as this process of querying such public records has become more accessible to novice investigation firms over time.

Similarly, the larger hedge funds that have been more successful at raising and retaining assets often have had many background investigations performed on them by many different firms at the request of the numerous hedge fund investors who were performing due diligence on their firms. As more assets have flowed into the hedge fund sector, experience suggests that the trend of multiple investors performing due diligence on the same fund has continued.

The result has been that, over time, each of these background investigation firms has constructed a private repository of hedge fund background investigation data. During the initial years of the hedge fund industry's resurgence in the 1990s, there were significant cost barriers to gaining access to this information. This was especially true since, at that time, a large number of background investigation firms would not allow their clients to review historical reports or even confirm whether they had performed work on a previous hedge fund or individual before. Rather, whenever a new report was ordered on a hedge fund that a background investigation firm had previously investigated, the background investigation firm would ostensibly perform this research from scratch. In practice, this "new" research would generally not include a reverification of certain already-verified information, such as previous employer of a certain individual, but only a search for records that may have changed over time.

From the background investigation firm's perspective, there are two primary arguments for not allowing clients to use historical investigation reports. First, the majority of background investigation firms will argue that by providing such reports to their clients they are effectively encouraging investors to act based on stale information. For example, if a hedge fund manager were arrested between the time of the completion of the historical report and the time an investor allocates, this would not be reflected in the old report. There is definitely some logic to this argument. An investor cannot be completely confident that something did not happen (e.g., a hedge fund manager's arrest for a crime), which would influence her decision not to allocate to a particular hedge fund in the interim time between when the old background investigation report was completed and when the investor allocated. A second reason for background investigation firms' initial hesitance to follow a model that provides historical reports is that they can generally charge higher fees for new work, or at least revalidating old work, than they can by simply providing an off-the-shelf historical report.

Despite these objections, there has been a trend lately for background investigation firms to sell copies of historical reports at reduced rates to existing clients. Some background investigation firms have opted to sell these historical reports only where they had performed previous investigatory work on a certain hedge fund or to those investors who had already allocated to a fund and are now interested in a background investigation. In the latter example, it could be argued that any negative information obtained from a background investigation after an investor has already allocated would come too late to be useful. However, if investors desire, they could submit a redemption request if something in a background investigation report alerts them to a potential problem or something else prompts them to do so.

To understand why the trend of allowing investors access to the library of reports created by background investigation firms has taken hold in recent years, we need to look at the economics of the background investigation industry. The nature of most background investigation firms' business models, depending on the comprehensiveness of the investigation process, is that there are large startup costs relative to the price charged for an individual final report. Examples of these costs include the various subscriptions required to numerous database services, the costs of requesting copies of documents from various governmental entities, certain travel expenses to physically visit courts in different jurisdictions in order to search onsite files, phone calls to references, and so forth. The way a larger background investigation firm makes this arrangement feasible is by serving large numbers of clients and therefore benefiting from economies of scale. Additionally, there are significant costs incurred in terms of the amount of time and effort required to research, review, and summarize the data collected during an investigation. It is not very cost effective for a small background investigation firm to perform a onetime-only search into a certain hedge fund or its principals. Instead, such firms can realize substantial profits be reselling these reports, or slightly updated versions of them, to multiple clients in order to generate a higher return on their initial investment. This model is even attractive for larger background investigation firms, which can realize additional profits from their existing work.

Many background investigation firms have begun to follow this library model, where clients are provided with existing lists of previously performed work and the dates that the work was performed. Under this scenario, it is up to the background investigation firm's clients (e.g., the hedge fund investor) to determine whether the report is too old or stale to be used or whether it will suffice. From the client's perspective, certain types of information, such as the confirmation of whether a certain individual graduated from a particular university, are static. Once confirmed as part of one search, these items need no further confirmation. Other items, such as litigation searches, will produce different results if any new litigation has been brought since the time of the last investigation. It is in these items that change over time that the *decay* of the value of the background investigation takes place. Consequently, the onus is on the background investigation firm to generate as much income from these reports as possible before these items are determined by investors to be so decayed as to be virtually useless.

More background investigation firms are beginning to accept this library approach, and it has begun to signal a trend of commoditization of background investigation data and reports. What does this trend mean for hedge fund investors? It means that, compared to the early days of the industry, an investor can purchase a hedge fund background investigation report for a relatively low price. The brunt of the expense of such reports is borne by the first investor who orders reports on a particular subject; the subsequent purchasers of the report gain the cost savings of the typically cheaper price charged once the report is complete and it begins to age. Additionally, these off-the-shelf reports, if purchased from a reputable vendor, will generally contain the same standardized information as reports from other similar quality vendors.

There is another impact of the acceptance of the library model by background investigation firms. Any first-mover advantage to a hedge fund investor of materially negative items that had been uncovered by a background investigation firm, on behalf of their hedge fund investor clients, when they initially did the work is more quickly eroded under the library approach than otherwise. Two scenarios can demonstrate this point. First, consider a background investigation performed into a newly launched hedge fund. An investor who is the first to perform an investigation into this fund using a particular background investigation firm will be the first of this background investigation firm's clients to learn about any negative items uncovered as part of this search. Under the library approach, this report would now be sold to other investors sooner than if seemingly new work needed to be completed from scratch, as if it had never been performed before for the new investor. The second scenario is where an investor has background investigation work performed into an individual whom the background investigation firm had *not* examined previously. If any materially negative information were uncovered during this search, it would also be available to other investors more rapidly.

Turning to the investor's perspective, there are three primary reasons why the trend of commoditization has taken hold. First, the cost benefits are apparent to investors who do not have the resources to request that investigations be performed from scratch. There are also significant time savings in purchasing off-the-shelf background investigation reports. The typical timeframe to complete an entirely new background investigation, contingent on the comprehensiveness of the report, can be six weeks or longer, whereas historical, off-the-shelf reports are immediately available.

Finally, most investors have tended to view the background investigation process, similar to the way they have viewed the operational risk process, as a stopgap. Background investigations were performed to determine whether there was anything materially negative in anyone's background that would prevent an investor from allocating to a fund. If nothing were found, the investor would generally proceed. There was not necessarily any informational or tactical advantage associated in the minds of investors for being the first to obtain or protect such data. As the trend of commoditization takes hold, it can be predicted that, beyond the basic screening for obvious materially negative items (e.g., criminal violations, regulatory sanctions, etc.) or blatant fraud (e.g., claiming false employment or educational credentials), the truly innovative hedge fund allocators will begin to realize the information advantages of mining the results of background investigations to facilitate such techniques as independent reference checking (discussed in Chapter 6).

It is certainly feasible that leading hedge fund allocators will cast a broader net when performing background investigations to cover more employees and affiliated entities of a particular firm. The motivation behind a broader dragnet is that when the same firms' and same principals' backgrounds are examined over and over again by investors, those hedge funds with any material issues in their background will likely go out of business. If the issue is severe enough, or becomes well-known in the marketplace, it will certainly come up in a background investigation report. Less common, however, is for investors to examine more-junior individuals at a firm who may have items in their background that could prove to be just as damning. For example, while most investors will perform a background investigation on a hedge fund's chief financial officer, perhaps no one has previously performed an investigation on its controller.

This leads us to the final trend in the commoditization of background investigations, which is related to the broadening of the background investigation process—the ownership of the background investigation process by allocators. Protection or ownership of the process relates to the notion of maintaining a strategic informational advantage over other allocators. Returning to our example, let us assume that this controller had pleaded guilty to a series of misdemeanors related to the use of illegal drugs and shoplifting. Let us further assume that the controller has hid this from his employer. The investor performing this background investigation might be the first in the financial community to uncover this information. As such, this investor would possess an informational advantage over other investors. This investor could use this information, if he felt it to be material, either to avoid allocating to this manager, or, if he had already invested, to redeem or scale back existing investments. Investors without this knowledge, who, if they had known, would not have invested, might allocate to this fund. In an increasingly competitive environment for client assets among allocators such as funds of hedge funds, an information advantage can be very valuable. Consequently, more sophisticated hedge fund allocators are beginning to realize the benefits of either bringing the background investigation function in-house, or entering into agreements with background investigation firms to protect for as long as possible the proprietary nature of any data that is uncovered on their behalf by a background investigation firm.

A similar trend of commoditization has also begun in the area of operational due diligence reports. As discussed in Chapter 3, in addition to the emergence of a number of operational risk rating agencies, where the hedge funds are traditionally the clients, there are a number of third-party firms that investors hire to perform third-party operational risk reviews of hedge funds. Similar to the background investigation model, many of these third-party operational risk reviewers have begun to accept the library approach and resell previously completed, generic, off-the-shelf (*canned*) operational risk reviews to other clients. Here, too, many large allocators have begun to realize the value of maintaining ownership of the entire operational due diligence process as well as the informational advantages of mining and controlling operational risk data. Consequently, there has been an increasing trend toward the creation of dedicated operational due diligence departments among larger hedge fund allocators, and it can be expected that such a trend will continue as funds continue to face a changing and more challenging operational environment.

INCREASED RELIANCE ON SERVICE PROVIDER CONSULTING SERVICES

As the minimal standard of overall operational competency that investors expect from hedge funds has slowly risen over time, increased pressure has been put on both established and nascent hedge fund organizations to hone their internal processes with an eye toward the implementation of cost-effective, operationally efficient processes that are transparent enough to demonstrate to investors. Realizing this desire, and seeking to provide a continued stream of value-added services, such as capital introduction, in order to distinguish themselves from other firms in the increasingly stiff competition for trade commissions, prime brokers, and to a lesser extent other service providers, have begun positioning themselves as consulting partners with regard to a host of operational issues. This guidance can come in many forms.

One such circumstance is the traditional consulting model, where a hedge fund will approach a prime broker with a specific issue or problem in mind. A common example is when an established hedge fund contemplates an upgrade to its internal accounting system or a new fund is attempting to determine which accounting system it should select. The fund may or may not have begun to investigate such systems on its own. If the fund had already begun to vet systems, they might come to the prime broker with a short list and ask for a recommendation. However, if the fund had done no prior investigation into the issue, it might ask the prime broker to provide a recommendation.

Another example of the consulting services provided by a prime broker is assistance in conducting issue-specific operational audits. These audits are health checks into the status of a particular operational competency of a hedge fund. Once complete, a prime broker typically identifies any potential areas of operational weakness and provides a list of recommendations. Additionally, a prime broker generally works with the fund to assist it with implementing these recommendations via such methods as recommending service providers and software packages. Examples of operational areas where a hedge fund may ask a prime broker to conduct an audit would be overall technology competency and trade placement and processing.

There are a number of benefits for hedge funds in leveraging preexisting relationships with prime brokers, and other service providers, to gain additional consulting services. The primary benefit to these funds is that they can leverage the considerable knowledge and experience of service providers who often have deep institutional knowledge about certain operational practices. Additionally, the larger service providers, such as prime brokers, have the distinct advantage of ongoing dialogues with their large hedge fund client base. These service providers provide valuable perspectives to hedge funds regarding operational trends and best practices throughout the industry. Finally, by using consulting services, and many of their features, which are often provided at no additional charge to hedge fund clients, these funds get more for their commission dollars, in the case of prime brokers, and save on costs.

There are also a number of potential drawbacks and concerns that both hedge funds and investors should be conscious of in relation to the use of consulting services. One such drawback is the threat that a hedge fund will become too reliant on the advice of third-party service providers. This could lead to a hedge fund effectively outsourcing its decision-making authority and oversight of certain operational areas to these third parties. With a lack of internal operational competency, a hedge fund may be hesitant to discontinue the relationship with the service provider providing the consulting services and utilize the services of nonrecommended service providers or software platforms. One way that hedge funds can protect themselves against such a risk is to maintain internal knowledge and oversight concerning any operational issues for which they seek consulting services. Additionally, hedge funds can protect themselves against risks by diversifying their business among several service providers, such as prime brokers, so they are not too reliant on any one service provider.

CAPTURE OF HEDGE FUNDS BY SERVICE PROVIDERS AND EMPLOYEES

Similar to the risks that hedge funds run in becoming too reliant on their service providers as a result of the use of additional services such as consulting advice, a trend has emerged in recent years that relates to the practice of hedge funds hiring away employees from their service providers. This phenomenon is not specific to any type of service provider and runs the gamut from legal counsel to administration personnel. From the perspective of hedge funds, these hiring decisions are often prompted when an employee from the service provider announces his intention to depart the service provider to pursue another career opportunity. Fearing it will lose access to this individual, the hedge fund will often extend to this person an attractive offer and bring him in-house.

Such an arrangement is attractive from a hedge fund's perspective for several reasons. First, the hedge fund manager typically hires an individual with whom he is very familiar and with whom he has worked for a number of years. These individuals are generally intimately familiar with the operational practices present at the hedge fund in a particular area. Consequently, once they are hired, they hit the ground running and require very little, if any, training to get up to speed. The hedge funds also may be able to realize a substantial savings by bringing these individuals directly onto the payroll as opposed to paying them through the service provider, which is usually very attractive to both parties.

There is nothing inherently wrong with hedge funds hiring individuals with whom they have a preexisting relationship via their service provider. However, there are several potential risks that this scenario presents, of which both hedge funds and investors should be conscious. A common example of a risk associated with this situation relates to the hedge fund continuing the relationship with the service provider from which the individual employee was hired. Consider an example where a hedge fund hires away the attorney it has worked with for the past few years from the law firm that serves as its primary domestic general counsel. Once hired, assume that the attorney decides to continue the relationship with her former law firm as the hedge fund's general counsel since she is familiar with the senior partners at this firm and considers their work to be of high quality. Over time, as the needs of this hedge fund grow, let us further assume that this attorney continues to give more legal work to this law firm. The risk that is present in such a scenario is that the law firm in question may not have the particular expertise or the details for new issues that have come up, or its fees may not necessarily be competitive. However, the person providing internal guidance to the fund, in this case the lawyer who was hired away, may simply be comfortable with this firm, and also may not wish to damage the relationship with her former colleagues. That is not to say that this scenario will take place in every situation. However, it could be argued that the potential risk of overreliance on a service provider, when it may not be necessarily prudent, is more prevalent when a preexisting employment relationship exists between the service provider and the person who is the primary decision maker concerning the firm's continued use of that service provider. Additionally, the hedge fund runs the risk of being effectively unable to fire the attorney, should the need arise, since she essentially controls the relationship with her former employer. The point could be raised that the third-party law firm would likely continue the relationship with the hedge fund; however, such a relationship would most likely be damaged by the hedge fund's firing of the law firm's former colleague and main point of contact at the hedge fund. As we have illustrated, with such increased reliance, hedge funds run the risk of essentially being *captive employers and clients*. Both hedge funds and investors alike should be conscious of the threat of being overly reliant on such individuals and service providers as well as of the need to maintain diversification, both of service providers and internal shared operational competency.

HEDGE FUND PURSUIT OF AUDIT CERTIFICATIONS

With the continued flood of assets into the hedge fund space, there has been a Darwinian evolution of hedge funds that have continued to thrive and those that have gone the way of the dinosaur. Those naturally selected to survive and thrive have served to facilitate the standardization of baseline operational practices throughout the industry. This is fueled partly by the increased infusion of large institutional capital into the space. Such institutionalization has relegated the traditional concept of the lone hedge fund manager trading from a hotel room in Monaco to ancient history. Today, the vast majority of successful hedge fund managers, those with large asset bases, established track records, and detailed and time-tested investment practices, are supported by full-scale operational networks.

With an eye toward seeking independent third-party confirmation of the fortitude of such operational infrastructures and best practices and the operational competency of a particular hedge fund, there has been a recent trend among larger, more operationally complex hedge funds to seek formal audit certifications of their practices. Previously, it was commonplace for only large hedge fund service providers such as administrators to undergo such detailed operational review processes.

In the United States, the most common example of audit certification being pursued by hedge funds is the Statement on Auditing Standards (SAS) No. 70, Service Organizations, commonly known as an *SAS 70 report*. The Auditing Standards Board of the American Institute of Certified Public Accountants (AICPA) issues the auditing standards. Technically, today, the majority of such SAS 70 audit firms conduct audits not only in adherence to SAS 70, but also in adherence to the subsequent amendments known as

SAS 88, Service Organizations and Reporting on Consistency, and SAS 98, Omnibus Statement on Auditing Standards. These reports are generally titled "Report on the Processing of Transactions by Service Organizations," but may also be referred to as "Report on Controls Placed in Operation and Tests of Operating Effectiveness," or some variation thereof.

Formally, a SAS 70 can be defined as a report "where professional standards are set up for a service auditor that audits and assesses internal controls of a service organization."[1] SAS 70 reports come in two forms: A Type I report details the auditor's opinion as to the fairness of the presentation of the organization's description of controls as well as the suitability of the design of such controls to achieve the specified control objectives. A Type II report contains all of the information in a Type I report, as well as the auditor's opinion as to whether the specific controls had operated effectively during the period under review.

In Canada, a report similar to SAS 70 is known as *Section 5970*. Another example of these types of reports is found in the United Kingdom. It is the guidance issued by the Audit and Assurance Faculty of the Institute of Chartered Accountants in England and Wales. This institute provides guidance to reporting accountants on undertaking an assurance engagement and on providing a report in relation to internal controls of a service organization.[2] This updated guidance paper supersedes the earlier one known as *FRAG 21/94*. Many of the U.S.-based service organizations that provide services to financial services companies are now required to undergo SAS 70 review in order to comply with the requirements of the Gramm-Leach-Bliley Act. With the recent discussion in the marketplace regarding increasing the regulatory oversight of hedge funds, such SAS 70–type reviews may become commonplace for hedge fund organizations as well. Many investors and operational due diligence professionals alike view such audit certifications not as replacements for, but as complements to, the operational due diligence process.

OPERATIONAL ACTIVISM

The traditional view toward the hedge fund operational risk function can be likened to that of a bouncer outside of a night club. It lets only those funds meeting certain operational criteria into a particular investor's investable universe. If a hedge fund does not make it in, that is usually where the relationship stops. In certain cases, as with startup hedge funds, there is a certain key or strategic investor who serves as mentor to a young hedge fund when certain issues come up. Similar to the role of the board of directors or a consultant, the role of these key strategic investors is to assist the firm in developing over time from both an investment and operational perspective.

Traditionally, these mentoring roles were reserved for early stage strategic investors who had typically provided seed capital to help foster startup funds. As the hedge fund industry has evolved, and competition has increased for certain types of brand-name institutional capital or access to certain distribution platforms, the nature of this mentoring relationship has broadened and evolved into a new breed. We can label this new breed of mentoring relationship with the umbrella term *operational activism*. Under an operational activist approach, similar to the stance taken by certain types of activist investors, hedge fund investors who have substantial investments in certain funds will seek to make their voices heard by senior management to recommend certain operational changes within hedge fund organizations. It is not that the hedge fund is necessarily below the minimum operational threshold established by the investor; if it were, the hedge fund investor would likely not have allocated in the first place. Rather, it is the hedge fund investors who have begun to leverage the knowledge gained by performing continuing operational due diligence on hedge funds who feel that certain aspects of a hedge fund's operations could be improved or enhanced. This improvement can take the form of such things as new processes with respect to certain operational issues, the implementation of new systems or technology, or the upgrading of talent by either the replacement of existing personnel or the addition of new, more experienced personnel in certain operational areas of the firm.

Operational activists may be a hedge fund's existing investors who are seeking operational improvements at hedge funds to which they allocate, or prospective investors who will not allocate to a hedge fund unless certain operational changes are implemented. Focusing on the example of existing fund investors, an operational activist approach may be the outgrowth of minimum operational requirements for third-party hedge fund investors within a particular investor's organization. For example, a certain hedge fund allocator may have certain internal risk reporting requirements that require that the underlying hedge funds to which they allocate provide certain types of data, which they may not normally provide, or provide data that they provide to other investors in a certain format that is easier for the investor to integrate into his specific systems. Investors who adamantly require such specific reporting may seek to have these requirements spelled out in a side letter. Problems arise when the hedge funds do not have the capability to provide such reports at the behest of investors. Consequently, continuing our example, if a hedge fund wants a capital allocation from this investor, it must make an internal operational change. This becomes more of a strategic business decision from the perspective of the hedge fund as to whether the benefits of making such a change (e.g., receiving a capital allocation from the investor) outweigh any costs associated with providing reports in a particular format. Of course, the hedge fund should factor into its cost-benefit analysis the fact that being able to provide this information in this format may be an improvement over the existing way this is done, and may be able to be leveraged across all of the firm's investors. Additionally, the hedge fund should consider that other investors might begin to request new reporting formats. Therefore, not making the appropriate operational changes to facilitate these investors could lead to larger losses, or more missed opportunities, than merely the client in question.

When dealing with investors who take this activist approach toward operational risk management, hedge funds must walk a delicate tightrope. On the one hand, they do not want to lose control of internal operational decision-making authority by kowtowing to investors' every beck and whim. On the other hand, by developing dialogues with their larger investors about operational issues, combined with other efforts that may be in play, and following the trends previously discussed, such as the recommendations of third-party consultants, operational risk rating agencies, or third-party auditors, hedge funds may be able to significantly improve their operational competencies. In addition, these hedge funds might realize operational efficiencies and capitalize on opportunities they would not have been aware of had they been functioning in a state of operational isolation. Furthermore, operational dialogues with investors generally serve to foster stronger relationships with these investors and lead to stickier capital allocations that are beneficial to the hedge fund organization.

AU 332 AND FAS 157

In recent years, there has been an increase in the participation in more illiquid instruments by hedge funds. In line with this continued foray into illiquidity has come a growing wave of concern among investors and regulators alike who have seen the percentage of fair-valued instruments held by hedge funds increase over time. Investors and regulators have begun to take steps to increase scrutiny of the pricing methodologies and procedures utilized by hedge funds to mark such instruments.

We can first discuss the marketplace's general reaction toward the responsibilities of hedge fund auditors, hedge fund allocators, and hedge funds regarding who should determine what the term *fair value* means, how to determine fair value, how to document fair values, and how to independently confirm these fair values. Two of the primary auditing standards for investments are AU section 332, "Auditing Derivative Investments, Hedging Activities, and Investments in Securities" and AU section 328, "Auditing

Fair Value Measurements and Disclosures." While these sections were not specifically designed to apply to hedge funds, they do have significant relevancy for the auditing of the valuation techniques in place at hedge funds, with particular emphasis on fair valued instruments.

To facilitate auditors in the application of these standards to hedge funds, in 2006, the AICPA issued Interpretation No. 1 of AU section 332, "Auditing Investments in Securities Where a Readily Determinable Fair Value Does Not Exist." This interpretation was accompanied by a companion technical practice aid issued by the AICPA's Alternative Investment Task Force that provided guidance with respect to "existence and valuation assertions, because of the lack of a readily determinable fair value for these investments and the limited investment information generally provided by fund managers."[3] In essence, AU section 332 and AU section 328 state that an auditor must consider both the intricacy as well as the liquidity of the hedge fund's investments when determining the amount of audit evidence required. The guidance on these standards has particular implications for the auditors of clients who hold investments in hedge funds, such as a fund-of-hedge-funds auditor. This guidance, can provide valuable aid for hedge fund investors attempting to determine the controls and processes in place at a hedge fund with respect to fair value determination.

A step toward the standardization of the treatment of these internally marked instruments is the fair value measurement standard issued by the Financial Accounting Standards Board, *FAS 157*, which took effect on November 15, 2007. This new standard will need to be implemented for audited financial statements issued by hedge funds for the 2008 fiscal year. Hedge fund investors will formally see the results of the implementation of FAS 157 in 2009, when the hedge fund vehicles in which they invest produce their 2008 financial statements.

Specifically, the following excerpt from the Financial Accounting Standards Board's Summary of Statement No. 157 outlines the reasons for issuing this statement on fair value measurements:

> *Prior to this Statement, there were different definitions of fair value and limited guidance for applying those definitions in GAAP. Moreover, that guidance was dispersed among the many accounting pronouncements that require fair value measurements. Differences in that guidance created inconsistencies that added to the complexity in applying GAAP. In developing this Statement, the Board considered the need for increased consistency and comparability in fair value measurements and for expanded disclosures about fair value measurements.*[4]

FAS 157 seeks to accomplish three main goals:

1. Create a uniform definition of fair value.
2. Establish a fair value measurement framework under generally accepted accounting principles (GAAP).
3. Broaden the disclosure requirements for those fair value observations.

FAS 157 clarifies fair value as the price a hedge fund would receive if it were to sell the asset in the market (i.e., exit price). This represents a significant departure from the previous general thinking that fair value was the price a hedge fund would pay to acquire an asset (i.e., entry price). This distinction between the use of exit price versus entry price is important, because different hedge funds may use different reference marks when determining the exit price. Additionally, contingent on a number of factors, including timing of the calculations and the types of assets involved, entry prices and exit prices can differ substantially.

FAS 157 outlines a framework for fair value measurement that categorizes assets into three distinct buckets. Each bucket correlates to the ease or certainty with which the value of an asset may be obtained. Specifically, assets that fall into the Level 1 category are those whose prices are easily available in the market. An example of a Level 1 asset would be a stock traded on the NASDAQ or New York Stock Exchange.

Level 2 assets are those whose prices are not readily observable but whose valuations are based on observable inputs of similarly traded assets. An example of a Level 2 asset would be the common stock of a public company restricted from sale under Rule 144.

Level 3 assets are those whose values are not observable in the market. Examples of Level 3 assets include certain mortgage-linked assets, private equity investments, and certain long-dated options. When reviewing FAS 157's impact on hedge funds, it is the classification and subsequent disclosures surrounding Level 3 assets that will likely have the biggest impact on the way in which a hedge fund goes about marking assets to internally developed models.

FAS 157 will require hedge fund managers to provide specific additional disclosures regarding certain amounts of information. Included in these disclosures will be information concerning the segregation of assets into each level (i.e., Level 1, Level 2, or Level 3). Additionally, for Level 3 assets, hedge funds will need to disclose details such as a description of the input used to determine the mark, and the information utilized to develop this.

To ensure compliance with FAS 157, many hedge funds will have to make a number of changes in the way in which they track, monitor, and retain support documentation for certain types of internal pricing information.

These changes could require the upgrading or customization of a hedge fund's internal trading and accounting systems. There could be a number of changes needed to internal valuation policies and procedures. Additionally, many hedge funds, depending on the proportion of Level 3 assets held, will need to be proactive with their auditors and administrators in addressing the new valuation challenges presented by FAS 157. When performing initial operational due diligence or ongoing monitoring of hedge funds, investors should be conscious of a number of different issues with respect to FAS 157, including:

- Developing an understanding of the approximate percentage of assets in each respective vehicle classified as Level 1, Level 2, and Level 3 as well as whether this classification coincides with the investor's understanding of the investment strategy (e.g., a fund that primarily trades highly liquid instruments such as managed futures should not have a high percentage, if any, of Level 3 assets).
- Whether there have been any disagreements between the fund's auditor or other service providers, such as administrators, with regard to the classifications of assets among each level.
- What technological and systems changes, if any, the fund has had to implement in order to properly comply with tracking assets for FAS 157.
- What valuation policy changes, if any, the fund has had to make to properly comply with FAS 157. Specifically, investors should question which of the three generally accepted valuation techniques (market approach, cost approach, or income approach) a hedge fund manager is utilizing with respect to certain assets. FAS 157 allows for differing approaches to be utilized, but stresses consistency of approaches. If a change is made, a certain amount of underlying support information is required. Investors should be inquiring as to how the fund has thought about these differing approaches and how it has dealt with any ambiguity in the valuation process.
- If the hedge fund trades any restricted stock, whether the firm anticipates having to make adjustments to quoted prices, as FAS 157 outlines, to the extent that market participants would consider the restriction in their pricing. If so, has the firm addressed such adjustments in its pricing policies? Has the fund developed a plan for how to document such adjustments?

DEVELOPMENT OF HEDGES TO OPERATIONAL RISKS

Investors like to know that their investments are protected and are willing to pay a price for peace of mind. This is the basis of the insurance industry.

The same is true for hedge fund investing. Portfolio managers are often willing to sacrifice some of their gains by hedging out certain types of risk. Some hedge fund investors apply similar concepts to their investments in hedge funds. Those hedge fund investors seeking to take on more risk, for the return of potential higher profits, can lever up their investments via such things as structured products. Those seeking to give back some profits to protect against uncertainties such as currency movements can enter overlay currency hedges on top of their hedge fund investments. These techniques apply to financial or investment-related risks. Traditionally, investors had no means of diversifying or hedging against operational risks. Consequently, it was very important to be extremely thorough when performing operational due diligence reviews.

While not seeking to limit the importance of performing operational due diligence reviews, certain hedge fund investors are looking to gain additional assurances against potentially large losses due to blatant fraud. Recognizing this need, several new insurance products have been announced recently that cater to investors by providing protection against fraud. While this is an evolving area of the insurance sector, these policies are generally designed to kick in once a regulator or court becomes involved.

Certain questions have yet to be tested by the marketplace. For example, what common definition of fraud will be settled on among insurers, courts, and hedge fund investors? Will it simply be manipulation of NAVs? What if a portfolio manager misrepresents his credentials, and something is later revealed to the public that causes a fund to liquidate and an investor to lose her initial investment? Will this be covered? Does the policy protect the investor's original investment amount, or the value of the investment at the time the court case proceeds or the regulator becomes involved? If it is the latter, what NAV will be utilized to determine the amount that the investor should be paid by the insurance company? Such a question becomes extremely important if the fraud resulted in a fund reporting inflated NAVs. Will the providers of the insurance policy be able successfully to go after (typically via a legal procedure known as *impleader*) other hedge fund investors who redeemed before the fraud was detected, and force them to disgorge profits?

This fate befell a number of investors, including celebrities such as Sylvester Stallone and John Cusack, when they redeemed their money, at a substantial profit, from the Lipper Convertibles fund. "A portfolio manager had inflated profits by at least 40 percent, Lipper discovered in 2002."[5] The fund's remaining investors subsequently sued Stallone, Cusack, and others, claiming they were unjustly enriched at the other investors' expense and sought the return of more than $100 million from those investors who got out early. It is still unclear how hedge fund fraud insurance will fare in such instances. As these types of coverage gain traction among hedge fund investors, the answers to our questions will likely begin to approach some semblance of clarity.

LINKS BETWEEN OPERATIONAL RISK AND CREDIT ANALYSIS

A series of recent market events, such as the subprime mortgage crisis and the subsequent credit crunch, felt throughout the capital markets, coupled with the meltdown of household names such as Bear Stearns, has led those analyzing the credit markets to revisit questions of analysis methods and valuation techniques. Because of these types of events, there has been an initial outcry among policy makers for increased transparency in financial markets. Specifically in regard to valuation techniques, the markets are currently witnessing a three-way struggle between regulators, auditors, and hedge funds. This discussion directly relates to how a hedge fund should appropriately classify and mark certain instruments under FAS 157. These classification questions also invite further inquiry into how to effectively compare valuation techniques of hedge funds under FAS 157 against those that use other accounting standards, such as International Financial Reporting Standards (IFRS). For several years, European IFRS users have had the equivalent to FAS 157 in the form of International Accounting Standard No. 39, but it does not have the same prescriptive approach.[6]

With regard to hedge funds that invest in the credit markets, such as managers who focus on acquiring thinly traded distressed debt, there has been higher scrutiny as a result of the failures mentioned earlier. Operational risk considerations are seen as possessing a greater amount of gravitas, in both the original investment decision and the subsequent valuation of any distressed debt on the books of the hedge fund manager. This has marked the transition from a traditional silo approach, between investment analysis and operational risk evaluations, into a more holistic approach to risk management. Herein lurk a series of unique conundrums for both the hedge fund manager and the fund's investors, especially in situations where there is a very thinly traded market, if any at all, for these types of securities. Part of the difficulty in answering these questions is the combination of a lack of specific regulator guidance regarding the newly implemented FAS 157, the differing opinions of auditors and valuation consultants, and a host of differing policies and procedures for valuing such securities among hedge funds. Consider the following outstanding questions:

- Should the hedge fund value distressed securities at cost until sold?
- Does the hedge fund manager have any strict guidelines or policies that dictate how often such distressed securities need to be revalued? If yes,

what are the guidelines? Is it with any sort of frequency (e.g., every quarter), or is it when a credit event takes place? If the latter, how does the manager define *credit event?*

■ In what situations is it appropriate for the hedge fund manager to bring in third-party valuation consultants? Will different consultants, with different areas of expertise in relation to different industries, be used for different types of distressed debt?

■ Does the hedge fund manager have strict guidelines that require that a third-party valuation be performed (e.g., if the manager owns a certain percentage of the outstanding market share of a distressed security; or if the value, however defined, of the distressed security exceeds a certain dollar value)?

■ How does the firm's auditor evaluate the marking of a certain security? Does the auditor review the manager's internal models, or the work of any third-party valuation consultants, or does the auditor use any of his own models?

■ If an auditor has another client that holds the same thinly traded distressed security, will the auditor compare, and perhaps use, the valuation of the other client for the particular hedge fund in question? What if this valuation is more conservative than the hedge fund feels is the case, based on its models?

PROPOSED REREGULATION OF THE HEDGE FUND INDUSTRY

There has been a reinvigorated discussion in Washington, D.C. toward restructuring the model under which investment firms, including hedge funds, have previously been regulated. Several factors are fostering this movement toward the latest reincarnation of the U.S. financial regulatory regime, including the recent blowup in the subprime market, the subsequent credit crunch, and the massive trading losses posted by Société Générale. The seminal event to date that seems to have brought these lingering regulatory discussions to a head was the near failure and subsequent bailout of Bear Stearns with the assistance of the Federal Reserve's $30 billion credit line.

The emerging champion of this new cause seems to be Treasury Secretary Henry Paulson Jr., the former head of Goldman Sachs Group Inc., who recently proposed a new blueprint for regulatory reform. Paulson originally would have seemed an unlikely candidate for the leader of this new regulatory revolution, particularly in light of his former Keynesian stance that investors and creditors rather than regulators best handle hedge fund regulation. One of the main proposals outlined in this blueprint is the consolidation of regulatory power with the Federal Reserve as the new official market stability regulator. In this role, according to Paulson, "a market stability regulator would have the authority to review certain private pools of capital, such as hedge funds and private equity, which have the potential to contribute to a systemic event."[7] Hedge funds may also be exposed to the further oversight of other newly proposed regulatory groups outlined in Treasury's blueprint. More specifically, these newly proposed regulatory groups may take on the role of business regulators and would adopt many of the roles of both the SEC and CFTC.

Several groups have come out in favor of this new regulatory model. Among the leading proponents is the Securities Industry and Financial Markets Association (SIFMA), which represents the interest of securities firms, banks, and various asset managers. Tim Ryan, President and CEO of SIFMA, stated in part, "Treasury has delivered a thoughtful and sweeping plan...."[8]

Opponents of this proposed regulation have voiced a number of concerns. Among the dissidents are New York Senator Charles Schumer, and William F. Galvin, Secretary of the Commonwealth of Massachusetts. Galvin criticized the new plan as "a disastrous backward step that would put the investor in jeopardy because it would pre-empt state regulation of securities and insurance."[9] Others are less critical; House Financial Services Committee Chairman Barney Frank "called Paulson's proposal a 'constructive step' but said it wouldn't give the Fed enough authority."[10]

While it seems that in restructuring the system it will take at least a year for the specific details of the new regulations to be reviewed, and most likely revised, by the U.S. Congress, whatever the outcome, a change in the way in which hedge funds are regulated, at least in the United States, is highly likely. Whether this change is implemented via such methods as revised hedge fund registration guidelines, increasing reporting requirements, more frequent disclosures on certain types of information, increased regulatory audits, or any combination of the above still remains to be seen. Stricter regulation will never be able, with total certainty, to predict or prevent fraud or the failure of a hedge fund because of operational issues. At least on the surface, increased regulation and transparency requirements imposed on hedge funds may facilitate the ways in which operational information about hedge funds is collected. This increased regulation may also help standardize the way in which operational information is presented to investors and prospects. However, increased regulation will never remove the burden on investors and hedge funds to effectively diagnose and monitor operational risks.

Notes

1. www.tech-faq.com/sas-70.shtml.
2. For further details, see "Assurance Reports on Internal Controls of Service Organizations Made Available to Third Parties," Technical Release AAF 01/06, Institute of Chartered Accountants in England and Wales, 2006.
3. "Alternative Investments: Audit Considerations," American Institute of Certified Public Accountants, 2006.
4. Summary of Statement No. 157: www.fasb.org/st/summary/stsum157.shtml.
5. Ianthe Jeanne Dugan, "Failed Hedge Fund Haunts Celebrities," *Wall Street Journal*, August 22, 2006.
6. Alex Chambers, "Valuation Crackers," *Euromoney*, March 2008.
7. Remarks by Secretary Henry M. Paulson Jr. on "Blueprint for Regulatory Reform," March 31, 2008, www.treas.gov/press/releases/hp897.htm. *Source:* IBD News Services, "Paulson's Broad Regulatory Revamp Plan Faces Criticism from Dems and Industry," March 31, 2008; www.investors.com/editorial/ IBDArticles.asp?artsec=16&issue=20080331.
8. Travis Larson, "Treasury's Regulatory Reform Plan 'Thoughtful,' 'Sweeping,' Says SIFMA," March 28, 2008, www.sifma.org/news/65873847.shtml.
9. Boston.com, "Administration Unveils Sweeping Plan to Overhaul Financial Regulation," March 31, 2008, www.boston.com/business/articles/2008/03/31/ paulson_proposes_sweeping_overhaul_of_financial_regulations/?p1=Well_Most Pop_Emailed5.
10. IBD News Services, "Paulson's Broad Regulatory Revamp Plan Faces Criticism from Dems and Industry," March 31, 2008, www.investors.com/editorial/ IBDArticles.asp?artsec=16&issue=20080331.

Index

Printed and bound by CPI Group (UK) Ltd, Croydon, CR0 4YY

23/04/2025

14661005-0002